US elections t

MANCHESTER
UNIVERSITY PRESS

US elections today

New edition of *Elections USA*

Philip John Davies

Manchester University Press

Manchester and New York

distributed exclusively in the USA by St. Martin's Press

First edition (*Elections USA*) published 1992 by Manchester University Press

This edition published 1999 by
Manchester University Press
Oxford Road, Manchester M13 9NR, UK
and Room 400, 175 Fifth Avenue, New York, NY 10010, USA
http://www.man.ac.uk/mup

Distributed exclusively in the USA by
St. Martin's Press, Inc., 175 Fifth Avenue, New York,
NY 10010, USA

Distributed exclusively in Canada by
UBC Press, University of British Columbia, 6344 Memorial Road,
Vancouver, BC, Canada V6T 1Z2

British Library Cataloguing-in-Publication Data
A catalogue record for this book is available from the British Library

Library of Congress Cataloging-in-Publication Data applied for

ISBN   0 7190 4507 X *hardback*
         0 7190 4508 8 *paperback*

This edition first published 1999

06 05 04 03 02 01 00 99   10 9 8 7 6 5 4 3 2 1

Typeset by Ralph J. Footring, Derby
Printed in Great Britain
by Biddles Ltd, Guildford and King's Lynn

For Rosamund Sarah Davies

Contents

Tables

Preface

The US election process provides a lens through which to observe the history and contemporary structure of American politics and government. Popular sovereignty is an underlying principle of American politics, but this is both supported and constrained by a historical fear of tyranny, both majority and minority, and this results in a system with a complex machinery of representation.

The study of American elections and political campaigns takes the observer from the sometimes stylised, but not always calm, counterpoint of the founding debates to the calculated, but not necessarily cynical, rough and tumble of contemporary campaigns. American political life at every level can be seen through the election process – federal, state, county and municipal governments depend on the willingness of candidates to stand and campaign, and on the electorate to vote for them. Executive, legislative and judicial offices are filled in this way, providing officeholders whose constituencies and functions then check and balance each other while exercising shared powers in ways that confirm the operation of US constitutional principles every day in American political life.

In chapter 1, this book examines the contemporary US ballot in various forms as a way of examining the underlying constitutional and historical principles of American government – checks and balances, separation of powers, the articulation of the executive, legislature and judiciary, and the existence of federalism. The chapter goes on to examine the importance of the ballot, of the opportunity to vote, and of actual participation in contemporary elections.

Taking up the historical thread, chapters 2 and 3 concern themselves with developments over the past 200 years of political campaigns. Chapter 2 analyses the amalgamation of campaigning, public interest and the use of technology and design by candidates, interests and political organisations to spread the political word. Most important among those organisations have been political parties. While there has always been a vein of suspicion in the American electorate about political parties, they have consistently performed the role of aggregating public opinion, providing alternative policies for public choice and organising government throughout America. Chapter 3 examines the genealogy and current status of America's party systems.

The parameters of the current campaign system were set by legislation in the 1970s. In chapter 4, the regulations and practices underpinning the modern political system, especially surrounding contemporary campaign finance, and political party activity are reviewed. This system provides the context for the entrepreneurial style and candidate-focused campaigns, the subject of chapter 5, that had become the norm by the end of the twentieth century.

State and local government is closest to, and most appreciated by, the American public. It consists of about 86,000 governments with roughly half a million elected officeholders. It is the least glamorous level, with essential services to perform, policy to create and laws to enforce. Chapter 6 sheds light on this relatively understudied area of the American polity.

Congressional and presidential elections attract more public, journalistic and scholarly attention, and the process of campaigning and electioneering at these levels forms the content of chapters 7 and 8. The amount of attention devoted to these elections does not necessarily result in any great consensus of analysis, and the changing fortunes of political parties and their candidates when facing the electorate have left things delicately poised at the beginning of the twenty-first century.

I have been helped and supported by many friends in the collection and analysis of materials for this book. I have been welcomed into homes, taken to campaign events, pointed at useful contacts and indulged outrageously with feigned (and much appreciated) interest when I have still been talking long after everyone really wanted to go to sleep. During the 1996 campaigns, the help of the Nuffield Foundation, De Montfort University and the United States Information Agency (USIA) in affording me the opportunity to make several visits to the USA was much appreciated. An invitation to visit Wartburg College, Iowa, gave me the two last weeks of the caucus campaign to race around the state chasing the candidates.

The aid of the USIA was invaluable in getting me into the Democratic National Convention, and Creighton University's support gave me another three weeks as a visiting professor to watch campaigns and give incorrect predictions to the media in yet another region. Television station KWWL, Waterloo, Iowa, and anchor woman Liz Mathis nonetheless gave me the chance to comment by outside broadcast from the Iowa caucuses throughout an evening that thoroughly satisfied my vanity, however negligible its value may have been to the viewers.

Thanks to my many welcoming hosts, including my cousins Jonathan and Mary Mitchell, and old friends Ruth and Keith Cox in Chicago; Mike

Bradley and Arlene Wergin in Maryland; Skip Atkins and Maureen Colton in Massachusetts; Fred and Edie Waldstein in Iowa; Clarence and Mary Stone in Washington; and Linda Cox and John Robinson in New York. Most exhilarating and amazing of all, these and other old friends and new continue to listen and talk to me, and to offer help, in spite of this obsessional interest. For these many acts of friendship, thanks also to Mary Chitty, Bob Turner, Kate Bateman, Mike Dukakis, Bryan and Chris Le Beau, Jim Ralph, Graham Ramsden, Ernie Paicopolos, Ed Sullivan and John White. Their regard and support give meaning to the tap, tap of my keyboard. There are undoubtedly more who should be listed here. If you can remember being systematically bored in pursuit of this publication, add your name above.

Carolyn and Andrew Davies are increasingly independent, making their fond support ever more valued. Rosamund Davies amazes me by having the clear ability to run the whole world, but choosing instead to concentrate on the little bit where I live.

Leicester, UK
May 1999

Abbreviations

AFL–CIO	American Federation of Labor–Congress of Industrial Organizations
CNN	Cable Network News
FEC	Federal Election Commission
FECA	Federal Election Campaign Act
GOP	Grand Old Party [Republican Party]
GOTV	get out the vote
MTV	Music Television
NVRA	National Voter Registration Act
PAC	political action committee
S&Ls	savings and loan associations
USIA	United States Information Agency

1

The US ballot: the symbol and reality of participation

Election day, 1996

On Tuesday 5 November 1996, voters all over the USA went to the polls to help elect a President. These voters had known for some time when the election would take place. Article 2, Section 1, Clause 3 of the US Constitution gives Congress the authority to 'determine the time of choosing' the nation's President, and early in the history of the USA Congress opted for the Tuesday after the first Monday in November as its preference for election day. The voters had also known for some time that they would be choosing between an incumbent and various challengers to be President.

Bill Clinton's first term as the nation's chief executive was coming to a close. He had first been elected President in November 1992, defeating the incumbent, George Bush, and he had taken office at noon on 20 January, the date and time specified by the Constitution for the beginning of the presidential term of office. Since the Constitution stipulates that an individual elected to the presidency 'shall hold this office during the term of four years' (Article 2, Section 1, Clause 1), Clinton had been required to present himself to the public for re-election in 1996. Once re-elected, President Clinton would not be eligible to stand for the office again, since the Twenty-Second Amendment to the Constitution states that 'No person shall be elected to the office of the President more than twice.'

It has been fairly common in recent years for the electorate to be called upon to choose between candidates when one of them was the incumbent, or sitting, President. Thirteen of the seventeen presidential elections from 1932 to 1996 featured an incumbent as one of the candidates. The exceptions were in 1952, 1960, 1968 and 1988 (table 1.1). The history of the USA before 1932 saw a much lower proportion of presidential elections featuring incumbents – slightly fewer than half from 1792 to 1928. Given the two-term limit on Presidents, a tradition that was later written into the Constitution, and the received wisdom that incumbents have an advantage in elections, one might expect a tradition of two-term

1

presidencies followed by an election between non-incumbents. This pattern would appear to have been more typical during the first two-thirds of nation's history than it has been in the late twentieth century (table 1.1).

The explanation comes in two main parts. In 1932 Franklin Delano Roosevelt beat an incumbent, then, with the nation under pressure from the double crisis of massive economic depression and involvement in the Second World War, broke with tradition to stand for re-election three times. This was unique, and subsequently the Constitution was amended to stop its repetition. Since Roosevelt's death, an unusual proportion of incumbents have been renominated by loyal party members, only to lose to a challenger from another party – a fate that befell George Bush in 1992, Jimmy Carter in 1980 and Gerald Ford in 1976. Roosevelt's success, and other candidates' failures, have combined to provide a series of elections unusual for the proportion featuring incumbents as candidates.

In all elections voters exercise both retrospective judgement, considering the actions of the outgoing administration, and prospective judgement, balancing the promise of the competitors. When there is no incumbent standing, the electorate will be able to draw on its knowledge of the party affiliation of candidates and administrations. A presidential election in which an incumbent is pitted against a challenger gives voters a special chance to exercise both retrospective and prospective judgement, since an incumbent is the personification of the outgoing administration. Some recent incumbents have found the test very hard.

Both major party candidates and one minor party candidate were well known to the voters in 1996. William Jefferson Clinton, Democrat, was approaching the end of his first term as President. Robert Dole, Republican, had been a US Senator since 1968, rising to Majority Leader of the Senate. Ross Perot, now of the Reform Party, had gained almost one in five votes with a quixotic independent candidacy in 1992, and hoped, four years later, to break the mould of American party politics. All three candidates had run vigorous and long election campaigns so that by the time the voters entered the polling booths there were hardly any who could claim that they did not know something of these candidates.

The voters of the township of Leicester, Vermont, for example, had, along with their compatriots, plenty of warning of the date of the election, ample time to realise that in this election they would have to choose a President, and had been subjected to a goodly amount of expensive campaigning to increase their awareness of the major competing candidates for that office. Nevertheless, those voters, regardless of their comprehension of election regulations, or of their attention to the campaigns, may well have had some surprises when faced with the ballot. Voters looking at the ballot found that the election for President was not a simple run-off between Republican Bob Dole with his running-mate Jack Kemp, and Democratic incumbent President Bill Clinton and Vice-President

Table 1.1. *Main candidates for the presidency, 1932–96*

Year	Candidate	Elected
1996	William Jefferson Clinton (Democrat – *incumbent*) Bob Dole (Republican candidate) Ross Perot (Reform Party candidate)	elected
1992	William Jefferson Clinton (Democrat candidate) George Bush (Republican – *incumbent*) Ross Perot (independent)	elected
1988	George Bush (Republican candidate) Michael Dukakis (Democrat candidate)	elected
1984	Ronald Reagan (Republican – *incumbent*) Walter Mondale (Democrat candidate)	elected
1980	Ronald Reagan (Republican candidate) James Earl Carter (Democrat – *incumbent*) John Anderson (independent)	elected
1976	James Earl Carter (Democrat candidate) Gerald Ford (Republican – *incumbent*)	elected
1972	Richard M. Nixon (Republican – *incumbent*) George McGovern (Democrat candidate)	elected
1968	Richard M. Nixon (Republican candidate) Hubert H. Humphrey (Democrat candidate) George C. Wallace (American Independent candidate)	elected
1964	Lyndon B. Johnson (Democrat – *incumbent*) Barry Goldwater (Republican candidate)	elected
1960	John F. Kennedy (Democrat candidate) Richard M. Nixon (Republican candidate)	elected
1956	Dwight D. Eisenhower (Republican – *incumbent*) Adlai Stevenson (Democrat candidate)	elected
1952	Dwight D. Eisenhower (Republican candidate) Adlai Stevenson (Democrat candidate)	elected
1948	Harry S. Truman (Democrat – *incumbent*) Thomas Dewey (Republican candidate)	elected
1944	Franklin D. Roosevelt (Democrat – *incumbent*) Thomas Dewey (Republican candidate)	elected
1940	Franklin D. Roosevelt (Democrat – *incumbent*) Wendell Willkie (Republican candidate)	elected
1936	Franklin D. Roosevelt (Democrat – *incumbent*) Alfred Landon (Republican candidate)	elected
1932	Franklin D. Roosevelt (Democrat candidate) Herbert Hoover (Republican – *incumbent*)	elected

Al Gore (each party's presidential and vice-presidential candidates run as a team). Nor was the Reform Party team of Ross Perot and Pat Choate the only alternative. There were more. Harry Browne and Jo Jorgensen were on the ballot representing the Libertarian Party; the Natural Law

Party's John Hagelin and Mike Tompkins were there; James E. Harris and Laura Garza were standing for the Socialist Workers Party; the Liberty Union Party was represented by Mary Cal Hollis and Eric Chester; the Green Coalition Party by Ralph Nader and Anne R. Goeke; Dennis Peron and Arlin D. Troutt Jr were the Grassroots Party candidates; and the US Taxpayers Party team was Howard Phillips and Albion W. Knight Jr. The voter could mark the presidential ballot with any one of ten available choices. In addition, there was a 'write-in' space for the voter to add any other choice felt preferable. That was not the end of things.

A moderately aware voter would already have known that this election was not merely about the presidency. All states now schedule elections for the US Congress on the national election day, and many conduct elections for other offices on the same day. Vermont, along with all other states, has two Senators in Congress, but neither of these Senate seats was up for election in 1996. All members of the US House of Representatives were up for election in 1996, as they are every two years. The whole of Vermont has a population of less than 600,000, with the result that it contains only one US House constituency. Therefore, in common with all other Vermont voters in 1996, the electorate of Leicester found seven candidates on the ballot, six under the auspices of party labels, and one, Bernie Sanders, the incumbent Vermont member of the House of Representatives, standing as an independent. A write-in space was provided for this, as for all the other offices. The opportunity to vote did not stop there.

The presidential and congressional elections all determine members of the federal government – the victors will be 'sent to Washington' – but more localised competitions take place simultaneously. Our 1996 Leicester, Vermont, voter was also called upon to help elect the state's Governor (seven candidates), Lieutenant Governor (five candidates), Treasurer (four candidates), Secretary (five candidates), Auditor of Accounts (six candidates) and Attorney General (four candidates). Except for one independent candidate for Governor, all these candidates were nominated by political parties, with Natural Law, Liberty Union and Vermont Grassroots party candidates appearing in every race, and Libertarians in three of the contests. In three cases (Secretary of State, State Treasurer and Attorney General) a single candidate was nominated by both the Democratic and Republican parties, and appeared with both party labels by their names.

Two state Senators were to be elected along with one state Representative, to represent local constituencies in the government at the state capital, Montpelier. Each of these races just had competing candidates nominated by Democratic Party and the Republican Party. One High Bailiff was to be chosen, whose 'duty, if the need should arise, is to arrest the sheriff because of some criminal or other problem, based on a writ ... issued by some creditable officer ... [and to serve] as an interim sheriff while the real sheriff is confined.'[1] There was only one candidate for High Bailiff, supported both by the Republican and Democratic parties.

The township of Leicester had to select five Justices of the Peace, for which positions there were five Republican candidates and no others. Two vacancies for 'Listers', 'responsible for appraising all personal and real property which is subject to taxation at its fair market value [on which valuations] Property taxes are based',[2] attracted one non-partisan nominee each. There was also one non-partisan candidate to be elected as the Director of Otter Valley School (see table 1.2).

Altogether our Leicester voter was asked to cast her vote up to twenty times. The ballot included the names of seventy-three candidates, representing a total of ten political parties together with a couple of independents. Voters unhappy with any candidate may legitimately write in the name of an alternative. Candidates have on occasion campaigned for and won election on the write-in vote. The formidable ballot has the potential to imbue the voter with a genuine sense of drama and occasion. Our Leicester voter entered the polling booth and drew the curtain behind her, to face all these choices for all these offices. Had she used all her votes, at no point abstaining or using the write-in option, she could have combined her choices of government personnel in 14,112,000 different ways.

This is not an untypical ballot in its presentation of a variety of options at many levels of government. Different states and communities adopt a variety of approaches to the ballot, so that there will be further options available to voters elsewhere in the USA. On election day 1996, the voters of Montgomery County, Maryland, were faced with a ballot that included elections for seven judges to three different state courts. Members of the Board of Education were elected through the same ballot. But most space on this ballot was taken up by six questions on proposed amendments to the Maryland State Constitution, two questions on amendments to the Montgomery County Charter proposed by the county council and three questions on amendments to the Montgomery County Charter proposed by public petition. Each question presented the voter with a paragraph describing the proposed amendment, then requested a vote for or against the proposal (see table 1.3).

In Falmouth, Massachusetts, on 5 November 1996, voters could help choose the President and Vice-President, a Senator and Representative to the US Congress, and a state Senator and state Representative. Candidates appeared for the Workers World Party and the Conservative Party, as well as for many of the parties already mentioned. In addition, there were races for Governor's Council, and for the Barnstaple County offices of Register of Probate, County Commissioner and Assembly Delegate. Along with all voters in Massachusetts, they could vote on Question 1, 'A Law Proposed by Initiative Petition'. This was effectively a referendum on a publicly

Table 1.2. *Candidates and offices as listed on the Leicester, Vermont, ballot, 5 November 1996*

Office/candidate	Party
For President and Vice-President of the United States (vote once):	
Harry Browne and Jo Jorgensen	Libertarian
Bill Clinton and Al Gore	Democratic
Bob Dole and Jack Kemp	Republican
John Hagelin and Mike Tompkins	Natural Law
James E. Harris and Laura Garza	Socialist Workers
Mary Cal Hollis and Eric Chester	Liberty Union
Ralph Nader and Anne R. Goeke	Green Coalition
Dennis Peron and Arlin D. Troutt, Jr	Grassroots
Ross Perot and Pat Choate	Reform
Howard Phillips and Albion Knight, Jr	US Taxpayers
For Representative to Congress (vote for one)	
Peter Diamondstone	Liberty Union
Norio Kushi	Natural Law
Jack Long	Democratic
Robert Melamede	Vermont Grassroots
Thomas J. Morse	Libertarian
Bernie Sanders	Independent
Susan W. Sweetser	Republican
For Governor (vote for one)	
Bill Brunelle	Natural Law
Howard Dean	Democratic
John L. Gropper	Republican
Mary Alice Herbert	Liberty Union
Dennis 'Denny' Lane	Vermont Grassroots
Neil Randall	Libertarian
August St John	Independent
For Lieutenant Governor (vote for one)	
Dona Bate	Natural Law
John Carroll	Republican
Bill Coleman	Vermont Grassroots
Murray Ngoima	Liberty Union
Douglas Racine	Democratic
For State Treasurer (vote for one)	
Dylan Bate	Natural Law
Randy Bushey	Vermont Grassroots
James H. Douglas	Republican/Democratic
Richard F. Gottlieb	Liberty Union

table continues opposite

Office/candidate	Party
For Secretary of State (vote for one)	
Christopher D. Costanzo	Libertarian
Jimmy 'Iceman' De Pierro	Vermont Grassroots
Jerry Levy	Liberty Union
Jim Milne	Republican/Democratic
Toni M. Wilder	Natural Law
For Auditor of Accounts (vote for one)	
David A. Baker	Libertarian
Charlet Ann Davenport	Liberty Union
Edward Flanagan	Democratic
William C. McLaud	Natural Law
Gerry Morrissey	Republican
James L. Sweet	Vermont Grassroots
For Attorney General (vote for one)	
Jeffrey L. Amestoy	Republican/Democratic
Aaron Diamondstone	Liberty Union
Henry H. Huston, Jr	Natural Law
Tom Kingston	Vermont Grassroots
For State Senator (vote for not more than two)	
Joe Acinapura	Republican
Tom Bahre	Republican
Gerry Cossens	Democratic
Elizabeth M. Ready	Democratic
For State Representative (vote for one)	
Diane G. Drake	Republican
Patricia 'Patty' Smith	Democratic
For High Bailiff (vote for one)	
Robert E. Grant	Republican/Democratic
For Justice of the Peace (vote for no more than five)	
Thomas Barker	Republican
Diane Benware	Republican
Penny Eastman	Republican
Bonnie L. Johnson	Republican
Peggy Oliver	Republican
For Lister, term expires March 1997 (vote for one)	
Gary Pfenning	
For Lister, term expires March 1998 (vote for one)	
Harold A. Smith	
For Otter Valley School Director, term expires March 1999 (vote for one)	
Sid S. Glassner	

Table 1.3. *Abbreviated version of the Montgomery County, Maryland, ballot,*
5 November 1996

President and Vice-President of the United States (vote for no more than one pair):
[Six choices listed on the ballot]

Representative in Congress, Eighth Congressional District (vote for no more than one):
[Two candidates listed on the ballot]

Judge of the Circuit Court, Sixth Judicial Circuit (vote for no more than five):
[Five candidates listed]

Judge, Court of Appeals, Seventh Appellate Circuit (vote yes or no for each Judge):
Irma S. Raker   For continuance in office
                                                                Yes/No

Judge, Court of Special Appeals, At Large (vote yes or no for each Judge):
Ellen L. Hollander   For continuance in office
                                                                Yes/No

Board of Education, At Large (vote for no more than one):
[Two candidates listed]

Board of Education, District 2 (vote for no more than one):
[Two candidates listed]

Board of Education, District 4 (vote for no more than one):
[One candidate listed]

Question No. 1 Constitutional Amendment
Judicial Disabilities' Commission
Altering the membership of the Commission on Judicial Disabilities; establishing
requirements for public members of the Commission; limiting the number of terms
that Commission members may serve; providing that the Commission reflect the
racial, gender, and geographic diversity of Maryland; and establishing certain
provisions of limited duration to implement these Constitutional Amendments.
                                                                For/Against
Question No. 2 Constitutional Amendment
Executive Department appointments
[Paragraph of description]   For/Against

Question No. 3 Constitutional Amendment
Dual offices – exceptions
[Paragraph of description]   For/Against

---

table continues opposite

Question No. 4 Constitutional Amendment
Charter counties – elections
[Paragraph of description]   For/Against

Question No. 5 Constitutional Amendment
Harford County – elections
[Paragraph of description]   For/Against

Question No. 6 Constitutional Amendment
Harford County – property
[Paragraph of description]   For/Against

Question A Charter Amendment by Act of County Council
Ethics code
Amend Section 410 and repeal Section 411 of the County Charter to retain the
requirement that the Council adopt a code of ethics applicable to all County
officers and employees and explicitly require that the code must include certain
provisions; to delete from the Charter certain specific restrictions on the activities
of County employees and contractors; and to expressly allow the Council by law to
create an ethics commission to enforce and interpret the law and to allow the
commission to retain its own legal counsel without the approval of the County
Attorney.   For/Against

Question B Charter Amendment by Act of County Council
Biennial capital improvements program
[Paragraph of description]   For/Against

Question C Charter Amendment by Petition
Property tax – relation to income tax
Amend Section 305 of the County Charter to:
– require the County Council, when setting rates for the real property tax, to
reduce the total revenue produced by that tax in any fiscal year by the amount of
revenue received during the preceding fiscal year from the county income tax
which exceeds the revenue that would have been received if the income tax rate
were 56 per cent of the state income tax; and
– allow property and income tax rate restrictions to be overridden only in an
emergency by a unanimous vote of all Council members.
                                                                              For/Against

Question D Charter Amendment by Petition
Budget adoption – majority vote
[Paragraph of description]   For/Against

Question E Charter Amendment by Petition
Fire and Rescue Department
[Paragraph of description]   For/Against

initiated proposal that would oblige the state government to change the law – in this case to ban the use of leg traps in hunting. The Falmouth ballot also contained an advisory question. In this case the public decision on the issue would not automatically lead to changes in the law but, clearly, elected officials would consider the public mood in subsequent legislative decision-making. In Boston, Massachusetts, a further binding referendum, on 'A Law Providing for the Election by the People of Members of the School Committee', appeared on the ballot. The Secretary of State in Massachusetts presented the information in Spanish as well as English, reflecting the existence of a substantial ethnic mix.

The voter might well choose to vote by following a particular party line. In New York, however, candidates may be endorsed by more than one political party, and one finds that the minority Liberal and Conservative parties on occasion split their support between Democrats and Republicans standing for different offices. In such cases it is clear that the party line may not have been a foolproof method of ensuring the accurate representation of one's opinion. Political parties issue sample ballots with their recommendations imprinted. But many races are non-partisan, and parties may not have a position on some questions. In Montgomery County, Maryland, the Republican Party in 1996 offered guidance on exactly half the voting opportunities on the ballot. A further option, available in Nevada and being promoted in other states, is to register a protest against all the candidates by voting for 'none of the above'.

If faced with the type of voting machine commonly used in the United States, our voter could pick her way through the listed offices, press down the little levers beside the candidates of her choice and, when confident she had chosen to her satisfaction, finish with a flourish by swinging across the face of the ballot the large lever that both records her votes and automatically pulls open the booth's curtain, making way for the next voter. If presented with the more modern and increasingly popular punch-card style of ballot, she might cheerfully stamp holes in the cards to express her approval of candidates and positions. In a very small community, or if using an absentee ballot, she might be indicating her votes in time-honoured style, with crosses in the appropriate spaces on the fairly large ballot sheets that are needed to list all the alternatives.

On the other hand, she might feel confused by the range of choice, stressed by the detail of the proposals, bemused by the expected range of knowledge, deterred by the election technology and, fatigued by the size of the ballot, fail to complete it for any other than the major election races. The electoral system which faces our voter combines the political dreams of the nation's Founding Fathers with the pragmatism of history and the reality of contemporary life. Its roots lie in the Constitution.

The constitutional background

The Founding Fathers who met in Philadelphia in 1787 to consider the future form of their national government did not face the problem of constructing a constitution for the United States totally devoid of precedent. The United States lays claim to have the first written national constitution in the world, but these men were well aware of the power and value of earlier political documents. They accepted the merits of English common law and they examined England's history and practice in order to adopt valuable elements of its political forms and traditions. In addition, they could learn from the colonial experience.

The early settlement of the colonies was accomplished by a wide variety of wealthy entrepreneurs, religious dissidents, ex-convicts and others driven to life overseas by personal needs. These groups sometimes established their own dominance over particular areas, or on occasion learned to live and mix with other settlers. Nominally under the control of London, the distance and slow communications meant that these colonies developed to some extent independently of its influence. At times this freedom of development had unfortunate consequences. Abuse of power by landowners and their representatives was well known, religious intolerance divided some communities and the southern colonies gradually enshrined African-American slavery in their statutes.

At the same time there was experimentation with new political forms. On 30 July 1619 the Virginia Assembly, made up of twenty-two burgesses, was elected to represent the local planters in meetings with the English-appointed Governor and his council. All men aged seventeen and over were eligible to vote. Just over a year later, on 11 November 1620, the *Mayflower* anchored in the harbour of Cape Cod, off what is now Provincetown, Massachusetts. Having strayed off course during a rough transatlantic passage, these colonists were well outside any legal jurisdiction. In response to this legal limbo, the forty-one men on board agreed and signed the Mayflower Compact, a document outlining a form of majoritarian government to be used until a permanent structure could be created. Between this time and the War of Independence there were to be many more examples of at least partial self-determination. The colonies developed their own forms of administration, consultative assemblies were set up, the law was enforced with the help of local juries, ideas of civil rights were discussed and, to a limited degree, implemented. These were not exercises in radical democracy by modern standards, but they set the direction towards a time when political structures could be organised by citizens of their own free will, through the election of their peers to direct policy, under the guidance of a form enshrined in the laws.[3]

The issue of representation was central in the manoeuvring that preceded the American War of Independence. 'No Taxation Without Representation'

shifted from political demand to battle cry in the face of English intract-
ability. The Declaration of Independence proclaimed that all men were
'created equal', that they had certain 'unalienable Rights' and that 'whenever any Form of Government becomes destructive of these ends, it is the
Right of the People to alter or abolish it...'. The early attempt at national
government, the Articles of Confederation (1781), proved too weak and
the members of the Philadelphia Convention undertook the daunting task
of designing a system that responded to both the radical demands of the
revolution and the pragmatic operation of a nation state. The delegates
debated all aspects of government institutions, appointment and election.
Terms of office, forms of election and the extent of, and limits on, popular
control, all formed part of this debate.

While there appeared to be a general feeling that the new American
government should be held accountable for its actions, and should govern
only with the consent of the governed, there were broad differences as
to how this accountability should be effected and by whom. In the event,
a relatively small percentage of the population had the vote immediately
after the adoption of the Constitution. 'Negroes were excluded, women
were denied the right to vote. In order to vote in some states, a person
had to own a certain amount of property, or pay a certain amount of
taxes. A few states even had religious tests.'[4] The legal bedrock of these
limitations was gradually eroded by changes in the laws and the Constitution over the next two centuries.

To the Founding Fathers of 1787, even an electorate limited to qualified
white males seemed pretty broad, and the proponents of this degree of
democratic involvement clashed with those who feared 'the mob'.
Compromise resulted in a national election system where only US Representatives were elected directly 'every second Year by the People' (Article
1, Section 2, Clause 1). US Senators were to be chosen for their six-year
terms 'from each State, chosen by the Legislature thereof' (Article 1,
Section 3, Clause 1), with one-third of Senate members coming up for
election every two years. The President and Vice-President were given four-
year terms, and were further isolated from direct public control by the
invention of an Electoral College which was given the responsibility for
choosing the nation's executive officers. The members of this College were
in turn to be chosen in a manner prescribed by the state legislatures,
thereby creating a kind of 'three-tier democracy' that remains a com-
plicating factor today in spite of subsequent changes in practice.

The qualifications needed by citizens in order to vote were set by the
individual states, although Congress has retained the right to pass laws
regulating the conduct of federal elections, and over time there has been
a move towards more uniform qualifications for voting. The different terms
of office and the staggering of elections meant that the government would
be receiving regular indications of public, or at least state legislative,

opinion. But radical response to swings of public mood would be moderated by the fact that at no time would all national government politicians face election simultaneously.

These constitutional mechanisms form the basis of the rights of the contemporary US electorate. Nevertheless, there have been many changes since the Constitution was ratified. Organisational changes to do with elections and office-holding have prompted four amendments to the Constitution. The clumsy operation of the presidential election process in 1800 led to a redesign instituted in 1804 by the Twelfth Amendment. The Twentieth Amendment, ratified in 1933, moved the starting dates for presidential and congressional terms of office to the January following the elections. The Twenty-Second Amendment (1951) limited Presidents to two elected terms of office and the Twenty-Fifth (1967) attempts to deal with the problem of succession and transfer of authority in the executive branch.

A further seven Amendments are wholly or partly concerned with the extension and protection of the right to vote. The Fourteenth and Fifteenth, passed in the aftermath of the Civil War, contain an inclusive definition of American citizenship ('all persons born or naturalized in the United States') and guarantee the right to vote regardless of 'race, color, or previous condition of servitude'. In 1913 the Seventeenth Amendment introduced the direct election of US Senators throughout the nation, and the Nineteenth (1920) extended the vote to all American women. Direct election of Senators was already operating in practice, and women were already voting in some states, but these practices were not confirmed and protected nationally until enshrined in the US Constitution. Washington, DC, is a federal district, not part of any state, which left all of this city's electorate in the anomalous position of being unable to vote in any elections to the federal government until the Twenty-Third Amendment (1961) gave Washington, DC, a place in the presidential Electoral College. The Twenty-Fourth Amendment (1964) abolished the imposition of a poll tax as a qualification for voting, thereby eliminating one of the few remaining vestiges of state attempts to reduce the electoral participation of African-American and poor people. The most recent extension of the franchise was by the Twenty-Sixth Amendment (1971), which reduced the voting age to eighteen years.

The role of the Supreme Court

While the US Constitution provides the foundation of electoral practice, the laws passed by the US Congress and by the states build the structures on that foundation. Regulation of voter eligibility, voter registration and the management of elections are the subjects of a network of federal and state laws that has built up over the years, with the result that there are no simple definitions of electoral practice that apply to all states. This complex web of laws nevertheless has to fall within the parameters set by the Constitution. Occasionally there is dispute as to the appropriateness of these laws, and over time major cases resulting from these disputes have reached the Supreme Court. This is the country's senior court of law, with the power to declare laws unconstitutional, if this is appropriate, in deciding cases coming to the Court. The Court's power to interpret has at times given it the chance to remould the constitutional foundation of electoral practice. Some decisions crucial to the definition of the electorate have been taken by the Supreme Court, among the most important being cases involving the rights of African-American voters, and the principle of each person's vote carrying equal weight.

That votes had become unequal in value was mainly a consequence of the changing distribution of America's population. The nation's cities grew, but in many states the legislatures failed to redraw constituency boundaries either for state or for congressional districts. Over time this gave minority rural representatives disproportionate power in states and in Congress, a power that they were unwilling to give up. Meanwhile, urban areas, with their relative concentration of poor, ethnic and African-American voters, were growing in population, but being awarded no more legislative representation, thereby having their votes devalued. In the landmark case of *Colegrove* v. *Green* (1946), the Court decided that it did not have the authority to rule, even though Illinois, the state being challenged, had some constituencies with over eight times the population of others.

This appeared to commit the Court to a 'hands-off' stance, until 1960, when, in the case of *Gomillion* v. *Lightfoot*, the state of Alabama had to defend its decision to redraw the boundaries of the city of Tuskegee from a simple quadrilateral to a strange twenty-eight-sided figure in a clear attempt to counter the voting power of that city's black voters. This racist gerrymander was tackled by the Court and helped supply a precedent for dealing with other cases involving the unfair distribution of electoral representation. Subsequently, in the case of *Baker* v. *Carr* (1962), the Court invalidated Tennessee legislative apportionment that had been unchanged for sixty years; in *Wesberry* v. *Sanders* (1964) it invalidated the unequal apportionment of Georgia's congressional districts; and in *Reynolds* v. *Sims* (1964) 'Earl Warren announced that population had to be the starting point and the controlling criterion for judgement in legislative apportionment cases'.[5] These decisions extrapolated from the US Constitution the principle that constituencies should be designed to give the members of a state's electorate votes of equal value. They also had a direct effect in that the institutional reforms prompted by these decisions altered immediately the potential power of different groups of voters.

The right of African-Americans to vote appeared to be clearly established by the Fifteenth Amendment, but this met resistance in some states, where legislatures used their ability to set the criteria for voting in such a way as to undermine the participation of blacks. The infamous 'grandfather clause' of Oklahoma discriminated against those whose ancestors had not been eligible to vote in 1866, a clear attack on the descendants of unenfranchised blacks. This law was declared unconstitutional in the case of *Guinn* v. *United States* (1915), but was rejigged by the Oklahoma legislature and did not finally bite the dust until *Lane* v. *Wilson* (1939). In other states African-Americans were excluded from the primary elections in which party organisations often used to nominate their candidates prior to general election campaigns, on the grounds that party primaries were private affairs, not subject to the strictures of the Fifteenth Amendment. This was especially disadvantageous to blacks in those southern states that had become effectively dominated by the Democratic Party and where, therefore, victory in the primary was tantamount to victory in the general election. In the 1944 case of *Smith* v. *Allwright*, the Court dismissed the 'private club' argument, declaring that in running a primary the political parties were effectively 'an agency of the state' and therefore subject to the Amendment. Two years later, in 1946, the *Williams* v. *Mississippi* decision declared invalid a Mississippi state constitutional amendment requiring as a condition for voter registration the ability to interpret any article of the US Constitution, when it was clearly shown that in practice this rule had been used to give local poll officials the opportunity to disfranchise black citizens.

While these decisions removed some barriers to those systematically excluded from voting, they still left to the individual the responsibility to claim a place on the electoral roll. Given the strength of anti-black feeling in many areas, it was often an act of bravery to insist on these rights, and many exclusionary practices continued even after having been declared illegal. In 1964, for example, the official Mississippi delegation to the Democratic national convention was still an all-white body. It was not until the civil rights movement rose to challenge such discrimination, and the federal government began to pass civil rights legislation beginning with the Civil Rights Act of 1957, and most particularly the Voting Rights Act of 1965, that African-American electoral participation began to increase substantially.

As is clear from these examples, the constitutional and legal environment of elections in the United States does not stand still. Nor can the Court always be seen as adapting the Constitution towards the progressive demands of modern times. Supreme Court Justices look towards legal principle for the bases of their decisions, and at times they find these principles unchanging even in the face of societal change. The moves outlined above often reversed or adapted different, sometimes diametrically opposed, positions taken in response to earlier cases. In turn these precedents, while not being overruled, have been adapted and refined by later decisions. Nevertheless, through these decisions, and many others, there has been a gradual shift over time towards broader representation in the US electoral system and, with a few limited exceptions, for example convicted felons, any citizen of the United States over the age of eighteen years is now eligible to register and vote.

The ballot: visualising the political system

As eligibility to vote has expanded to its present breadth the number of offices to vote for has also grown. In 1996 the US Bureau of the Census, reporting the latest reliable figures, counted 85,006 different government units in the United States, encompassing between them over half a million elected positions and employing almost nineteen million people.[6] By far the majority of these governments operate at the local level, including 3,043 counties with almost 60,000 elected officials, 35,935 townships, towns and municipalities with over a quarter of a million elected officials, 14,422 school districts with around 90,000 elected officials and 31,555 special districts with a further 84,000 elected officials, responsible for other services, such as public housing, irrigation and power. The rest of the elective offices are at state level (for example governors, state legislatures) and to the federal government in Washington, DC. Terms of office and election dates vary, and within the different states and communities of the United States different patterns of government units are in place, but over time any US citizen can expect to have the opportunity to vote on ballots listing offices from a wide variety of these categories. For example, the average central city dweller is subject to the US national government, the relevant state government and, in addition, an average of over four layers of local government.[7] The appearance of so many offices, representing all levels of government, makes the ballot an illustration of some major elements of the American political system.

The federal system comes alive on the ballot, with each level of government being represented. Opportunities to vote for President and Vice-President, US Senator and US Representative express in action the individual voter's contribution to forming the US national government. The voter participates in state government when voting for Governor, Lieutenant Governor and any of a number of other state-wide offices that may appear, as well as for members of the state legislative body. Local government participation may be requested in the form of a contest for mayor of a city, executive of a county, membership of a school board or of some general municipal government. The constitutional structure of the nation and of its constituent states determines the make-up of the ballot.

The casting of one person's vote may be a modest and limited contribution to the edifice of American government, but the commitment of the nation to this form of participatory democracy has developed to give the voter a wide variety of opportunities to make that contribution. This, in turn, encapsulates another feature of the American political system, a pluralism afforded by the provision of multiple points of access.

Different communities and different interests of voters may be more completely represented at different levels. Issues may belong clearly to the local, state or national sphere, and voters have the opportunity to express an opinion at each of these levels as long as there is a candidate expressing relevant policy stances. The variety of this access is reflected not just in its expression of the levels of the US federal system, but also in the way it feeds into another prized feature of US constitutionalism, separation of powers, and its complement, checks and balances. At the national level this input is most clearly seen in the simultaneous votes being cast for the President and Vice-President, or executive branch, and for the US Congress, or legislative branch. Appointment to the federal judiciary is by executive nomination overseen by the legislature, but at lower levels that third branch of government is also subject to election, and state and county judgeships appear on the ballot alongside state and local executive and legislative offices. Categorical distinctions are not always crystal clear, especially at the state and local level, where there has been a twentieth-century explosion in the number of elective offices, as well as the addition of referendums and similar questions, but the general point is indisputable, that the ballot represents every citizen's entry into every branch of government at every level of the US political system.

The citizen's involvement, by voting, in the institutional structure and the internal tensions of US government is not merely theoretical. The evolution of the ballot into a patchwork of discrete opportunities to make political choices enables the application of discrete criteria by a citizen when making each separate choice. With such a variety of opportunities to participate, and with those opportunities already categorised by level and function, the voter's decision-making can be similarly refined. Judgements applied to the different offices can take into account the varied character of the problems faced by incumbents of the different offices and of the range of policy alternatives available to the holder of that particular office. The individual voter is encouraged by this system to consider separately national, state and local problems, in effect, to subdivide his or her citizenship, responding as a citizen of nation, state or local community where relevant.

Citizens aware of the countervailing powers of levels and branches of government can make their choices with this in mind. While one voter may be entirely satisfied to simplify the necessary decision, for example by following loyally the lead of party affiliation, others may subscribe to the opinion that competing institutions are better occupied by officeholders from different, competing parties. In some cases partisan direction may not always be available and, even where it is, many voters may feel they wish to compare qualities of the candidates for the relevant offices apart from the signal of party identification. The citizen of nation, state and community is likely to want at each level an elected representative committed to the vigorous promotion of the interests of that constituency. But the interests of these constituencies may not always coincide, so it is not altogether surprising if any one voter's chosen officeholders do not necessarily always see eye to eye. The differentiation within the ballot is inviting the voter to respond in a way that may, from the individual citizen's point of view, form a coherent pattern of choices, but is at the same time atomising the single citizen according to the different constituencies to which he or she belongs in casting each individual vote for each individual office.

In 1992, the citizens of Gloucester, Massachusetts – almost 18,000 of whom were registered voters in November of that year – took part in elections for national, state and local offices. At the national level, these were for President of the United States and for the US Representative from the sixth district of Massachusetts; at the state level, for Governor's Councillor from the fifth district, state Senator from the first Essex and Middlesex district, and for state Representative from the fifth Essex district; and, at the local level, for Sheriff for Essex County and County Commissioners for Essex County. The victors in each of these elections were, respectively, President Bill Clinton (Democrat), Representative Peter Torkildsen (Republican), Governor's Councillor Edward Carrol (Democrat), state Senator Robert Buell (Republican), state Representative Bruce Tarr (Republican), Sheriff Charles Reardon (Democrat), and County Commissioners Marguerite Kane and John O'Brien (Democrat). In each case, Gloucester formed part of a larger constituency (e.g. county, US congressional district, state), but with the exception only of the state Senate race, a majority of voters in Gloucester cast their votes for the eventual winner.

There were undoubtedly voters who followed a consistent party line on these offices, but there were enough voters who disregarded such affiliations to help return a varied body of candidates to office. While the community opted for a wholly Democratic team at the county level, at the state level they returned a mixed team, electing Republicans as state Representative and state Senator, but a Democrat as Governor's Councillor. At the national level, Gloucester voted for a Republican to be sent to the US House of Representatives in Washington while supporting the Democratic ticket for the White House. Clearly, some Gloucester voters chose quite consciously to be represented at different levels and in different offices by candidates of different political stripes.

Certainly, those elected, when engaged in subsequent political discourse and conflict, would be tempted to claim that they had a mandate for their particular point of view from constituencies that included the people of

Gloucester, and this may reflect the voters taking an atomised view – judging the attractions of the candidates with respect to their relative positions in the federal system. Hence, Representative Torkildsen might claim electoral support to challenge President Clinton's policies from the same electorate that Clinton would feel formed a justifiable part of his own mandate. The voter becomes atomised in retrospect, claimed by office-holders at all levels as having endorsed various, often competing, policy positions. This interpretation of the ballot by the winners, for the purposes of governing, consistently reasserts the living nature of federalism, separation of powers and checks and balances in contemporary US government, and gives voters a role in keeping those constitutional concepts alive.[8]

Promoting the voting

'Don't Just Not Vote. Do Something About It' proclaimed the headline over a letter published in the *New York Times* in the run-up to the 1996 election. Robert Richie of the Center for Voting and Democracy in Washington, DC, accused legislators of drawing constituency boundaries to reduce the number of competitive elections, but hoped this would be 'a clarion call to reformers'.[9] In the period immediately prior to a major election in the United States, a substantial number of messages appear in the media that are not associated with any particular candidate but are apparently designed to encourage electoral participation. Sometimes these messages are issue oriented, for example the campaign sponsored by the National Rifle Association under the slogan '"Never Disarm" – Register to Vote – Your Gun Rights Depend On It!' Other 'get out the vote' (GOTV) messages come from business organisations and unions. For example, Members Only, makers of clothing and other products, combined with the League of Women Voters to produce a video featuring images of Hitler, Stalin and an absurdly posturing Mussolini, finishing with the slogan, 'There is no excuse not to vote'.

In music and video stores shortly before the 1996 election, customers found a leaflet saying, 'You don't let other people choose your music. Why let them choose your future?', with information on the issues of the moment and on the positions of five presidential candidates. This was sponsored by 'Rock the Vote', a non-partisan organisation aiming to increase political participation among the young, and by 'Choose or Lose '96', a political awareness campaign of Music Television (MTV). MTV's full-page advertisement in the *New York Times* on 1 November 1996 claimed that the channel had 'devoted more than 100 hours in air time worth over $72 million to election issues ... [and] the Choose or Lose Bus has toured some 80,000 miles through 48 states, bringing more than 100 live events'; now it said, 'Make Sure You Vote'. Telephone numbers and

Internet addresses for more information were given. MTV continued this effort with hours of 'Votefest' programming during the weekend before the 1996 elections. But there has been non-partisan GOTV advertising aimed at young voters before. The Hawaii state elections office used a controversial scene in 1990 featuring a couple in bed. 'Tim, wait,' says the woman, 'before we go any further, I have to ask. Are you registered to vote?' Furthermore, each major network plugs the election for civic and audience purposes. 'Be sure to vote and watch your vote count on NBC News,' intones Tom Brokaw. And now there is more competition for the election audience. 'Cable Brings It To You,' says a CNN promotion.[10]

Cartoonists joined in. In 1994, in Johnny Hart's *BC* strip a sleepy electorate remained in their caves, put off by a rainy day, leaving one voter to 'Vote me a pay raise and a pension, while I'm at it.' *The Wizard of Id* (Parker and Hart) was gloomily confident that 'You can fool ... all of the people some of the time ... and that ... is usually enough to get you re-elected.' The October/November 1996 issue of *Washington Woman* used its cover and a major article to promote voting. Printed over a stylised US flag, the cover said: 'Most politicians still think women should be seen and not heard. In the last election fifty-four million women agreed. On November 5th, don't be one of the women no one hears.' *Veterans' Vision*, a publication of the Center for Homeless Veterans, devoted most of an issue to 'Campaign '96', endorsing some candidates, but carrying articles from all sides and encouraging readers to 'Please register to vote today so your voice can be heard!'

Officially sponsored voter education takes many forms. A 1996 photograph in the *Des Moines Register* shows the launch of a 'Head for the Polls' effort, with Tom Parkins, the incumbent auditor for Polk County, Iowa, presenting voter registration cards to Mr and Mrs Potato Head, full-sized, costumed versions of the traditional children's toys. The press release extended the tortured metaphor, claiming that 'All "eyes" were on a unique voting campaign with fresh "a-peel" today.'[11] Also in Iowa, somewhat more conventionally, the Black Hawk–Bremer Counties League of Women Voters attracted the financial backing of locally based business to produce a 1996 voters' guide in the form of a handy leaflet that listed all elected officials, and gave information on voter eligibility, registration and absentee voting. Around election time the state secretary of Iowa organises 'Kids' Caucus', a mock election process that is used in schools to increase knowledge of that process as well as of the issues and candidates.

A 'Vote: Be Counted' game, designed to stimulate elaborate role-playing exercises in schools and colleges, is also used by the Elections Division of the Massachusetts State Secretary's Department as part of its voter education process. The support materials give examples where a very small number of votes made a difference, for example, 'Marcus Monton was elected Governor of Massachusetts in 1839 by one vote out of 102,066 cast.' The examples are not confined to voting at general elections: 'One vote saved President Andrew Johnson from impeachment conviction in 1868' refers to a vote among US Senators; 'One vote kept Aaron Burr from becoming President' refers to the very unusual presidential election of 1800 when the final decision was made in the House of Representatives; and 'One vote elected Rutherford B. Hayes to the presidency' refers to the fairly dubious behaviour of the Electoral College in the 1876 presidential election. Nor are the examples confined to America. 'One vote made Adolph Hitler head of the Nazi Party (1923)', we are told, and 'One vote caused Charles I to be executed (1649)'. These examples are given greater local and contemporary relevance by the inclusion of a list of recent Massachusetts state and local races that have been close. The research is not always perfect – one example claiming that John F. Kennedy would have lost the 1960 presidential election had he failed to get his very slim majority in Illinois is wrong – but the point is clear: voting is a civic responsibility not to be avoided lightly. The attempt by this state elections office to reach out to its electorate has included printing some materials in Spanish, French, Portuguese, Greek, Italian, Polish and Chinese, and is just one of the more vigorous official pursuits of the received wisdom that the vote is an important instrument.

There have been vigorous statements of the power of the vote during America's history, especially during the debates over the extension of the franchise. Women's suffrage faced considerable opposition even though small numbers of women have been able to vote almost throughout US history. After independence, New Jersey used property as a qualification for the franchise, and land-owning women as well as men had the vote, but the state's women were excluded in 1807 as part of the move towards universal male suffrage. In 1838 Kentucky ended the period of total exclusion of women from the electorate when it extended strictly limited voting rights to widows. Some other communities followed suit during the rest of the nineteenth century, and the younger states entering the union were more likely to have extended the franchise than the older states. The willingness of a few territories and states to enfranchise women even on a limited basis gave an extra opportunity to organise against politicians who had not endorsed the passage of a constitutional amendment to establish women's suffrage nationwide. By 1916 both Democratic and Republican parties had declared in favour of women voting.[12] More recently, a witness before the US Senate Judiciary Committee opposed the reduction of the voting age to eighteen with the statement 'Callow youth is to be accorded the same privilege as grownups, at a time when we already have a mass of ignorance in the voting area.' In each of these cases the discussion was focused on the entry of a large group of voters to the electorate, and the fears expressed revolved around the expectation that this group would alter the balance of election decisions.

'From the vote, from participation in the elections, flow all other rights....
That was the key to opening the door ... in education, housing, jobs and
public accommodation,'[13] said Robert F. Kennedy, in 1964, about the
campaign to register African-American voters throughout the southern
states. And the opposition felt much the same: 'If you went into Mississippi
and talked about voter registration they're going to hit you on the side
of the head and that's about as direct as you can get.'[14] Perhaps the most
dramatic evidence for this opinion has been provided by the way that
increased African-American electoral participation has altered the political
status quo at local, state and national levels. For example, the racist
operation of the electoral system in Mississippi in 1964 meant that only
6.7 per cent of eligible African-Americans were registered to vote, whereas
in 1988 African-American presidential candidate Jesse Jackson won the
Democratic Party presidential primary in that state, backed by 45 per cent
of the 359,417 Democrats who voted. Jackson progressed no further than
the primaries in his quest for the presidency, and has made no attempt
on the presidency since, but the context of African-American office-holding
has changed dramatically, and by the 1990s there were more than 12,000
African-American officeholders in the United States.

While it is reasonable to expect the participation of a group, particularly
a group united by common concerns, to have a real effect on political
outcomes, it is less convincing to argue that the participation of any
individual will really make very much difference. The very fine works of
Anthony Downs and Mancur Olson have pinpointed some of the difficulties
inherent in trying to make any such argument.[15] If a person needs to feel
that her or his vote may truly make a difference in order to be convinced
to take part, then there is little chance that the argument can stand up.
It is immensely rare that elections are genuinely close enough that a single
vote, or even a handful of votes, would change the result – the hardworking
staff of the Massachusetts Elections Division had to include examples from
far and wide to develop its list. The costs to an individual in becoming
knowledgeable enough to make a choice, especially given the range of
choices offered on the US ballot, are real. There must even be a tangible,
albeit extremely small, risk in casting a vote. After all, the enthusiastic
voter might be hit by a car while crossing the road to the polling station.

Any individual's experience of elections is likely to indicate that one can
always rely on others in the electorate to do the job, producing a result
that would be most unlikely to have been altered by dint of one person's
involvement. Nevertheless, 'According to most democratic theory, widespread participation means responsive government, maximally gratifying
policies, and, consequently, greatest citizen contentment.... the exhortation
to vote is heard at every election time; people are expected to exercise the
franchise as part of a solemn duty.'[16] Certainly, a generalised belief among
voters that 'widespread participation' has these qualities could be expected

to encourage voting, since turnout itself would thereby be valued as politically efficacious, and it has been hypothesised that this and complementary motivations help account for voters' wish to be involved. At the same time, it is valuable for a regime to be able to present itself as providing responsive policy to a contented citizenry, and insofar as a broadly used franchise is considered synonymous with these qualities so turnout may become identified as an indicator of these other characteristics. The logic of the connection may not always be convincing, but its public relations value is undeniable. Witness, for example, the enthusiasm in pre-glasnost Warsaw Pact nations for elections with extremely high turnouts to justify regimes that tumbled just as soon as the election process was prized from the grip of the East European Communist Parties. A similarly corrupt enthusiasm might be indicated by the election result in West Virginia in 1888, when the reported turnout was 12,000 voters higher than the total eligible to vote.[17] Given that the received wisdoms of Western democracy and the legitimisation of political regimes mutually reinforce the idea that a substantial electoral turnout is to be valued, it is not surprising that a considerable effort is expended by government, private and civic organisations in the United States to promote the vote.

The League of Women Voters, formed in the year that the Constitution was amended to include female suffrage, has become a major non-partisan actor in many areas of electoral and policy research, and is a significant contributor to the GOTV effort, undertaking a wide variety of tasks aimed at getting non-partisan and practical information to the electorate. The League co-operates with many newspapers to produce free newspaper supplements immediately prior to elections containing a wide range of voter information. A supplement of this kind produced by the *Boston Globe* in 1996 filled twenty-four tabloid pages. General information included the news that 'polls may open as early as 5.45 a.m., but no later than 7 a.m., under the election laws of Massachusetts – all polls must close at 8 p.m.' Eligibility, registration and voting requirements were given, along with a four-page chart and two-page map from which the voter could establish her voting districts. The referendums were explained. Biographies of all candidates on the ballot for President and Vice-President were followed by twelve pages in which a total of 312 candidates for US Senate, US House of Representatives and the state legislature were given the chance to answer standard sets of questions.

Similar voters' guides appear throughout the United States, and not just in presidential election years. The *Boston Globe* also devoted twenty-four pages to this exercise in the 1994 mid-term elections. In that same year in California the *San Jose Mercury News* published a twenty-eight-page voters' guide, including information on candidates and issues, plus instructions (with pictures) on how to assemble the Pollstar portable voting booths used in Santa Clara County. Similar guides are sometimes delivered to households by state and local government elections offices. The official California ballot pamphlet for the 1994 general elections ran to ninety-six pages. In the same year the New Mexico official election guide, featuring no candidates for office, but simply covering those constitutional amendments and bond issues that were to appear on the ballot for public decision, filled fifty-six pages, the entire text being printed in Spanish and English. How successful are these efforts in producing a participatory election?

Tallying the turnout

Over ninety-six million members of the American voting-age population voted in the November 1996 presidential election, and a slightly larger number did not vote. The turnout expressed as a percentage of the voting age population was around 49 per cent, the lowest percentage at a presidential election since 1924. It was a dramatic fall from 1992, when over 104 million, or about 55 per cent, of the voting-age population had taken part, and was only the second time since 1944 that the actual number of voters declined from one presidential election to the next.[18] The 1996 election was only the latest in a series of low turnouts. From 1920, the first election allowing nationwide female suffrage, to 1960, turnout increased fairly steadily, from 42.5 per cent to 62.8 per cent. Since then it declined steadily until 1988, rising in 1992 before falling to a modern low in 1996. Mid-term elections, those held for Congress halfway through a presidential term, suffer even lower turnout. The whole of the US House of Representatives, and one-third of the Senate, are on the ballot at mid-term, but voter participation has averaged around 35 per cent since the mid-1970s.[19] In the years before 1960, factors such as the initial diffidence of some women in exercising the franchise and severe discrimination against African-Americans and others in some parts of the country could help account for low turnout, but one would expect these to have less influence in more recent years. An international survey of turnout percentages covering national elections in the 1980s placed the United States twenty-third on a list of twenty-four nations. Only in Switzerland, where central government has a modest role compared with the cantons, was turnout for national elections lower. France, one place above the United States, had a turnout more than 13 per cent higher, and turnout in most nations was between 20 and 40 per cent higher than in the United States.[20]

There is some controversy over the way these figures are calculated. One main caution is that American turnout is calculated on the basis of all the voting-age population, including non-US citizens, felons and other groups who are in any case not entitled to vote. Writing in the wake of the 1988 election, two leading CBS News analysts claimed that the supposed 'voting-age population' includes 'a lot of people – as much as ten percent – who are plainly not eligible to vote'.[21] Even if this claim is not exaggerated, it does not mean that US figures have to be corrected by 10 per cent for comparative purposes, since all nations have a certain margin of error in their electoral figures, as for example when the electoral register fails to keep up with population mobility. However, the inclusion in the United States of non-citizens and other ineligible groups is unusual and does lead to inaccurate comparative figures for US voter turnout. Nevertheless, even allowing for this, the United States would remain firmly fixed next to the bottom of the international table.

Another reason for the low US voter turnout figure has been that country's distinctive approach to voter registration. While the public ideology favours participation, the political apparatus has not always made it as easy as it might. According to Ruy Teixeira, 'The state, instead of keeping regulations and inconveniences to a minimum and actively assisting citizens in registration, makes qualifying to vote a time-consuming process contingent on individual effort.'[22] On the whole, the regulation of voter registration is left to the states, and state requirements vary a good deal. With the exception of North Dakota, which does not have voter registration, each state has a different voter registration form. In the 1990s there has been a conscious effort by national government to ease voter registration. One element of this was the production of a voter registration booklet to allow any US citizen the opportunity to register to vote. The booklet contained thirteen pages of instructions and two pull-out application forms. However, on page 1 it is pointed out that:

> Illinois and Mississippi will accept this form as a registration to vote only for federal offices (President, US Senator, and US Representative) unless their State laws are changed. New Hampshire town and city clerks will accept this application only as a request for their own absentee voter mail-in registration form. Vermont will accept this application only as a request for the State's mail-in voter registration form. Wyoming by law, cannot accept this form unless State law is changed.

Some states insist on having the applicant's social security number, some request it. Other states want to know instead a state driving licence number, or a date of birth, or nothing at all. The applicant may indicate a choice of political party, but while some states require an answer to allow participation in the political party's candidate selection processes, others do not. States vary according to whether they would like to know the race or ethnic group of applicants, or whether they would prefer not to. In Hawaii 'any descendent of aboriginal peoples inhabiting the Hawaiian islands which exercised sovereignty and subsisted in the Hawaiian islands in 1778, and which peoples thereafter have continued to reside in Hawaii' may indicate on the registration form that they are 'Hawaiian', and thereby gain the right to vote in the Office of Hawaiian Affairs elections. All states require applicants to hold US citizenship to register for the vote, but state residency requirements vary, as do the deadlines for acceptance of the application.

Voters in Mississippi must 'not have been convicted of murder, rape, bribery, theft, arson, obtaining money or goods under false pretense, perjury, forgery, embezzlement, or bigamy', while Massachusetts limits itself to prohibiting those who 'have been convicted of corrupt practices in respect to elections', Indiana to those 'currently in jail for a criminal conviction' and Georgia to those 'serving a sentence for having been convicted of a felony'. Most states, though not all, prohibit those they define as mentally incompetent, and these definitions too vary from state to state. In Wisconsin registrants must 'not make or benefit from a bet or wager depending on the result of an election'. Florida requires applicants to swear or affirm to 'protect and defend the Constitution of the United States and Constitution of the State of Florida' and Alabama requires further that the oath-takers 'disavow any belief or affiliation with any group which advocates the overthrow of the governments of the US or the State of Alabama by unlawful means' and concludes, in spite of the US Constitution's First Amendment separation of church and state, 'so help me God'.

The attempt to provide a nationally usable voter registration form was one consequence of the National Voter Registration Act (NVRA). Passed in 1993, to take effect in January 1995, this act was commonly known as the 'motor voter law', as, in an attempt to broaden voter registration, it obliged states to offer voter registration at state government facilities well used by the public, such as drivers' licence and motor vehicle offices. Some states responded more enthusiastically than others. Massachusetts, no more than averagely flexible on voter registration in the past, in 1996 advertised that applicants could register to vote:

> at any registration event, at any local election office, and at the following state agency offices: Registry of Motor Vehicles, Food Stamp Program, AFDC, WIC, Medical Assistance Program, Commission for the Blind, Commission for the Deaf and Hard of Hearing, Massachusetts Rehabilitation Commission, Department of Mental Health, Department of Mental Retardation, Secretary of the Commonwealth, or by mail.

Forty-three states implemented the NVRA, though some only after testing the law in the courts. In South Dakota, with no registration requirements, and in Maine, Minnesota and Wisconsin, with established laws to allow registration on election day, the new requirements did not apply. Idaho, New Hampshire and Wyoming, all states with turnout rates already higher than the national average, opted to introduce election day registration as an alternative to the NVRA.[23] Predictions as to the effect of the easing of voter registration have been varied. Turnout has been consistently higher in those states with easier registration requirements than in others, and research conducted at the University of Michigan's Institute for Social Research suggested 'that modified registration laws could increase overall voter turnout by about 9 per cent',[24] a figure roughly in line with a number of similar recent studies. Given that the 1996 turnout was the lowest in decades, it has to be asked whether these reforms had no impact or whether turnout would have been even lower without them.

Certainly voter registration was increased. According to the *Boston Globe*, 'about 20 million Americans will have registered or updated addresses'. The *Washington Post* reported that nine million of these were new voters, while other estimates were higher than this. Maryland electoral rolls increased by 413,000, or 19 per cent. In Virginia the rolls increased by 288,500, or 10 per cent, in spite of state-level resistance that delayed the implementation of the law until March 1996. The growth in registration would have been more had it not been for the resistance of states like Virginia, Illinois, Pennsylvania and California. But once the court battles were over and the NVRA was in place, groups such as the League of Women Voters, the National Association for the Advancement of Colored People, the Christian Coalition, and a range of other national and local groups worked hard within their target communities to register voters under the newly liberalised rules.[25]

Initial results suggest that turnout in 1996 would have dropped a little further without these voter registration modifications, but that this positive effect was very small. Those states with election day registration maintained a higher turnout than others, but the new states in this category did not notably improve their turnout rates. States with simpler registration rules had already shown better turnout rates and this effect continued, but did not accelerate, in 1996. Low voter turnout does not distribute evenly across the population. Findings by the Michigan researchers confirm that 'Blacks, Hispanics, and the poor are most likely to be discouraged', a conclusion that convinces some analysts that US elections may give a skewed impression of national opinion. It was expected that easier voter registration might improve turnout especially among these low voting groups and among young voters, another low turnout community. Early study suggests that any gains in turnout that were made were not among these groups, but instead among that part of the electorate already turning out in force, marginally increasing the bias already evident among participating voters.

These results appear disappointing, but they indicate that while reducing the barriers to registration may be a necessary condition for improving voter turnout, this alone is not sufficient to promote dramatic change. The Voting Rights Act of 1965 confronted the problem of racial discrimination and low turnout in the South, and both registration and turnout have increased dramatically in the states affected. Some citizens grasped their new voting opportunities quickly, but for many the removal of barriers alone did not overcome the previously enforced habit of non-voting. Only as it became clear that opportunities had improved permanently, and as citizens matured who had not felt the inhibiting restrictions of earlier years, did this growth in electoral participation put southern turnout within reasonable distance of the national average. This growth in turnout was felt as much in the 1970s and 1980s as it was in the immediate aftermath of the Voting Rights Act. It may be that the effect of the NVRA will also build over the long term.

The changes introduced since 1995 will take time to sink in. Initially those most likely to take advantage of the relaxed rules are probably the small number of motivated voters who previously slipped off the rolls for some reason, such as a change of address near to election time. Voting is habit-forming, and those newly on the rolls have no history of taking part. As voting opportunities repeat, a proportion of those finding themselves on the rolls may begin to take part – they will now be able to get involved even if they decide to do so very shortly before the election. Nonetheless, while lower barriers to registration reduce the limits on voting, they do not by themselves increase the motivation to vote. In a system that makes registration difficult, those motivated to register are very likely also to be motivated to vote, and on occasion much has been made of the high percentage of US registered voters who turn out, a figure given as 86.8 per cent by Nelson Polsby and Aaron Wildavsky. But with registration increased by the NVRA reforms, 1996 turnout as a proportion of registrants fell to about 66 per cent.[26]

Turnout has declined over the past thirty years in both 'easy' and 'difficult' registration states. Teixeira points out that changes in any of a range of socio-political characteristics (for example the citizen's feelings of partisanship and political efficacy) or social structural characteristics (such as education, age, residential mobility, race) might be expected to have some impact on electoral activity. He finds, for example, that while levels of education and economic achievement in the US population have improved considerably since 1960, and might be expected to prompt greater political involvement, feelings of partisanship and political efficacy declined over this period, more than counteracting the effects of socio-economic improvements on voting turnout. In 1996 low turnout may have been a reflection on the limited contextual incentives to vote. Professor Bill Adams argued that there was a lack of big Senate races, for example in California, to drive western voters to the polls, and the consistent Clinton lead in the polls provided no gripping finish to push voters to the voting booth.[27]

Designing effective policy to attack the low and declining voter turnout depends on developing an accurate explanatory model of the problem. Virtually all analysts consider that low registration has historically been part of the problem, although they would disagree as to how much positive effort to register voters should be made by the state, or how much should be expected from the efforts of registration drives sponsored by other organisations. Alterations of possible influencing factors other than these is more contentious and more complex, but some critics claim that even the most straightforward institutional stimuli to voting turnout are being purposely avoided. Certainly, the latest changes have not gone so far as Frances Fox Piven and Richard Cloward advocate: 'to win the principle that government has an affirmative obligation to register all eligible voters', a move that Piven and Cloward feel is hostage to political vested interests. After all, it is the unchanged electorate which put incumbents in office.[28]

On the other hand, America is a country where 'individualism' is as much part of the ideology as the drive to widespread political participation, and by no means everyone would agree that the state should remove from individuals the obligation to be independently responsible for their own electoral registration. One argument that has sometimes been put is that low turnout indicates a broad degree of satisfaction with the status quo, but the groups in which non-voting is most evident, for example the poor, the unemployed, racial and ethnic minorities, are not the groups one might expect to be most satisfied, so this explanation can at most be of very limited value. Another argument that has slipped a little out of fashion is that, given the concentration of low turnout among the poor, the less well educated and others from the nation's 'underclass', it might be a virtue of the US political system that it leaves them undisturbed, rather than stimulates them to act in what might be unpredictable and untoward ways.[29] More recently has emerged the idea that declining turnout is part of a general disengagement with institutions on the part of American voters, as Robert Putnam puts it, an increasing tendency for US citizens to like 'bowling alone'. While Putnam's critics argue that there is still plenty of evidence that Americans are enthusiastic joiners and networkers, those giving credence to his thesis feel that civic engagement is increasingly defined in personal terms and direct involvement in small, tangible projects, rather than activism within major party and campaign organisations.[30]

It is not clear what would be the partisan result of increased turnout. Given evidence that existing voters from those groups among whom turnout is low generally favour the Democratic Party, one might expect higher turnout to alter election results in that party's direction. But one cannot be sure. While some groups are disproportionately non-voters, there are substantial numbers of non-voters in almost all groups. Surveys of all non-voters have suggested that, in general, they hold political opinions very similar to those of the voting population, and that a broad-based increase in turnout would not therefore make much difference to the results. According to this argument, only an increase targeted on specific groups could be expected to make any difference at all. A 1996 poll by Northwestern University's Medill News Service may suggest a new way of identifying which group to target. Analysis of a survey of 1,000 non-voters led to their categorisation into five groups:

'doers' (29%)	well educated, informed, financially comfortable, see no need to vote;
'unplugged' (27%)	younger, less affluent, view government negatively, do not consider campaigns relate to them;
'irritables' (18%)	affluent, generally older, informed, but sceptical about politics;
'don't knows' (14%)	few political opinions, leave politics to others;
'alienated' (12%)	negative about politics, pay little attention to political news.[31]

The intriguing problem of pinpointing all the causes of low turnout remains. In the words of Teixeira:

at this point we do not know the precise origins of this political problem, though the hypothesised causes are many: the influence of the media and polls; the role of television advertising; the decline of the political parties; the conduct of campaigns; the quality of candidates; generalised disconnection from politics; decreased sense of civic duty; the erosion of traditional forms of political consciousness.[32]

Certainly, targeted mobilisation of voters is significant. Robert A. Bernstein and Edward Packard, building on the work of Steven Rosenstone and John Hansen, conclude that 'contact from mobilizers is nearly the most important single variable in determining electoral participation. Only level of education outstrips it in importance, and that is only because education has so many strong indirect effects on participation.'[33]

This has particular relevance as contemporary political campaigns move away from direct contact and towards greater reliance on mass communications. And it may be that turnout matters for US society regardless of the potential effect on partisan results. Support for the regime must be maintained, and it may be that democracy needs not just to happen, but to be seen to happen. With turnout steadily falling, there must be the possibility that the disaffected could claim they were becoming rather less visible than they should be. Research by Wendy Rahn, John Brehm and Neil Carlson suggests that elections do stimulate national solidarity and trust in government among those who take part, and speculate on the positive political leverage that could be generated. 'If we can improve our elections ... by, for example, increasing mobilization by the political parties and enticing quality candidates to run, such efforts may redound to civil society with higher levels of political efficacy, more trust in government, and greater social solidarity.'[34]

For now, the American electorate can be segmented into those more or less likely to vote, by all kinds of demographic factors, and according to their sense of involvement and political impact, or efficacy, and the ones most likely to turn out are now subjected to highly visible campaigns to attract their allegiance. The next chapter considers the historical development of those election campaigns in the United States.

Notes

1 Letter to the author from Lori M. Forrend, executive assistant to the Secretary of State of Vermont, 20 June 1997.

2 Letter from Forrend.

3 For a discussion of elections in the seventeenth and eighteenth centuries see Robert J. Dinkin, *Voting in Provincial America: A study of elections in the thirteen colonies, 1689–1776* (Westport, CT, Greenwood Press, 1977).

4 Edward F. Cooke, *A Detailed Analysis of the Constitution* (5th edn, revised, Totowa, NJ, Littlefield, Adams & Co., 1984), p. 17.

5 Richard Hodder-Williams, *The Politics of the US Supreme Court* (London, George Allen and Unwin, 1980), p. 152.

6 US Bureau of the Census, *Statistical Abstract of the United States: 1996* (116th edn, Washington, DC, 1996), pp. 295, 319.

7 See, for example, Philip Davies, *The Metropolitan Mosaic* (Durham, British Association for American Studies, 1980).

8 Election details for Gloucester are drawn from *Massachusetts Elections Statistics 1992* (Boston, MA, Office of the Massachusetts Secretary of State, n.d. [1993?]).

9 *New York Times*, 21 September 1996, p. 14.

10 'Hawaii ad touts horizontal voting', *Boston Sunday Globe*, 4 November 1990; the examples taken direct from campaign and election literature are from items in the personal collection of the author.

11 'Exactly as envisioned by the Founders', *Des Moines Register*, 9 February 1996, p. 2A.

12 R. Darcy, Susan Welch and Janet Clark, *Women, Elections and Representation* (2nd edn, Lincoln, NE, University of Nebraska Press, 1994), pp. 8–10; Hugh Brogan, *The Pelican History of the United States of America* (Harmondsworth, Penguin, 1985), p. 478.

13 Arthur M. Schlesinger, Jr, *Robert Kennedy and His Times* (New York, Ballantine, 1978), p. 312.

14 Quoted in Abigail M. Thernstrom, *Whose Votes Count?* (Cambridge, MA, Harvard University Press, 1987), p. 14.

15 Anthony Downs, *An Economic Theory of Democracy* (New York, Harper, 1957); Mancur Olson, *The Logic of Collective Action* (Cambridge, MA, Harvard University Press, 1965). See also Brian Barry, *Sociologists, Economists and*

Democracy (London, Collier-Macmillan, 1970) for a challenging critique of the literature. 'Solving the puzzle of rational participation', a paper by Sidney Verba, Kay Schlozman and Henry Brady presented to the 1997 Annual Conference of the American Political Science Association, argues that rational actor theory is useful in analysing how participants act, but not in predicting what motivates them to take part.

16 Dean Jaros, *Socialization to Politics* (New York, Praeger, 1973), p. 42–3.

17 Everett Carll Ladd, *The American Polity* (New York, W. W. Norton, 1985), p. 398.

18 Figures from *New York Times* election coverage, 7 November 1996; Gerald Pomper, *The Election of 1992* (Chatham, NJ, Chatham House, 1993), p. 137; Gerald Pomper, *The Election of 1996* (Chatham, NJ, Chatham House, 1997), p. 178; Carolyn Smith (ed.), *The '88 Vote – ABC News* (New York, Capital Cities/ABC Inc., n.d. [1989?]).

19 Eliza Newlin Carney, 'Opting out of politics', *National Journal*, vol. 30, no. 3, 17 January 1998, p. 108.

20 Nelson W. Polsby and Aaron Wildavsky, *Presidential Elections* (9th edn, Chatham, NJ, Chatham House, 1995), p. 4.

21 Warren J. Mitofsky and Martin Plissner, 'Low voter turnout? Don't believe it', *New York Times*, 10 November 1988, p. A31.

22 Ruy A. Teixeira, *Why Americans Don't Vote: Turnout decline in the United States, 1960–1984* (New York, Greenwood Press, 1987).

23 For detailed argument and early research results on the recent changes in voter registration I am indebted especially to two papers delivered at the 1997 Annual Conference of the American Political Science Association: Craig Leonard Brians, 'Voter turnout and election day registration', and Michael D. Martinez and David Hill, 'Did motor voter work?'.

24 Steven J. Rosenstone, quoted in *ISR Newsletter*, vol. 16, no. 1, 1988, p. 3.

25 'Interest groups moving to register new voters', *Boston Globe*, 1 October 1996, p. A28; Ellen Nakashima and Kathryn Wexler, 'Some area officials don't think motor-voters will jam polls', *Washington Post*, 29 October 1996, p. B1.

26 Nelson W. Polsby and Aaron Wildavsky, *Presidential Elections* (9th edn, Chatham, NJ, Chatham House, 1995), p. 8. The 1996 turnout is estimated by the author from figures given in Martinez and Hill, 'Did motor voter work?, and in Pomper, *Election of 1996*.

27 Quoted in Bob Minzesheimer, 'Turnout takes a record downturn', *USA Today*, 7 November 1996, p. 3A.

28 Frances Fox Piven and Richard A. Cloward, 'Government statistics and conflicting explanations of non-voting', *PS: Political Science and Politics*, vol. 22, no. 3, September 1989, pp. 580–8.

29 See, for example, William Kornhauser, *The Politics of Mass Society* (London, Routledge and Kegan Paul, 1960).

30 Carney, 'Opting out', pp. 110–11.

31 Quoted in Minzesheimer, 'Turnout takes a record downturn'.

32 Ruy A. Teixeira, 'Registration and turnout', *Public Opinion*, January/February 1989, pp. 12–13, 56–8.

33 Robert A. Bernstein and Edward Packard, 'Paths to participation in electoral politics: the importance of mobilization', paper presented to the 1997 Annual

Conference of the American Political Science Association, p. 21. See also Steven Rosenstone and John Mark Hansen, *Mobilization, Participation and Democracy in America* (New York, Macmillan, 1993).

34   Wendy M. Rahn, John Brehm and Neil Carlson, 'National elections as institutions for generating social capital', paper presented to the 1997 Annual Conference of the American Political Science Association, pp. 30–1.

2

Changing technology and
the art of campaign advertising

The early campaigns: from restraint to enthusiasm

The earliest presidential elections featured little public campaigning and virtually no direct candidate involvement. In fact, in 1789 the whole affair was more of a coronation or nationalist celebration than anything else. But, like most celebrations, it spawned a number of souvenirs. Metal tokens celebrating political events and celebrities had been in vogue in England for some time. It may have been these that gave the button makers of New York and Connecticut the idea to commemorate the first presidency on their wares. In any case, it is interesting to note that these first American political tokens were produced by entrepreneurs for commercial reasons, exploiting the cheap technology of the day. Among the 1789 buttons that have survived are one example bearing the inscription 'Long Live the President', another showing an endless chain of thirteen links, each bearing the initials of one of the thirteen original states, surrounding the initials of George Washington, and a third design, reputed to have been worn by Washington at his inauguration, picturing an eagle and a sunrise.[1]

Framed glass brooches containing a cameo or an engraved picture of the President were also popular in the late eighteenth and early nineteenth century. Many of these were imported – for example France was a source for glass brooches – as the technology of North America did not always match the public's appetite for, and the salesmen's ability to merchandise, political souvenirs. While these trinkets appear generally to have been souvenirs, rather than declarations of support, there was some evidence of the use of ephemeral emblems for political purposes. By 1796, for example, some Federalists had adopted a black cockade in their hats as a patriotic emblem, while the Democratic-Republicans countered with the colours of the French tricolour. Similarly, in one campaign the supporters of George Clinton sported bucktails in their hats as a declaration of their stance.

A number of political 'issue-based' items were being imported from England. Perhaps the most lasting image was that of the chained slave printed on to a Wedgwood plate in the 1790s and featuring the slogan 'Am I Not a Man and a Brother'.[2] The image was reused in many forms, and by the 1830s had been adapted to 'Am I Not a Woman and a Sister' on antislavery medallions then in circulation. Nevertheless, the production of campaign ephemera was still neither widespread nor large-scale. At the presidential level the striking of celebratory medals for the inauguration was fairly regular, but in 1820 the campaign was so quiet, and the re-election of James Monroe so unsurprising, that not even an inaugural commemorative medal was struck.

This presidential campaign calm was disrupted in 1824. Four candidates shared the Electoral College votes, no-one gained an overall majority, and the constitutional provision throwing the election into the US House of Representatives was triggered. The House took thirty-six ballots before making John Quincy Adams, who had received the second largest number of Electoral College votes, the next President. This Adams victory had depended on the co-operation of erstwhile supporters of another candidate, Henry Clay. Once in office Adams appointed Clay to the prize position of Secretary of State. Andrew Jackson, who had led in the initial count of Electoral College votes, was enraged by his failure to gain the presidency and by the Adams/Clay co-operation that had apparently taken the post away from him. Crying 'bargain and corruption', Jackson supporters readied themselves to challenge again in 1828.[3]

Adams' inauguration was commemorated by a medal, but 1824 may also have been the first presidential election when medals advertising support for a candidate were worn during the campaign. According to one account:

> By Resolution of Congress on February 27, 1815, General Andrew Jackson was awarded a gold medal for the 'brave and successful repulse' of British troops who had attacked New Orleans the month before. The execution of the medal was long delayed because of Jackson's tardiness in providing the engraver with a suitable portrait, but by the time Jackson became an announced candidate for President of the United States in the election of 1824, the medal had been executed and was formally presented to him by President Monroe on March 16, 1824. Shortly thereafter Jackson's supporters were sporting from their lapels small brass discs which bore the name and likeness of the General and a reference to his victory at New Orleans.[4]

Some scholars are leery of the claim that these were the first 'official campaign buttons', noting that contemporary newspaper reports and advertisements suggest that any such medallion production was likely to have been small-scale and still of the souvenir trade variety.[5] However, there is no disagreement that the bitter rematch election of 1828 stimulated the production of a substantial variety of medals and other trinkets aimed directly at the supporting camps of the major candidates. From now on the wearing of some token bearing the image of a candidate, and/or some apposite slogan, became a regular form of campaign 'advertising'.

Jackson's vigorous pursuit of the White House, the equally vigorous opposition he provoked, and the considerable extension of the franchise in presidential elections changed the face of campaigning. One review of surviving 1828 materials claims that 'Jackson's matrimonial affairs, his profanity, his gamecocks and race horses, his duels and brawls, were the subject of merciless campaign propaganda. Handbills with pictures of coffins of soldiers executed by Jackson were distributed by Clay.' Jackson's supporters replied in kind, painting John Quincy Adams as an unsavoury character who had installed 'a piece of gambling furniture' (a billiard table) in the White House, while portraying Jackson as the 'Protector and Defender of Beauty'. Adams himself (son of earlier President John Adams) was accused of being a 'Monarchist – John the Second', whose re-election would sound the death knell of Congress. And literature was even distributed attacking Mrs Adams.[6]

Before the next presidential election, in 1832, another lasting innovation was introduced by the Anti-Masonic Party, when it held the first national political party convention.[7] The other parties followed suit, and the national convention became a tangible focus of candidate and party activities in presidential election years. Jackson's support for the introduction of the convention was probably influenced by the belief that he could exercise his authority more easily over party followers at a national convention than would have been feasible through a more federalised system. In the event, Jackson was able to ensure the selection of his favourite and heir apparent, Martin Van Buren, as the Democratic presidential candidate in 1836.

Electioneering materials rapidly developed into varied forms, using the available technologies and reflecting the varied artisan skills of the nation to spread the candidates' words and images. As well as paper handbills and street banners, less expected sites were used for representations of the candidates' names or pictures, such as glass flasks and tin lanterns. The lithographed silk was a common campaign favourite at this time. Short ribbons of silk had printed upon them pictures and messages idolising or attacking candidates, and stating positions. Often used as bookmarks, they could also be pinned to a lapel. Household trinkets and small sewing boxes featured candidates' portraits, an interesting element of the campaign given that women would not be allowed to vote nationwide in presidential elections for almost a century. Some campaign symbols did not rely at all on what the salesmen had to offer; for example 'Old Hickory' Jackson's supporters carried hickory poles, and in 1832 Henry Clay's followers responded by brandishing poles of ash. Much of the material was produced by entrepreneurs, and some was home made, but campaign organisations were increasingly involved, and had to find the cash to underwrite the advertising effort. It is reported for example that 'Clay's managers issued a great deal of campaign literature which was largely financed by the United States Bank.'[8]

The opposition to 'King Andrew' coalesced into the Whig Party, and one striking effect of the increasingly partisan response was that pro- and anti-Jackson materials also appeared in the congressional elections of the Jacksonian period. The negative materials could be very brutal, parodying Jackson's egocentric presidential style, and featuring jackass and hog devices. The startled former President James Monroe wrote, 'We have to be a little vulgar in these Jackson times.' Looking back to the campaign of 1836, Senator Thomas Hart Benton spoke of the many medals and tokens that were created as 'pieces struck in imitation of gold and silver coins – made ridiculous by figures and devices, usually the whole hog, and inscribed with taunting and reproachful expressions. Immense sums were expended in these derisory manufactures, extensively carried on and universally distributed; ... and intended to act on the thoughtless and ignorant through appeals to their eyes and passions.'[9]

The nineteenth-century expansion of campaigning

The intervention of a newspaper helped step up the temperature in the 1840 campaign. The partisan editor of the *Baltimore Republican* lampooned Whig candidate William Henry Harrison, saying 'Give him a barrel of hard cider and a pension of two thousand a year, and ... he will sit the remainder of his days in a log cabin.' This contempt for simple pleasures and the hard life was unwelcome in the West, and gave the Whigs their slogan and symbols, especially when a genuine log cabin could be fabricated for candidate Harrison (he owned one, and his parents may have lived in one temporarily while their house was being built, but it was not his birth place, nor had it ever been his residence). The log cabin and hard cider motifs became a powerful complement to the campaign slogan linking alliteratively Harrison's battlefield success and his vice-presidential candidate's name, 'Tippecanoe and Tyler Too'. This campaign also featured the extraordinary fashion of rolling huge balls from one city to another, but this was just part of the panoply of parades, ersatz log cabins and innovative campaign trinkets used by Whig supporters. Harrison even dared to make a few overtly political speeches to his supporters, but candidates were still expected to stand clear of the razzmatazz of the campaign, and this innovation did not catch on generally for another generation or more. Meanwhile, Harrison's supporters could sing from the first printed political song sheets:

Let Van from his coolers of silver drink wine
And lounge on his cushioned settee,
Our man on his buckeye bench can recline,
Content with hard cider is he.

The Democrats attempted to undermine the Harrison appeal by revealing that he lived in a 'magnificent frame house surrounded with a princely estate', but they could not stop the ball rolling once they themselves had started it, and the defeated Martin Van Buren was left commenting that he had been 'lied down, drunk down, and sung down'. So put out was the Democratic Party that its 1844 platform contained a plank condemning 'factitious symbols' and 'displays and appeals insulting to the judgment, and subversive of the intellect of the people'. This does not seem to have had much practical effect, as political movements, campaigners and entrepreneurs continued to produce a wide variety of candidate- and issue-related novelties, though sometimes supply outstripped demand, and campaign materials have a very short shelf-life. One example was an advertisement on 10 November 1852 by a Hartford, Connecticut, store for a new medallion honouring the recently deceased Daniel Webster. A footnote referring to the general election that had taken place days before added 'Pierce and Scott selling at a discount'.[10]

In the mid-nineteenth century, the political entrepreneurs had plenty of candidates, parties and controversy to fire an interest in their goods. Dealers gave the profiles on their medallions a heroic quality, they created silks commenting on the issues of the day and they printed candidates' names directly on to the US flag to exploit nationalistic feelings. Sometimes, eager to get into the market, errors were made – for example Lincoln became 'Abram' on at least one piece – but still their simple tokens had a huge attraction. Materials were not always simple and direct, and posters sometimes carried a large amount of detailed material, but campaign medals and badges were becoming immensely popular. An article in *Harper's Weekly Magazine* in 1896 recalled the favours of 1860:

> The campaign medals of the times gone by were made in the shape of the coins of that time. They bore the busts of candidates and inscriptions. The customary way of displaying them was to bore a hole in them, through which a ribbon was run and attached to the wearer's coat or waistcoat, as he preferred. The medals were made from dies, like the coin of the country. They were made of different materials – the brighter ones of block tin; the darker ones of brass and copper.
>
> Occasionally a nickel-plated one would be found, and once in a while one of silver would make its appearance. The medals were turned out, ... by manufacturers, for sale to enthusiastic partisans. In the Lincoln campaign the manufacturers all made money because of so many candidates in the field and because of the intense interest. Nearly everybody wore a medal then and there was no difficulty in telling how a man stood.

The nearest approach to a button in the Lincoln campaign was the first appearance of a medal-like affair, which held in place tin-type photographs of the candidates. Lincoln, and his running mate, Hannibal Hamlin, were pictured on opposite sides of the republican medal. The names under the pictures were all the reading matter on the medals. The pictures were good. The same manufacturer also turned out these things for the other parties, presenting Douglas and Johnson, Breckinridge and Lane and Bell and Everett.[11]

A candidate's humble origins had been a reasonable campaign asset at least since 1828, and the 'log cabin' campaign of 1840 had given such an approach its generic motif. Lincoln's campaign could trade on his apparently humble origins, and Kathleen Hall Jamieson gives a fine example of image advertising in a heightened atmosphere when she describes the carrying into the 1860 Republican convention of a banner saying:

ABRAHAM LINCOLN
The Rail Candidate
For President in 1860

Then, seemingly referring to the poles supporting the banner, it went on:

Two rails from a lot of 3,000 made in 1830 by John Hanks and Abe Lincoln, whose father was the first pioneer of Macon County.[12]

Also in 1860, the street parades that had sometimes taken place in association with campaigns took a new turn with the formation of young supporters of Lincoln into 'Wideawake' clubs. The members gave a distinctive character to the processions, carrying torches, metal canisters containing fuel, with a lighted wick, and adopting a uniform of oil cloth capes and hats, perhaps also designed to protect them from the weather and any kerosene dripping from the torches. The Douglas campaign countered with its own uniformed paraders, dressed in orange and called, for their hero, the 'Little Giants'.[13] These torch-lit parades were a feature of campaigning through the rest of the nineteenth century. By 1876 the torch-light processions were such a fixture (and presumably so spectacular) that the Old Colony Railroad advertised an extra train, and cheap evening excursion rates, into Boston for a Hayes and Wheeler gathering. Torches took many shapes, eagles figured prominently, axes were present at the 'rail splitter's' parades (although by the turn of the century Cary Nation's efforts on behalf of prohibition had given the hatchet a different symbolic role), and rooster-shaped torches probably indicated support for General Hancock. Top hats appeared as torches as well as headgear in the 1888 campaign of Benjamin Harrison, whose supporters sang:

Grandfather's hat fits Ben
He wears it with dignified grace

So rally again, we'll put uncle Ben,
Right back in his grandfather's place.[14]

This brought echoes of that vigorous 1840 campaign of grandfather William Henry Harrison across the generations.

Identification of a candidate with the flag was not new, but the Civil War gave Republicans a particular opportunity to appropriate the union flag, and later to add the special banner of the 'bloody shirt'. In 1868 Democratic candidate Horatio Seymour called the Republican campaign a cheap 'stars and stripes canvass' conducted by 'those who claim to have a patent right for all patriotism'. But the Grant campaign was also careful to brush up other parts of his image, with posters emphasising his credentials as a 'working man', and images of him as a 'family man', as well as a military man. During the last quarter of the nineteenth century a wide variety of functional and ornate items became decorated with campaign emblems. Oil lamps, cast iron household goods, Japanese lanterns, umbrellas, canes, toys, razors and household china are examples of the mass-produced items on the election market. Silks as promotional items were generally in decline, although elaborate celebratory issues were still made (they are occasionally still replicated, though today they might better be called 'polyesters'). Tammany Hall, the controlling and corrupt political machine of New York City, produced particularly ornate silks. A particular item lampooning the less savoury and more venal aspect of Tammany Hall, however, was a metal moneybox which featured a Tammany politician seated in a throne-like chair. When a coin was placed in his outstretched hand he bowed graciously and deposited the coin in his pocket. Decorated bandannas were popular, although they were generally designed to be displayed, poster-style, rather than to be worn, until Cleveland's 1888 running-mate Allen Thurman showed a taste for wearing a red bandanna, thereby making its imitation a token of campaign support.

National party conventions generated their own excitement, with the number of delegates steadily rising from about 300 to around 1,000 over the second half of the nineteenth century. In 1884 James G. Blaine was nominated after a demonstration delivered a huge plumed helmet to the rostrum, an action echoed in 1964 when an immense 'cowboy hat' was paraded through the Democratic convention by Lyndon Johnson's supporters. Blaine, though, had not always had his own way at conventions. At the 1876 Republican convention, 'Robert G. Ingersoll's flowery nomination speech of James G. Blaine as "The Plumed Knight" created such unbounded enthusiasm that the managers of other candidates cut off the gaslights in order to force a recess, stalling the bandwagon that threatened to start rolling.'[15]

Newspapers had been important from the very early days of democracy in America, and valuable information about campaign developments can be gleaned from them. In a significant challenge to the status quo in 1871, *Woodhull and Claflin's Weekly* announced a woman candidate for the presidency. Victoria Woodhull declared her candidacy under the banner of the Cosmo-Political, or Equal Rights Party, apparently with Frederick Douglass as her running-mate. This challenge to norms then current was not a campaign for election but was rather designed to create awareness of women's demands for the right to vote. Woodhull found herself and her newspaper subject to harassment, and she eventually migrated to the United Kingdom and became active in the British suffrage movement. In 1884 James G. Blaine suffered from the attentions of a hostile press. A week before the election a Blaine supporter had attacked the Democrats as the party of 'rum, Romanism, and rebellion' and the same evening Blaine attended a banquet at the exclusive restaurant Delmonico's. The New York Democratic press conflated the two, banner headlined the story, and Blaine lost New York by 1,149 votes, and the presidential election to Grover Cleveland. But whatever the impact of nineteenth-century news sheets in individual cases, the most lasting legacy may be that provided by Thomas Nast's newspaper and magazine cartoons which attached the donkey and the elephant permanently to the two major parties.

Entering the twentieth century

Candidates were finding that they had to learn to manage their contact with the press carefully. In 1900 potential candidate Admiral George Dewey suffered from his inexpert handling of the press. A publicly acclaimed hero of the Spanish–American War, he had resisted blandishments to run for President until, on the night of 3 April 1900, Horace Mocke of the *New York World* called in on the Admiral, and was told by Dewey:

> Yes, I have decided to become a candidate ... I said that nothing would induce me to be a candidate for the Presidency [but] I have had time to study the matter ... I am convinced that the office of the President is not such a very difficult one to fill, his duties being mainly to execute the laws of Congress ... I would execute the laws of Congress as faithfully as I have always executed the orders of my superiors.

These comments were naive, but apart from that, by giving the *World* an 'exclusive' on his announcement, Dewey alienated the other leading newspapers. Having been scooped, they treated his comments and his candidacy with scorn and amusement, leaving the Admiral high and dry.[16]

If the second half of the nineteenth century was primarily a time when existing campaign technology was adapted and elaborated, the end of the century nevertheless brought a dramatic shift of gear. Campaigning for President was becoming expensive, but under the direction of Mark Hanna the 1896 McKinley general election campaign spent $3,350,000 (not including pre-nomination costs). Not until 1920 did a Republican again spend as much, and no Democrat reached this total before 1928. Indeed, it is only since 1952 that both candidates have consistently and simultaneously spent more than the 1896 McKinley total. Hanna was dedicated to a McKinley victory years in advance of 1896. He had shepherded McKinley on speaking tours; he had opened a 'McKinley for President' office on the fringes of the 1892 Republican convention; he had opened a permanent national headquarters in Chicago in spring 1895; he had arranged a speakers' bureau of 1,400 supporters of the 'Grand Old Party' (GOP); and, according to one report, the campaign he managed is reputed to have mailed or given out 200,000,000 pieces of literature in English, German, French, Spanish, Italian, Norwegian, Swedish, Danish, Finnish and Hebrew.[17]

One of the main technological breakthroughs, though, was the invention of the celluloid-covered campaign button. The Whitehead and Hoag company of Newark, New Jersey, secured the patent in 1896 for a button using thin, clear celluloid as a covering for paper designs.[18] The paper and celluloid were heat-bonded and mounted on a metal disc, with a pin back fitted inside the curl of the button. There was no better time for such an invention. With Hanna driving McKinley's campaign, and the 'Boy Orator of the Platte', William Jennings Bryan, using the railway to conduct the first 'whistle stop' campaign by a major party candidate, enthusiasm for campaign favours was high, and buttons were very cheap. Each candidate inspired hundreds of designs. According to a contemporary writer in the London-published *Strand* magazine, 'Citizens march thousands strong in torchlight processions to the music of countless bands; gay banners, with portraits of the candidates and the catchwords of the campaign are hung across the principal streets; and campaign buttons adorn the lapels of voters all over the land.' The author goes on to do a creditable job of describing some of these and translating their slogans. He manages to decipher GOP, but another symbol clearly had not yet received universal recognition, and leads to the complaint, 'What the elephant represents no one except the designer can tell.'[19]

The turn-of-the-century campaigns may have produced the greatest variety of genuine campaign items of any period. Continuing the nineteenth-century tradition of campaign novelties, one has ceramics, glass flasks, street torches, sheet music, silks and badge-sized mechanical toys. Especially popular in 1896 were 'gold-bugs' and 'silver-bugs'. These metal beetles could be pinned on the lapel to display one's stance on fiscal policy. When the carapace was pressed, the hidden wings flipped open to display pictures of the relevant presidential and vice-presidential candidates. The

1896 election also produced large numbers of silks commemorating the visits of the scores of delegations who tripped to the McKinley 'front porch' in Canton, Ohio, encouraged by the cheap rail fares sponsored by the Republican-supporting railway companies.

The nineteenth and twentieth centuries met in another way in the 1896 campaign. McKinley maintained, at least superficially, the candidate's traditional distance from the campaign, while Bryan went out vigorously on the stump, travelling 18,000 miles, making 600 speeches to a reputed 5,000,000 listeners. The technology for such a campaign had been in place for some time, but tradition militated against such direct candidate involvement. General James Weaver, People's Party candidate in 1892, had stumped the West, but Bryan, representing both Populists and Democrats, became the first major party candidate to do so. Within a couple of elections candidates were as active as they had previously been detached, with the vigorous three-cornered fight of 1912 perhaps setting the seal on this development, although later candidates for election and re-election have been known to stick close to their porches, or, as the case may be, their Rose Gardens.

Candidates had only just begun to use the railroads to get to the electorate when twentieth-century technology began to make startlingly large leaps. Radio came into people's homes – three million radios by 1924, ten times that number a decade later. And film newsreels emerged at a very early stage in the movie business. Eugene Debs, conducting his 1920 Socialist Party campaign from what might be considered the generally disadvantageous position of being Convict No. 9853 in the Atlanta federal penitentiary, indicates some of the usefulness of media's modern technologies in his own description of the campaign. 'Men had been nominated for President who were born in log cabins to testify to their lowly origin, but never before had such a nomination been conferred upon an imprisoned convict. It was indeed an unprecedented distinction which had been bestowed upon me.' Going on to describe the visit to the prison of the Socialist Party committee of notification, he continues:

> The representatives of the press were in the prison at the time of the notification ceremonies and gave good accounts to their readers of the very unusual proceedings at the prison. The film photographers were also in eager evidence, as is their wont, to pictorialize the event, and a few days later the scenes were reproduced on screens in thousands of motion picture theatres throughout the country.[20]

Debs, who received almost a million votes in 1920, sounds fairly sanguine about the film coverage he received. The same could not be said of Upton Sinclair. This crusading author and ex-member of the Socialist Party joined the Democratic Party of Franklin Roosevelt, and in 1934 gained the Democratic nomination for Governor of California, standing on a radical policy platform. His own account of the campaign catalogues many scurrilous tactics to subvert his candidacy, including one telling use of the popular technology. Film shorts in the manner of newsreels were made portraying him as rich, possibly debauched and supported by a rabble of alien socialists. The motion picture industry, anxious to avoid a Sinclair governorship, pressured cinema managers to show these films as a condition of staying in business.[21]

According to the Nineteenth Amendment to the US Constitution, ratified shortly before the election of 1920, 'The right of the citizens of the United States to vote shall not be denied or abridged by the United States or by any State on account of sex.' While the suffrage movement had produced material for decades, this legitimisation of the female role was even celebrated in mainstream women's publications. An article in the November 1920 issue of *Needlecraft* began:

> Surely there could not be a more effective and pleasing way of 'showing one's colors' than to have a 'comfy' pillow – or more than one – bearing the emblem of the political party favored, and the names of the presidential candidates, displayed invitingly on hammock, or piazza-chair, or couch. Such a pillow is almost certain to open the door to a pleasant discussion of party issues with friend or neighbor, and if we keep our temper, as of course we will, and present our views convincingly, who can say how many votes we may be able to win for 'our side'! And when the campaign is over, and the ballots counted, and we are ready to shake hands all round and valiantly support the winning ticket, whichever it may be, our pillow will yet remain a souvenir of the memorable contest in which woman cast her maiden vote for President of the United States.

The magazine published three designs, Cox/Roosevelt, Harding/Coolidge, and one based on 'the high cost of living', an issue 'we are all vitally interested in'.[22]

The age of electronic media

Radio came into its own in 1924, when the proceedings of the conventions were first broadcast live. The Democrats can hardly have been helped by this technological innovation as they staggered through 103 ballots to nominate John C. Davis. For many listeners the abiding memory of that convention must have been the ringing southern tones of Alabama Governor Brandon opening the ballot each time with 'Alabama casts twenty-four votes for Oscar W. Underwood' as that state's commitment to a failed candidate remained unmoved.[23] There were also paid radio advertisements in 1924. Some $120,000 was spent by the Republicans and $40,000 by the Democrats. Four years later this had jumped to a combined party expenditure of around a million dollars. The introduction of bought time on the electronic mass media signalled the beginning of the rapid inflation in campaign costs that continues today.[24] In 1940 the first television coverage of the political conventions was broadcast to an audience of 100,000 viewers. In 1948 Truman and Dewey purchased television time to broadcast speeches. By 1952 television had reached one-third of US households, and the first spot (i.e. short) advertisements were shown. The two parties spent $3,500,000 on electronic media in that campaign, with the Republicans massively outspending the Democrats, as they had when radio had first been used.

Traditional items were not eclipsed even in those campaigns where the electronic media became the dominant political message carriers. Buttons, handbills, posters and the self-adhesive bumper sticker (introduced in 1952) continued, and a look back at surviving materials reminds one of the candidates (also-rans as well as the successful ones), the divisions within parties, the issues of the moment, the political development of ethnic and other identifiable subgroups, the activities and dreams of minor parties, and other features of the campaigns. Banners were still to be seen, and the more extraordinary souvenirs still had a market, but the button was the main token used. Because they were cheap to produce (even cheaper after the introduction of lithograph pinbacks in 1920) they could be given away, and this made them attractive to cause groups and to minor party candidates as well as to the main challengers. Virtually any contribution they elicited was profit. They came in many designs and were easy to wear. Small groups and minor candidates can still afford this type of advertising, and the early campaigns of major candidates can ill afford to ignore it. The 1940 election provoked one of the largest and most inventive battles of campaign buttons, as Wendell Willkie stormed through thirty-four states in fifty-one days, attacking the allegedly monarchical designs of Franklin Roosevelt – in fact, attacking everything about Roosevelt. 'No Third Term' was the politest of the button slogans. 'Dr. Jekyll From Hyde Park' was pretty direct, 'We Don't Want Eleanor Either' confirmed the central significance of the 'first family' and, with a frankness that might perhaps have been surprising at that time, 'No Man Can Be Good 3 Times' came close to the bone. '100,000,000 buttons can't be wrong,' said one Willkie button. But they were: he took only ten states. Then again there had actually only been thirty-three million buttons for Willkie, and twenty-one million for FDR.

With the growing role of the electronic media, however, major election artists emerged, especially in television. The start was simple, homely and jaunty. The spots reflected the jingles common in early television advertising. But it was not long before substantial dramatic steps were taken. The most famous US election advertisement of all time was probably that commissioned by the Doyle, Dane, Bernbach agency for the Johnson campaign in 1964, and made by Tony Schwartz, 'The daisy girl'. The little girl plucks the petals from a daisy, counting inaccurately. The frame freezes, an echo-enhanced male voice starts a countdown. The camera zooms in on the girl's iris. As the camera reaches the black depths of the little girl's eye, the countdown reaches zero, and an atomic mushroom cloud erupts. Johnson, in a text borrowed in part from W. H. Auden, intones 'We must live together, or we must die.... The stakes are too high for you to stay home.' The advertisement was shown only once or twice before Goldwater protests resulted in it being withdrawn. But it was discussed repeatedly on the news broadcasts and in the print media. It fed well on public concern that one of the candidates might make a trigger-happy President if elected.

The expenditure of cash and care on television advertising, as well as simultaneous attempts to control, or at least influence, news reporting, reached new heights in 1968, when Joe McGinnis wrote of *The Selling of the President*. But in that year, the $20 million or so spent by the Nixon campaign on television and radio was backed up by millions of other campaign favours, including buttons, bumper stickers, balloons, straw hats, jewellery and clothing. The Federal Election Campaign Act (FECA) of 1971 and its later amendments have put some limits on presidential campaign spending. This has had the effect of concentrating official campaign spending into television, as it offers a cost-effective way of promoting a candidate in the market. This bias had been so severe in 1976 that campaign buttons and other similar items were in short supply. However, there have been further developments. Loopholes have been found to allow considerable 'unofficial' spending in presidential election years, and a 1979 amendment to FECA allowed political party organisations at national and state level to produce vast amounts of 'traditional' electioneering materials outside the rigid financial limits imposed on the main candidate campaigns. However, their effectiveness in the age of the modern, media-oriented, computer-aided campaign is open to dispute. Congressional candidate and political scientist Sandy Maisel refers to 'the "memorabilia" of politics, the buttons, bumper stickers, road signs, handcards, gimmicks.... Almost everyone I have talked to feels that these items are necessary but not effective.' The explanation given for this apparent oxymoron is that 'Campaign workers want and need them. How else can they feel that they are not alone, that there are others who are working for their candidate as well?... The goal is to find the critically minimum amount needed, the amount that will make workers happy but will not cost too much.'[25]

Meanwhile, the design of television advertisements has progressed since their initial use in the 1950s.[26] Tony Schwartz, of 'The daisy girl', produced a Mondale advertisement to the tune of Crosby, Stills and Nash's 'Teach your children', and featuring film of repeated military rocket launches. However, the public were not receptive to the idea that Reagan was trigger-happy and the technique did not work a second time. The Reagan campaign made new strides when its media arm, 'The Tuesday Team', went in for soft focus, symbolism and high production quality in 1984. Advertisements based on themes – such as 'Prouder, Stronger, Better: It's Morning Again in America'; a remarkable symbolic advertisement called 'The bear', drawing an analogy between US–USSR relations and the potential confrontation between a real bear and a human without ever mentioning the USSR; and 'The train', an advertisement filming the ersatz progression of the Reagans on a whistle-stop visit to small-town America, an image playing powerfully on Reagan's nostalgic representation of the 'good old days' – set new production standards for campaigners.

If the 1984 Republican presidential campaign lifted permanently the quality of campaign advertisement production, the 1988 Republican campaign set different standards. The Bush/Quayle campaign against Democratic candidate Michael Dukakis was one of the most negative and aggressive in American history. The Democrats learned that negative advertisements required rapid response, and in 1992 they were using the latest video and satellite communications technology to get their response on air so quickly that their Republican opponents were kept off balance. In the run-up to the November 1996 election, the Clinton team moved into pre-emptive mode, delivering millions of dollars worth of themed issue advertising to the public in waves starting in the summer of 1995.[27] Campaign advertisements and the teams that produce them can themselves become election news, as can candidates' sometimes volatile relations with their media team. In 1996 the *New York Times* 'Ad Campaign' column and the *Boston Globe*'s 'Ad Watch' were among many examples where newspapers used print space to describe television advertisements, and to analyse them for accuracy and style.[28]

Reagan's Tuesday Team made another breakthrough with their film 'A new beginning', an eighteen-minute hagiographic political film made at a cost of $425,000, and substituted for the traditional nominating speech at the 1984 Republican national convention. The television networks were hesitant to include this film within their convention coverage – speeches are news events, while this appeared to be the free national broadcast of a long and expensively produced campaign advertisement. NBC and CNN broadcast the film. ABC and CBS showed excerpts. But another technical and communications barrier had been breached. Since 1988 both parties have used films of this kind to introduce their presidential and vice-presidential candidates as a part of conventions that have become increasingly orchestrated for media consumption, and the television companies have carried them.[29] The television audience have reacted with their remote controls to turn away from recent national party convention coverage. The number of viewers for the last night of the 1996 Republican convention was 30 per cent lower than four years earlier, and the Democrats suffered a similar fall.[30] The major television companies have reduced their convention coverage in response to audience decline.

Ross Perot's 1992 independent campaign used thirty-minute 'infomercials' to deliver the message to the public. Such long advertisements were not a new idea. Fringe candidates had used them, delivered in the deep of the night, when both audiences and advertising rates were low, but Perot was unusual in buying peak viewing time for his lecture to camera. In a year when the electorate was seriously interested in his independent challenge, he attracted large viewing figures, but the attraction was at least in part the novelty value of such an approach. Perot's initiative did not set a trend, but it did help prompt the consideration of a range of media products aimed at different parts of the market. The Dole campaign used at least one five-minute advertisement in September 1996, and all campaigns used video in a variety of ways apart from the now standard thirty-second spot. In Iowa and New Hampshire especially, prospective voters in these important presidential caucuses and primary states find promotional video cassettes from the various presidential campaigns arriving in their mail alongside the usual fare of campaign leaflets.

The 1996 election was the first in which computer networked communications between candidates and voters became significant. The Internet had been a tool for scientists for many years, but libraries, universities and government at all levels increasingly used the system to enable contact between citizens and public institutions. The development of the World Wide Web broadened access to this form of communication, and by June 1996 about seventeen million Americans had access to the Internet, with the number increasing at an accelerating rate. The Voter News Service reported that 26 per cent of the respondents to its November 1996 election day exit poll reported that they regularly used the Internet. The time was ripe for the designers of Web pages to begin to have an effect. The Democratic hopeful Jerry Brown participated in an online 'chat' session in 1992, and four years later all the presidential candidates, as well as many candidates at other levels, had Web sites that 'offered voters not only issue papers, biographies and clips from speeches on the campaign trail, but also solicited volunteers and donations'. In some close congressional elections, such as California's tenth district, where a Democrat with a Web site achieved a 6,000 majority over a Republican incumbent without a Web site, claims were made that Internet presence may have made the difference. With so many voters using the Internet, the use of Web sites as an inexpensive method of communication between incumbents, candidates and citizens is a potential growth area, and is the latest expression of the use of developing, cost-effective technology in campaigns.[31]

Signs of conflict on the streets

There have been concerns that the shift to campaigns designed by consultants and delivered by television and other electronic media has devalued the role of the volunteer, and of materials traditionally used in campaigning at ground level. Certainly the domination by electronic media of major election campaigns will not be reversed. A Supreme Court decision in 1996 freed state party committees to spend more money on candidate campaigns, prospectively channelling an increased proportion of political money into television advertising, but other forms of campaign communications remain significant at presidential and non-presidential levels.[32]

With about half a million elected offices to fill, political parties floundering and entrepreneurial candidates all trying to establish a cadre of loyal camp followers and wider name recognition in the electorate, there is always likely to be a very important place for traditional materials. Posters and stickers will appear on city billboards, nailed to trees in rural areas, fixed to buses, pasted on buildings, propped in windows, strapped on to the tops of cars and fly-posted all over the place. In recent years it has been increasingly common to mount campaign posters on stakes in lawns and gardens, a practice that led to repeated complaints from some Maryland real estate agents during the 1994 mid-term elections: the resulting forest of campaign posters were accused of confusing potential home-buyers and undermining the realty business.[33] The importance of these items is shown in the repeated claims by candidates that their election chances are being damaged by opponents who remove or sabotage their posters. In a 1994 incident in Washington, DC, a candidate's son was found with a car full of his father's opponents' posters. The disappearance of posters during every election campaign, confirmed by the Local Elections Board, shows that someone believes they have an electoral value.[34]

The run-up to election days will bring the signs (and their proselitysing carriers) in force to public spaces. Increasingly, candidates and their volunteers can be seen in prominent spots on commuter roads within their constituencies, holding signs, waving, occasionally speaking and handing out buttons and leaflets when the traffic is halted. 'It reinforces that you're out there working,' said one candidate in Baltimore. 'People have seen me every Thursday morning on the same corner for three months,' said another, 'That's got to count for something. At a time when so much campaigning has become mass produced and impersonal, this use of traditional campaign materials creates an ersatz nostalgia, a sense, however false, of real contact.'[35]

Parades will continue to attract politicians eager to share the limelight and give away balloons. Candidates will continue to talk to the press, the punters, and to kiss babies and elderly ladies. Politicians, for the sake of their careers, and in the forceful pursuit of their ideas, will continue to adapt their style to the changing political, cultural and technological environment in which they campaign. They are competing in the market for public attention against rival politicians, and against all the other commercial, entertainment and news messages being projected, and will continue to exploit new opportunities as they arise.

Notes

1   Examples of these three items are held in the Museum of American Political Life at the University of Hartford, Connecticut. Professor Edmund B. Sullivan, former Director of the Museum, has published a number of books in the field, and has in addition written many exhibition catalogues. Professor Sullivan has been unfailingly helpful, and his work provides the source for many of the insights in this chapter. See, for example, Edmund B. Sullivan, *Hell-Bent for the White House* (Hartford, CT, Museum of American Political Life, 1988), and *Collecting Political Americana* (Hanover, MA, Christopher Publishing, 1991).

2   *Wedgwood Portraits and the American Revolution* (London and Washington, DC, National Portrait Gallery and Smithsonian Institution, 1976), pp. 116–17.

3   On these early campaigns see, for example, Michael J. Heale, *The Presidential Quest: Candidates and images in American political culture, 1787–1852* (London, Longman, 1982).

4   Edmund B. Sullivan, *America Goes to the Polls* (exhibition catalogue, 3rd edn, Hartford, CT, Travelers Insurance Company, 1964), p. 1.

5   Roger A. Fischer, *Tippecanoe and Trinkets Too: The material culture of American presidential campaigns, 1828–1984* (Urbana, IL, University of Illinois Press, 1988), p. 9.

6   Sullivan, *America*, p. 15.

7   Richard P. McCormick, *The Presidential Game: The origins of American presidential politics* (New York, Oxford University Press, 1982), pp. 136–7.

8   Sullivan, *America*, p. 16.

9   Sullivan, *America*, pp. 17, 18.

10 Sullivan, *America*, pp. 19–22; Robert M. Goshern, 'Come let us sing...', *Keynoter*, vol. 87, no. 2, 1987, p. 4.

11 '"Campaign medals: relics of political contests that were waged before the (civil) war", an article from *Harper's Weekly Magazine* – 1896', reprinted in *Keynoter*, vol. 86, no. 2, 1986, pp. 34–5.

12 Kathleen Hall Jamieson, *Packaging the Presidency: A history and criticism of presidential campaign advertising* (New York, Oxford University Press, 1984), p. 12.

13 Edmund B. Sullivan, *From Log Cabin to White House* (exhibition catalogue, Hartford, CT, University of Hartford, 1984), p. 10; Fischer, *Tippecanoe*, pp. 81–8.

14 Sullivan, *America*, p. 38.

15   Sullivan, *America*, p. 33.

16   William Alley, 'Adm. Dewey for President', *Keynoter*, vol. 86, no. 2, 1986, pp. 24–6, 35.

17   Stephen Wayne, *The Road to the White House 1996: The politics of presidential elections* (New York, St. Martin's Press, 1996), pp. 29, 32; Roger Fischer, 'Prosperity's advance agent: Wm. McKinley and the gold standard', *Keynoter*, vol. 84, no. 2, 1984, p. 9.

18   Fischer, *Tippecanoe*, pp. 144–5.

19   George Dollar, 'Campaign buttons', originally published in the *Strand* (1896), republished in *Keynoter*, vol. 84, no. 2, 1984, pp. 20–2.

20   Eugene V. Debs, 'My 1920 campaign for President', *Keynoter*, vol. 86, no. 2, 1986, pp. 16–18, a reprint of a chapter from *Walls and Bars* by E. V. Debs (Socialist Party Press, 1927; reprinted Montclair, NJ, Patterson Smith, 1973).

21   Upton Sinclair, *How I Got Licked and Why* (London, Laurie, 1935), published in America as *I, Candidate for Governor, and How I Got Licked* (Pasadena, the author, 1935).

22   'Attractive campaign pillows', *Keynoter*, vol. 86, no. 2, 1986, p. 17, reprinted from *Needlecraft*, November 1920.

23   George McAfee, 'Alabama casts 24 votes for Oscar W. Underwood', *Keynoter*, vol. 90, no. 3, 1990, pp. 20–5.

24   Robert J. Dinkin, *Campaigning in America: A history of election practices* (New York, Greenwood Press, 1989), p. 132.

25   Louis Sandy Maisel, *From Obscurity to Oblivion: Running in the congressional primary* (Knoxville, TN, University of Tennessee Press, 1982), p. 113.

26   See, for example, Edwin Diamond and Stephen Bates, *The Spot: The rise of political advertising on television* (Cambridge, MA, MIT Press, 1992).

27   Bob Woodward, *The Choice* (New York, Simon and Schuster, 1996).

28   'The Ad Campaign' series appeared regularly in the *New York Times*. For example see James Bennet, 'Explaining a 15 percent tax cut, in 30 seconds', 12 September 1996, p. 13, and Adam Nagourney, 'An attack in black and white on Clinton's drug policy', 21 September 1996, p. 8; Kenneth T. Walsh, Penny Loeb and Gary Cohen, 'Meet the puppetmasters', *U.S. News & World Reports*, 11 March 1996, pp. 28–30; James Bennet, 'The new campaign story: consultants steal the spotlight', *New York Times*, 9 September 1996, pp. 1, 12.

29   Joanne Morreale, *A New Beginning: A textual frame analysis of the political campaign film* (Albany, NY, State University of New York Press, 1991).

30   James A. Barnes, 'On to the hustings!', *National Journal*, vol. 28, no. 34, 24 August 1996, p. 1807; Tom Brokaw, 'Why you didn't watch', *Newsweek*, 26 August 1996, p. 25.

31   Graeme Browning, 'Please hold for election results', *National Journal*, vol. 28, no. 46, 16 November 1996, p. 2517; David Chandler, 'Politicking on the Web', *Boston Globe*, 10 June 1996, pp. 29, 32; E. Scott Adler, Chariti E. Gent and Cary B. Overmeyer, 'The home style homepage: legislator use of the World Wide Web for constituency contact', paper delivered at the Annual Conference of the American Political Science Association, 1997.

32   *Federal Election Commission (FEC)* v. *Colorado Republican Federal Campaign*

Committee. See James A. Barnes, 'New rules for the money game', *National Journal,* vol. 28, no. 27, 6 July 1996, p. 1501.

33 Adele Evans, 'Signs of conflict: campaign posters bad for business, realty agents say', *Baltimore Evening Sun,* 11 September 1994, p. K1.

34 Wendy Melillo, 'Skirmish on the campaign trail', *Washington Post,* 8 September 1994, p. D6.

35 Sandy Banisky, 'They who just stand and wave also run: candidates take to the streets', *Baltimore Evening Sun,* 9 September 1994.

3

Party systems in American history

The pressures on parties

The generally accepted wisdom regarding the political parties of the United States has for some time been that they are relatively weak when international comparisons are made. The American Political Science Association's report 'Toward a more responsible two-party system', published in 1950, displayed the professional concern of political scientists about the role of government and political parties facing the realities of the twentieth-century post-war world.[1] The report's authors favoured the development of more ideologically coherent parties with a more programmatic approach to government, and a greater collective responsibility for their administrations' actions. Criticism of the report pointed out that such a conception of party responsibility implied a commitment to majoritarian government that had never been part of the anti-majoritarian Constitution of the United States, and thereby called for changes that were hardly to be expected within the American political context.[2]

This apposite criticism indicates the uneasy position of political parties in relation to the US Constitution. From the time of the Founding Fathers there has been an intellectual antagonism to parties. James Madison's 'Federalist paper number 10' can be read as an attack on the potential for the development of large national political 'factions'. In 'Federalist paper number 1', Alexander Hamilton listed 'party opposition' as a motive comparable to 'Ambition, avarice, [and] personal animosity', and whenever he returned to the topic it was to say something in the vein of his comment in 'Federalist paper number 76', that 'it will rarely happen that the advancement of public service will be the primary object either of party victories or of party negotiations'.[3] George Washington, another of the Founding Fathers, did not change his opinion even after eight years as President, using his farewell address to warn his listeners 'in the most solemn manner against the baneful effects of the spirit of party generally'.[4]

American political parties developed nevertheless, if hesitatingly and subject to considerable transformations over time, but there remained in the American polity suspicions that the discipline implicit in party politics did not fit perfectly with the individualistic ideals of the American way. In reality, the political system showed signs of evolving to encompass the development of nascent political parties fairly quickly. An early example was the passage of the Twelfth Amendment to the Constitution in 1804. The Constitution originally placed the Electoral College victor in the presidency, and the runner-up in the Vice-Presidency, but after the omniscient George Washington had retired this led to two major problems in the space of the next two elections.

In the election of 1796 Federalist John Adams took the presidency by narrowly defeating his Democratic-Republican opponent Thomas Jefferson, who therefore became Vice-President. There was no partnership between these two, and the presence of Jefferson in the executive was of little use to either of these men, or to the nation. In the election of 1800 the Jeffersonian supporters were marshalled very efficiently, to vote for both of the Democratic-Republican candidates. In fact, so good was the organisation that both Jefferson and his running-mate Aaron Burr received exactly the same number of votes, under which circumstances the House of Representatives was called upon to break the tie. Burr, never having expected anything more than the vice-presidency, was now unwilling to give up his chance for the higher office, and Jefferson did not achieve victory until the House had voted thirty-six times. The Twelfth Amendment was a response to these difficulties, separating the voting of the Electoral College for President and Vice-President, and thereby allowing parties to present a team of candidates for the two offices, whose successful election would be a partisan victory without the danger of fomenting last-minute intra-party rivalry. Many other political adjustments have been made over the years as the role of parties, especially in the nominating process, has become recognised, and ultimately protected, by the law.

Such responses to political reality notwithstanding, the underlying air of disapprobation did not disappear, but continued to surface occasionally as part of the regular debate in the United States regarding limitations on party politics. Discussing the early-nineteenth-century party caucus system, Xandra Kayden and Eddie Mahe point out that the development of organisations that even approximated political parties caused a kind of psycho-political tension 'characteristic of American political life throughout our history ... we want to think of ourselves as united, as having a common view and a common purpose. The very idea of parties is an anathema to those who believe the nation is best served by dedication to the highest, and therefore most united, objective.'[5] But in the ideal world this national unity should be achieved by uncompromised individual decisions, rather than 'slavish' responsiveness to party leadership. The ideology of independence is supported by what Richard Merelman calls America's political culture of 'mythologized individualism', which 'invites

Americans to question all impositions of group power', but which comes with real costs: 'the heavy burden which it places on the individual ensures that much of the time most Americans cannot realize their cultural ideals in action.... Indeed, avoidance may itself become culturally legitimate.'[6] Kayden and Mahe pinpoint the early-twentieth-century 'Progressive era' as a period when antagonism to party politics produced particularly restrictive responses, with the introduction of nomination and election regulations designed to undermine the authority of party leadership, to which may be added reforms in state and local practice to reduce the delegation of authority to elected political leaders and to minimise the effectiveness of ward-based political organisation. Other factors have served to erode party strength during other periods of US history, but concern in recent years has concentrated most clearly on those changes in campaign law, campaign practice and campaign technology in the television age.

The genealogy of the parties

Criticism, suspicion and changing pressures notwithstanding, political parties have become formidable actors on the American scene. In recent years the holders of partisan elective offices in the United States have been almost exclusively from the ranks of two major political parties, the Democrats and the Republicans. The Republicans come complete with a venerable nickname, GOP, though if anything the Democratic Party is the senior of the two, at least in name. The Democrats can claim a heritage back to the presidential election of 1828, when Andrew Jackson's defeat of incumbent John Quincy Adams seemed to clarify matters at a time when America was emerging from a brief period of very indistinct party politics. The Republican Party was founded in Ripon, Wisconsin, in 1854, emerging from a variety of dissident and activist groups, but depending for much of its talent on members of the recently collapsed Whig Party. The Whigs had a relatively brief life, but they too had been stimulated into life as a political force by the 1828 election of Andrew Jackson, developing in the 1830s to oppose what they perceived as the autocratic nature of 'King Andrew's' administration, and signifying this stance by their adoption of the traditional name of Britain's anti-monarchist party.

Both Whigs and Jacksonian Democrats had emerged as factions within the Jeffersonian party (confusingly named the 'Democratic-Republicans'). Dating from the late eighteenth century, the Jeffersonians had come together to challenge the influence of America's first political grouping, the Federalists, and had done so with such success that by the 1820s the Federalists had disappeared as an organisation, and the Jeffersonians had become such a broad church as to be virtually meaningless as a politically unifying force.[7] Factional division created the conditions for the re-emergence of organised competition, and this formed the basis of modern party politics. The two modern parties can each claim to have family trees almost as old as the nation itself, and the two modern party labels have been around for well over a century, but in the journey from those early roots the nature of the parties, and of party competition, has undergone very significant changes. The birth and development of American political parties have been stimulated by the wish to bring order to the challenge for electoral victory and subsequent organisational authority in government, and the important stages in party development are parallel to significant phases in the history of US elections.

America's party systems

Even while the Founding Fathers were expressing a fairly generalised antagonism to political parties, their differences were helping to divide the politically informed citizenry of late-eighteenth-century America into loosely organised groups distinguished from each other by their opinions on the preferred nature of the new American nation. The more vigorous proponents of increased power for central government under the new Constitution formed the backbone of Federalist opinion, while those sharing Thomas Jefferson's suspicions about this centralising tendency evolved into the Democratic-Republicans. These groups became the major combatants in America's first party 'system', first visible in the mid-1790s and finally disintegrating in the mid-1820s.[8]

Transported back to those years, we might not easily recognise these early political parties. Politics was still largely a concern of the social elite at the beginning of the nineteenth century, with property requirements on voters in some states, no general commitment to toleration of opponents' opinions and only a gradual lifting of restrictions on direct public involvement in presidential elections. With the nation established on a firm footing, and the Jeffersonians in the White House and apparently comfortable with central authority so long as it was under their control, the issues that sustained the Federalists faded in significance, and by the early nineteenth century the party had ceased to be a considerable force in presidential politics. In the non-party vacuum that resulted, members of Congress nominated the presidential candidates of the next twenty years in a period commonly called the Era of Good Feelings, but more correctly perceived as the breeding time for factionalism. The party political system became fluid just as national expansion and changing electoral rules were leading to growth in public political participation, bringing with it new dynamics to electoral style, party response and significant issues.

Andrew Jackson was perfectly placed to take advantage of this shift. Born in South Carolina, settled in Tennessee, military hero of New Orleans and instrumental in the withdrawal of Spanish claims to Florida, he was identified with the aspirations of citizens on the frontier and in those states newly entering the union. His defeat in the election of 1824 was the last gasp of America's early, elite system. Jackson had won most states, most Electoral College votes and a higher proportion of the popular vote than any other challenger in 1824, but the field of candidates was large, Jackson did not have the required absolute majority in the Electoral College and constitutionally the final decision reverted to the House of Representatives, who selected John Quincy Adams to be President.[9] The nature of this defeat was exploited by the Jacksonians as evidence that the common man must organise to defend his common interests, and in 1828 Jackson swept to power on a wave of popular support.

During this second party system, built on the bickering foundation of the Era of Good Feelings, political parties made steps towards a structure more recognisable to modern viewers. Given the collapse of presidential nomination by congressional caucus, another structure had to be found, and the national nominating convention was born, proposed for the Democrats in 1827 by Jacksonian political organiser and then US Senator Martin Van Buren, but first used by the small Anti-Masonic Party, who held their meeting in a Baltimore saloon in 1831. The structure was rapidly assimilated by the Whigs, and then the Democrats, who also chose Baltimore as the site of their initial conventions.[10] The national party convention provided a forum for the various elements of a political party, centred around competing regional, issue or other foci, to meet, bargain and compromise in the search for a national candidate for President, and a national appeal to the electorate. It also took central decisions over presidential succession away from Congress, establishing instead a truly separate power base for presidential candidates within the structure of the political party.[11]

Candidate nomination at all levels became a central and lasting function of American political parties, but the national convention met only quadrennially to concern itself solely with the presidential election. The federal nature of American government, reflected in the developing structure of the political parties, protected the representation of differing regional interests both at the non-presidential level, by the operation of local decision-making, and at the presidential level, by the operation of compromise at the convention. This system of 'brokered' conventions lasted for well over a century.[12] Another aspect of the mid-nineteenth-century institutionalisation of the political party was the gradual formalisation of the ad hoc system of grassroots support into a system of state and local party committees, and the establishment in 1848 of the Democratic National Committee to co-ordinate national party affairs. While the parties institute structural changes at least in part to defend and stabilise their positions as legitimate conduits of public opinion, the changing issue bases of political debate and the changing nature of the electorate do not always buttress these structures. Regional divisions over the competing demands of the agricultural and manufacturing sectors, national development policy and slavery acted independently and in combination to make the divisions of Jacksonian America irrelevant. Conventional party loyalties were again fundamentally weakened, and in this atmosphere of change the Republican Party rocketed from its founding in 1854 to take the presidency in the multi-candidate election of 1860, simultaneously signalling the beginning of America's third party system.

By this time the major features of the modern political parties were in place. The Democratic and Republican parties had risen to dominate national politics, and these names were destined not to follow some of the earlier major parties into extinction. The parties organised nationally, bringing together a variety of groups each identifiable by regional, demographic, social or other features, and motivated by a variety of issues, and forging from them a coalition willing to compromise, bargain and co-operate in the pursuit of electoral victory. The parties had a network of committee structures to help this co-ordination, with a national committee acting as a forum for regular contact between elements of the coalition. Power in Congress and at state and local level was important, but the party structures were federalised, and electoral strategy for these offices was generally left to the state and local parties, which responded to a wide variety of policy stimuli, and which developed individually across a broad ideological spectrum, even under the umbrella of a shared party name. Presidential victory was the main national prize, and at the national conventions local, state and regional party leaders faced the real, and sometimes unpalatable, need to accept compromises in order to achieve national party unity behind an electable candidate. Through these structures the parties attempted to respond to, and control, changes that affected their election opportunities. While the continuity of party labels gives an appearance of stability, there are changes over time as some major issues decline in importance and others emerge, and as new groups enter the electorate. Sometimes these changes overwhelm all attempts by the party structures to maintain their electoral appeal.

America's third party system, which lasted from 1860 to 1896, showed these pressures in action. While the issue of slavery helped redefine the system to the advantage of the new Republican Party, within a few years Republican leaders had found that there was no political gain to be made out of further concern for African-American people, and the Democrats, regaining political control in the South, concentrated mightily on efforts to reduce African-American participation to the absolute minimum. Dominated initially by the intense pain of those issues central to the American Civil War, this era was also a period of mass immigration to the United States, of immense commercial and industrial growth, and of confrontational rivalry between the agricultural and financial sectors for control of fiscal policy. The major parties adapted slowly, and minor parties, most notably the People's (or Populist) Party, emerged to challenge their authority. The Democratic Party, which captured the White House only to face a nation-wide economic depression to which it had no response, fractured on regional and economic policy divisions, and the Republican Party sloughed off any remnants of its post-Civil-War radicalism to take instead the mantle of 'Prosperity – Sound Money – Good Markets and Employment for Labor – A Full Dinner Bucket', slogans that endeared them simultaneously to business interests and urban workers.[13] This reorganisation of party support and central issues presaged the fourth American party system, which would last from the turn of the century to the Great Depression of the 1930s.

The structural changes of this period are often interpreted as being anti-party, reflecting popular unease with militant and disciplined political organisation, but an alternative interpretation is that the reforms were stimulated by a middle-class Republican reaction to the electoral threat posed by the recruitment in the late nineteenth century of immigrants and unskilled workers into Democratic-dominated urban political machines. The practice whereby party organisations distributed ballots for their supporters to present at the polling places gave way in the late nineteenth century to the modern, or 'Australian' ballot, printed by a government agency and presenting a choice of candidates. Primary elections were introduced, including the first presidential primaries, as a way of wresting control over candidate selection from the hands of small groups of party activists and putting it in the hands of a broader community. Some state and local offices were made non-partisan in an attempt to eliminate the value of a party label, and the number of offices on the ballot increased in order to reduce the dependence of government officeholders on the patronage of strong political leaders.

Party political dominance of the policy agenda was challenged by the use of proposition initiatives and referendums. The precise mechanisms varied from state to state (see chapter 6), but in general terms the former invited voters to initiate policy proposals through the ballot, while the latter obliged certain categories of legislation, for example items that re-quired government to raise money by the issue of bonds, to be put on the ballot for public approval. In some parts of the country local govern-ment structures were redesigned to reduce the influence of subgroups within the community by substituting ward-based elections, which could reflect the geographical diversity of opinion within a city, with community-wide elections, which could be uniformly dominated by the overall majority. The recall election, whereby citizens could petition for a public vote on the removal of an officeholder even before the term of office expired, was designed to act as a sanction against politicians regarding electoral victory as an opportunity to slide into bad habits. Even the development of the voting machine to replace paper ballots, first used in the late nineteenth century in New York, was in part a reaction to the fears of electoral corruption in areas with entrenched local party structures. As well as being a move towards the simultaneous and efficient counting of votes for numerous offices, it was thought that the mechanisation of voting would make the control and falsification of results more difficult. In addition, the design of ballots was altered in many states to remove the simple option of voting for one or other complete slate of party candidates, requiring voters instead to indicate each voting decision for each office independently.

These reforms were patchy in their implementation and effectiveness, but when effective, and in combination, they served to reduce the impact of party political guidance and to increase the challenge to voters individually to find their way through the ballot, making choices on offices from the President to the County Register of Wills, a shift to complexity that generally served to increase the political strength of established, educated, politically efficacious groups, while subverting the participation of those with fewer personal skills and weaker linguistic ability to bring to electoral decision-making. Even getting to the polls was increasingly subject to a similar sorting process, as registration on the electoral rolls, introduced as a reasonable anti-corruption device, was made generally more complex, with the addition of literacy tests and other barriers, and with the responsibility to register being shifted to the individual, rather than being undertaken by a government agency.

The progressive urge to moderate perceived political, social and economic excesses by regulation went beyond electoral matters, and it was not solely a Republican issue. The electoral impact of political parties was one of the major concerns of the late-nineteenth and early-twentieth-century progressive reformers. Political battles are waged over many categories of policy, but political battles over the rules of politics are particularly significant. Any group that wins the opportunity to define the rules of engagement for the political battlefield can be expected to have an advantage in subsequent skirmishes. The structural reforms generally bolstered Republican Party domination in the early twentieth century, although the exasperation of some within the party did help stimulate Theodore Roosevelt's 1912 challenge for the presidency under the banner of the breakaway Progressive, or 'Bull Moose' Party, dividing the Republican electoral coalition and allowing Democrat Woodrow Wilson to occupy the White House as a result. While there have been many modifications since, the changes made to the political environment of party activity in this period had a dramatic effect on party political activity in American elections, in a way that some analysts see as permanently hobbling the ability of parties to act successfully as intermediaries between the electorate and government administrations, and that others interpret as stimulating further the development of a unique American party system that continues to exist by adaptation to the present day.[14] Certainly the attack on parties led to a regulation and formalisation that, perhaps contrarily, provided the two major political parties with extraordinarily strong legal foundations. Laws regulating the freedom of parties to act, in particular those concerned with primaries, simultaneously institutionalised the parties as part of the electoral process. From now on, in John Bibby's words, 'Parties become quasipublic agencies subject to legislative control.'[15]

While dominant parties may be tempted to reform political structures in a way that is likely to support their continued dominance, no amount of such tinkering can still the electoral reverberations of major national catastrophes. With the Wall Street collapse of 1929 and the subsequent slide into mass unemployment and the Great Depression, the reputation of the Republican Party for sound economic policy that benefited business and workers alike was shattered, at least among workers. Democrat Franklin D. Roosevelt won the 1932 presidential election and went on to be the longest serving American President, winning four successive elections before he died in office in 1945. Before then Democratic dominance for a political era which would become the nation's fifth party system had been guaranteed by the forging of an electoral coalition dedicated to the defence of the New Deal policy. The population groups that coalesced in support of Democratic candidates may all have supported active government intervention to face economic crisis, but otherwise they made strange bedfellows. Southern conservative Democrats, loyal to the party since the Civil War, were in a party that also attracted the support of ethnic and religious minorities in the urban north, that was strongly supported by labour unions and that had succeeded in persuading the African-American population to abandon its traditional allegiance to the party of Lincoln.

While the precise point at which one party system ends and a new one begins is difficult to determine, it is true that each of America's party systems had lasted roughly for a generation, about thirty-six years. Thirty-six years after 1932 came 1968, and political commentators have been examining the entrails of elections ever since in the attempt to determine whether America has entered the sixth party system.

The current party system

Analysts like to identify single critical elections as the foci of the realignments from one party system to the next, although, as Paul Kleppner points out, these electoral discontinuities generally take place 'over a short sequence of elections rather than as an event occurring at a single point'.[16] Such realignments can happen quickly, or may be more protracted. Kleppner identifies the shift from the second to third party systems as spreading over

Table 3.1. *Changing electoral domination in the American party system, 1789–1998: the number of times the presidency was held by each party, and the number of elections that produced party control in other branches of government*

Branch of government	Party system					
	First (1789–1824)	Second (1826–58)	Third (1860–94)	Fourth (1896–1930)	Fifth (1932–66)	Sixth(?) (1968–98)
Presidency	7DR 3F	6D 2W	2D 7R	2D 7R	7D 2R	3D 5R
US Senate	13DR 6F	15D[a] 2W[a]	3D[a] 15R[a]	3D 15R	16D 2R	10D 6R
US House	14DR 5F	13D 2W 2R	8D 10R	5D[b] 13R	16D 2R	13D 3R
Governorships[c]				7D[d]	12D 3R[d]	4R

Key to parties: DR – Democratic-Republicans (Jeffersonians); F – Federalists; D – Democrats; W – Whigs (National Republicans); R – Republicans. I have simplified in places, including early pro-administration officeholders as Federalists, Quincy Adams factionalists as Democratic-Republicans, and Civil War Unionists as Republicans.
[a] No party had a majority in the US Senate after the elections of 1832 and 1880, but in each case the Democrats ended up in effective control of the Senate.
[b] The 1930 election resulted in a majority of one for the Republicans, but the untimely deaths of members before Congress met allowed the Democrats to take control and organise the House.
[c] Party control of the majority of state governorships is calculated for the elections of 1946–90, even-numbered years only.
[d] No party held a majority of governorships after the elections of 1966.
Calculated from data in Carolyn Smith (ed.), *The 88 Vote* (New York, Capital Cities/ABC Inc., n.d. [1989?]); US Bureau of the Census, *Statistical Abstract of the United States: 1996* (116th edn, Washington, DC, 1996); and Charles O. Jones, *The Presidency in a Separated System* (Washington, DC, Brookings, 1994), p. 13.
Tables 3.2 and 3.3 from these same sources.

a twenty-year period, while the step from the third to fourth systems appears to have been complete in about six years. The discontinuity of realignment is followed by a period when partisan support in the electorate is relatively predictable and generally shows consistent favouritism towards one party. Realignments have generally been identified with a shift of electoral success from one party to another. In the case of the third and fourth party systems, however, the Republicans maintained office, the difference being that an electoral shift towards the Republican Party changed the nature of its support, and altered its position from being the

Table 3.2. *Presidential party domination of the US Congress, 1789–1998: the percentage of election results*

	First (1789–1824)	Second (1826–58)	Party system Third (1860–94)	Fourth (1896–1930)	Fifth (1932–66)	Sixth(?) (1968–98)
Presidential party controls Senate and House	95	59	50	83	78	19
Presidential party controls Senate or House	5	23	39	11	0	19
Divided control: presidency faced by Senate and House of a different party	0	18	11	6	22	62

consistent leader in closely fought elections to being the dominant force with comfortable to landslide majorities.

Tables 3.1 and 3.2 identify the dominant parties during the various party systems. Table 3.1 records the number of times each party won the presidency, and the number of times each could celebrate holding a majority in Congress after election day (and latterly the majority of state governorships). It can be observed immediately that the five commonly accepted party systems are all typified by a fairly uniform domination of office-holding by the major party of that era. This pattern has not been evident since 1968, which has been a period of Republican domination at the presidential level, competitive Democratic victory at the Senate level, and uninterrupted Democratic majorities in the House of Representatives.

Table 3.2 shows the percentage of election results during each party system when the administration party, that is the party of the elected President, was also dominant in the Senate and the House of Representatives. All of the first five party systems are typified by administration party domination of the federal government. In each case the majority of elections resulted in the party controlling the executive branch (the presidency) also controlling the legislature (the Senate and the House of Representatives). Throughout this time the electorate tended to vote for a government united by political party, and when electoral opinion shifted, even for short periods, the effect was generally felt on all parts of federal government simultaneously. A significant number of elections in the first five party

Table 3.3. *Comparison of party control of the presidency, Senate and the House of Representatives in the fourth party system, and in the period 1968–98*

Fourth party system				Since 1968		
Presidency	Senate	House		Presidency	Senate	House
1896	R	R	R	1968[b]	R	D	D
1898	R	R	R	1970[b]	R	D	D
1900	R	R	R	1972[b]	R	D	D
1902	R	R	R	1974[b]	R	D	D
1904	R	R	R	1976	D	D	D
1906	R	R	R	1978	D	D	D
1908	R	R	R	1980[a]	R	R	D
1910[a]	R	R	D	1982[a]	R	R	D
1912	D	D	D	1984[a]	R	R	D
1914	D	D	D	1986[b]	R	D	D
1916	D	D	D	1988[b]	R	D	D
1918[b]	D	R	R	1990[b]	R	D	D
1920	R	R	R	1992	D	D	D
1922	R	R	R	1994[b]	D	R	R
1924	R	R	R	1996[b]	D	R	R
1926	R	R	R	1998[b]	D	R	R
1928	R	R	R				
1930[a]	R	R	D				

R – Republican, D – Democrat.

[a] Presidential party controls only one legislative chamber.

[b] Divided control: presidential party controls neither Senate nor House.

systems did result in the administration party controlling one, but not both, chambers of the legislature, but relatively few election years resulted in a President of one party being confronted by a legislature where both chambers were controlled by another party. The pattern since 1968 has been quite different. The starkly divided government model of a President faced by a legislature united in party opposition has been the majority form. Table 3.3 contrasts these patterns, comparing the fourth party system with the post-1968 election years.

This evidence suggests at least that the fifth party system has been disrupted, although it has not been replaced by a system of party competition in elections that resembles the earlier examples. The lack of a clear equation with earlier systems has provoked considerable debate, but there has been other evidence suggesting that a realignment, or something like it, has occurred in recent years.

Earlier periods of party political dislocation have often been accompanied by some or all of a number of features. Minor parties have developed, introducing, expressing and exploring opinions that the major parties have avoided adopting; voters' party attachments have weakened, with a growth of political independence, split-ticket voting and an increase in shifts of loyalty between parties; new groups, sometimes with a policy agenda challenging the contemporary political norms, have entered the electorate in large numbers (such as the late-nineteenth-century wave of European immigrants, or the post-1920 entry of women into the electorate), de-stabilising existing electoral coalitions; new political issues have emerged, often prompted by unforeseen crises.

Examples of similar developments can certainly be found in the late twentieth century. The brave and self-disciplined re-entry of a large pro-portion of the African-American population into the electorate, supported by the passage and operation of the Voting Rights Act, the reduction of the age for voting eligibility to eighteen years and the elimination of some of the more complex voter registration regulations brought about twenty million citizens into the electorate in the late 1960s and early 1970s. The proportion of the electorate claiming to cast their votes independent of party influence rose from an average 22 per cent from 1952 to 1964 to 30 per cent in 1968, reaching 38 per cent ten years later, with the number of 'true' independents (claiming to be without even the weakest party leanings) almost doubling from 8 per cent in 1964 to 15 per cent in 1974. In the 1996 presidential election, an exit poll found 26 per cent of voters reporting themselves as independents, with a further 13 per cent of the sample voting against their usual party preference. On the same election day, the slightly fewer congressional voters were somewhat less inclined to independence (24 per cent), or to voting against their tradi-tional party affiliations (9 per cent).[17]

Republican Richard Nixon made some inroads into traditionally Demo-cratic blue-collar voting groups in his presidential election of 1968 and eroded further the Democratic grip on the southern states, which had shown signs of strain ever since the Democratic national convention of 1948 began to make gestures towards civil rights for African-Americans. No Democratic presidential candidate gained a majority of southern white votes after Lyndon Johnson's landslide victory of 1964. By 1996 Demo-cratic presidential candidates were writing off their electoral chances in some of the southern states, and even an all-southern team of Clinton (Arkansas) and Gore (Tennessee) found the competition stiff across this region.

Minor party activity was strongly evident in 1968, when George Wallace's American Independent Party took five states, and in 1980, when John Anderson's National Unity Coalition attracted almost 7 per cent of the popular vote. This period also saw the growth of the Libertarian Party, which did not win more than 1 per cent of the presidential vote but did have a small number of victories in local elections, and the emergence in some states of the Right-to-Life Party, highlighting the significance of an issue that the major parties found difficult to confront. In 1992 Texan billionaire Ross Perot ran an independent campaign for President that attracted almost 19 per cent of the vote. He went on to form the Reform Party, and received 8.5 per cent of the 1996 vote as its candidate. These Perot figures are the best consecutive results for a minor party or independent candidate at presidential level in US history but, like earlier parties inspired by the personality of particular leaders, appear not to have formed the foundation of a long-lasting political party.

In the late 1960s the conduct of the war in South-East Asia struck a raw nerve in American politics, but the actions of the antiwar movement were exploited by its critics as examples of domestic disorder and urban and social crisis rather than as contributions to the policy debate. Richard Scammon and Ben Wattenberg believed they could identify a redefining 'social issue', while Kevin Phillips wrote of an *Emerging Republican Majority* based on that party's response to the developing ideological and policy needs of southern and western voters.[18] The revelations of Watergate, the resignation of President Nixon, and the subsequent 1976 presidential election elevating Democrat Jimmy Carter to the presidency only interrupted Republican control of the White House for four years, after which Ronald Reagan, then George Bush, gained election by promising to attack government spending, reaffirm moral values and re-establish the nation's international reputation, and by attracting significant proportions of votes from some of the ethnic, religious and economic groups previously loyal to Democratic candidates. Bill Clinton's presidential victories of 1992 and 1996 brought a Democrat back to the White House, but his victories were based on unusual voting patterns. The intervention of Ross Perot in these elections provided an alternative that many voters found attractive. The three-way split of the vote in these two elections left Bill Clinton with victories based on the support of only 43 per cent and 49 per cent of those turning out.

The rearrangement of voting loyalties has had an impact at the non-presidential level. The South in particular has become a region where Republican candidates are in a more competitive situation than they have been for a hundred years, and some research supports the idea that a racially linked realignment occurred in the South in the late 1960s.[19] In the 1994 mid-term elections, the Republicans took control of both US Senate and US House of Representatives, with the once solid Democratic South now giving a majority of its seats in both chambers, and the majority of its governorships, to the Republican Party candidates. When the Republicans retained control of the House and the Senate in 1996 it was the first time that the party had been able to organise both chambers of Congress twice in succession since 1928. That was when Herbert Hoover won the presidential election, the US population was around 120 million (well under half the 1996 figure), Mickey Mouse made his debut on screen and Amelia Earhart became the first woman to fly the Atlantic.

Up to now the changes of the post-1968 period have not resulted in the kind of party domination that was evident in earlier party systems. Some analysts conclude that the contemporary changes are of a different order to earlier realignments. One possible conclusion is that the South is not so much signalling a new realignment as catching up with the socio-economic alliances of the fifth party system, albeit a generation late.[20] This has a certain appeal, given that even within the broad ideological spectra of US political parties there was something anomalous about an alliance between the culturally conservative elements of southern politics and the much more liberal Democratic activists outside the South. Another interpretation of this convergence has been that the rest of the country has moved towards the southern model of cautious liberalism on social welfare, and cautious conservatism on cultural values.[21] Nevertheless, one of the long-term strengths of the American political party has been a federalised structure that can accommodate major differences of opinion. This may dilute national ideological unity, but it preserves operational bonds in the attempt to improve the chances of electoral victory.

Democratic self-identification has declined among many groups. Bill Clinton is the first Democratic presidential candidate to win consecutive elections since Franklin D. Roosevelt, and some of the groups voting in strength for the Democratic candidate form a litany of disadvantage – the poor, African-Americans, Hispanics. Even within these groups it is dangerous for any party to take for granted uniform national support. Regional and other divisions exist within these groups that will have localised electoral effects. For example, while Hispanic voters nationally lean towards the Democratic presidential candidates this has not generally been so in Florida, where US relations with Cuba are of prime importance to a Hispanic community primarily Cuban in heritage. Cuban-Americans are predominantly anti-Castro and vote for the Republicans, being the more vigorously anti-Castro party. However, this party loyalty can be undermined by the Republican's stand on other issues important to this minority group. During the 1996 campaign harsh views on immigration and the rights of non-citizens emanated from the Republican Party, and there appears to have been a reaction among Hispanic voters. The Hispanic share of the national vote rose from 2 per cent in 1992 to 5 per cent in 1996, and 72 per cent of these voters voted for Clinton, including a majority of the Florida Hispanic vote.[22]

In the 1996 presidential election the Jewish vote maintained its liberal history, with 78 per cent for the Democratic Party, and the support of members of labour unions and their families lifted back to 59 per cent, a level for a Democratic candidate not reached since the Jimmy Carter victory of 1976. Clinton also drew particular support in 1996 from women voters (54 per cent, as opposed to his overall 49 per cent of the electorate), voters up to twenty-nine years old (53 per cent), voters with family incomes lower than $30,000 (about 55 per cent overall, with particularly strong support in the lowest income groups). African-Americans (84 per cent) continued a long tradition of huge Democratic support, while Catholics (53 per cent) returned in numbers to the Democratic candidate for the first time in twenty years. Bob Dole, the Republican candidate, drew strength among voters over sixty years of age, men, voters with annual family incomes over $50,000, holders of an undergraduate degree and white voters, especially white Protestants.

At the congressional level in 1996 the voting patterns were very similar, but some of the party differences were more marked. Republicans held an 8 per cent advantage among male voters (54–46), while Democrats were 10 per cent ahead with women voters (55–45). Republicans held a 10 per cent lead among white voters (55–45), which, given that whites made up 83 per cent of the voting population, is an apparently formidable asset. Almost half of 1996 voters in the US House elections were white Protestants, and among those the Republican advantage is a huge 24 per cent (62–38). The South, with 30 per cent of all voters, was in the Republican camp by a 10 per cent margin (55–45), and while the Democrats held a good lead in the East (56–44), this region contained a smaller pool of voters (23 per cent of the national vote). The other regions were, overall, closely balanced in 1996, although in the 1994 congressional elections the Republicans had shown an ability to achieve support approaching that of their southern strength.

While the overall voting balance between the two main political parties in the 1996 House elections was about even, the areas of particular Democratic strength were small portions of the electorate. In 1996 only 10 per cent of voters were African-American, 5 per cent Hispanic and 11 per cent with incomes under $15,000, with many Democratic voters appearing in all three groups. The Republicans' solid strength among white Protestants alone more than balanced those groups making up the Democratic bedrock. Very important to both parties is the potential establishment of lifetime voting habits among young voters. In the presidential elections of the 1980s, and again in the congressional elections of 1994, a majority of eighteen- to twenty-nine-year-olds voted Republican. In 1992 more of these voters chose Perot or Bush than voted for the Democrat, Bill Clinton. Clinton's victory in 1996 attracted the majority support of young voters to a Democratic presidential candidate for the first time in twenty years. If the partisan voting habits of the young are resistant to major change during that generation's voting lifetime, then Democratic candidates face the difficult job of having to convert a proportion of voters as they mature.

During the 1980s it appeared that the nation was locked in a face-off between an executive branch dominated by Republicans and a Congress where Democrats held the whip hand. In the six presidential elections from 1968 to 1988, twenty-one states were consistently for the Republican candidate, while the Democratic nominee had been able to place absolute reliance only on the support of the District of Columbia. This foundation of support gave Republican candidates a flying start at election time and, given that this strength was concentrated in areas of high population growth, some observers felt that the Republicans had acquired a 'gridlock' on the presidency.[23] On the legislative side the Democrats had controlled the House of Representatives continuously since 1930, the longest period of one-party control in US history. Democratic control of the Senate had lasted from 1932 to 1980, and in 1986 they were back in control. The elections of 1992–8 maintained the pattern of divided government, but shook the state of the parties, with the Democrats taking the presidency in 1992 and 1996, and the Republicans taking Congress in 1994, 1996 and 1998, the first time in American history that the Republicans have maintained control of Congress during the administration of a Democratic President.

In spite of the Democratic presidential victories of the 1990s, the eight presidential elections from 1968 to 1996 show a regional pattern to the foundation of Republican success during this period (see tables 3.4 and 3.5). The agricultural Midwest, together with some states in the West and the South, have given Republican presidential candidates a solid bedrock of support. In the South we can see that the Carolinas, Texas and Mississippi have swung to the Republican candidate even while the Republican record in other states has been disrupted by the Clinton victories. The Republicans can only recently claim to have gained consistently in the other branches of federal government. Richard Wirthlin, a Republican pollster, considers this to be evidence of a 'rolling Republican realignment' – moving through the regions of the country, and through the levels of the federal system, rolling relentlessly to a realignment favouring the Republicans. A Democratic counterpart, Paul Maslin, does not concede the point, saying that, regardless of the local success of Republican presidential candidates, there continues to be 'a state and local system in which the Democrats still prosper'. While the 1996 elections left the Republicans with thirty-two of the fifty state governorships, one of their best performances ever, the Democrats still held a majority, albeit reduced in recent years, of state legislative seats (by 3,883 to 3,470).[24] After the 1998 elections Republicans held thirty-one governorships, losing the prime state of California to the Democrats while picking up Florida, and made sweeping gains at lower levels in some major states, in particular Texas, but the Democrats slightly increased their overall representation in state legislatures.

The modern party system appears to be typified by a complex redefinition of partisan loyalties that is not uniform throughout the political

Table 3.4. States supporting the Republican candidate in eight presidential elections, 1968–96 (state Electoral College values[a] for 2000 in parentheses)

No. of times supported a Republican candidate	Northeast	Midwest	South	West
8/8		Indiana[b] (12) Kansas[b] (6) Nebraska[b] (5) N. Dakota[b] (3) S. Dakota[b] (3)	Oklahoma[b] (8) Virginia[b] (13)	Alaska[b] (3) Idaho[b] (4) Utah[b] (5) Wyoming[b] (3)
7/8			N. Carolina[b] (14) S. Carolina[b] (8)	Arizona (8) Colorado (8) Montana (3)
6/8	New Hampshire (4) New Jersey (15) Vermont (3)	Illinois (22)	Alabama (9) Florida (25) Mississippi[b] (7) Texas[b] (32)	California (54) Nevada (4) New Mexico (5)
5/8	Connecticut (8)	Iowa (7) Michigan (18) Missouri (11) Ohio (21)	Kentucky (8) Tennessee (11)	Oregon (7)
4/8	Delaware (3) Pennsylvania (23)	Wisconsin (11)	Arkansas (6) Georgia (13) Louisiana (9) Maryland (10) W. Virginia (5)	Washington (11)
3/8	New York (33)			
2/8	Massachusetts (12) Rhode Island (4)			Hawaii (4)
1/8		Minnesota (10)		
0/8			District of Columbia (3)	

[a] The presidential election is decided by the allocation of the Electoral College votes of each state to the candidate who wins most of the popular vote in that state. The national total of Electoral College votes is 538. A candidate needs to accumulate 270 Electoral College votes to win.

[b] These states voted Republican in the five consecutive presidential elections from 1980 to 1996.

Table 3.5. *Distribution of current Electoral College vote, by states won by Republicans in eight presidential elections, 1968–96*

No. of times supported a Republican candidate	Northeast		Midwest		South		West		Total	
8/8	0	(0.0%)	29	(5.4%)	21	(3.9%)	15	(2.8%)	65	(12.1%)
7/8	0	(0.0%)	0	(0.0%)	22	(4.1%)	19	(3.5%)	41	(7.6%)
6/8	22	(4.1%)	22	(4.1%)	73	(13.6%)	63	(11.7%)	180	(33.5%)
5/8	12	(2.2%)	57	(10.6%)	19	(3.5%)	7	(1.3%)	95	(17.6%)
4/8	26	(4.8%)	11	(2.0%)	28	(5.2%)	11	(2.0%)	76	(14.1%)
3/8	33	(6.1%)	0	(0.0%)	10	(1.9%)	0	(0.0%)	43	(8.0%)
2/8	16	(3.0%)	0	(0.0%)	5	(0.9%)	4	(0.7%)	25	(4.6%)
1/8	0	(0.0%)	10	(1.9%)	0	(0.0%)	0	(0.0%)	10	(1.9%)
0/8	0	(0.0%)	0	(0.0%)	3	(0.6%)	0	(0.0%)	3	(0.6%)
	109	(20.2%)	129	(24.0%)	181	(33.7%)	119	(22.0%)	538	

Note: the Electoral College value of states is as at the presidential election of 2000.

structure, together with a general decline in the strength of party allegiance. If traditional alignments are changed, but then do not form the basis of an easily recognisable new party system, can a realignment be said to have happened at all? In an attempt to encompass the almost consistent modern division of power in Washington between one party in the White House and the other controlling Congress, commentators have characterised this as a real, but 'hollow', 'weak', 'casual', 'soft', 'interrupted' or 'rolling' realignment. Some expect this yet to mature into a hard-and-fast party realignment, and Walter Dean Burnham has declared that America is already in the sixth party system, that 'Its origins are located in the vast general crisis of the late 1960s' and that the weakness of parties is a significant feature of this system, as the historic structure of party coalitions has given way to a 'divided-government, permanent-campaign regime'.[25] John Kenneth White is not so convinced, referring instead to the 1980s as providing 'parity, American-style: parity of a very strange sort', 'the New Deal coalition is moribund.... At the same time, the Republicans do not have enough pull to command a majority', and quotes appositely from Gramsci: 'The crisis consists precisely in the fact that the old is dying and the new cannot be born; in this interregnum a great variety of morbid symptoms occurs.'[26]

As Everett Ladd points out, some observers posit that 'the contemporary electorate is being guided by a kind of cognitive Madisonianism', that is a conscious commitment to divided party control of government such that their own wish to check and divide governmental authority persuaded them positively to vote for candidates of different parties at different levels of government.[27] This appears to suggest a high level of voting sophistication and an almost ideological commitment to a theory of government structure, but should not be easily dismissed. Morris Fiorina concludes that while there are multiple causes of divided government, 'Some of the aggregate features of election results are consistent with the notion that electorates want the kind of government they have and may even be voting in such a way as to produce it.'[28] Fiorina feels that a problematic element in the current system is why the Democrats were not able to capitalise on the clear support shown in congressional elections through to 1994, while James Campbell has concluded that the Democratic majority in Congress was itself based on 'cheap seats', or party strength unevenly distributed into areas of modest turnout, thereby giving the Democrats more results for their electoral investment.[29] Byron Shafer and William Claggett posit that there has developed a political order in the United States organised around two clusters of issues, an economic/welfare cluster (social welfare, social insurance, civil rights) and a cultural/national cluster (cultural values, civil liberties, foreign relations). The salience of these clusters at election times, and the ability of the parties to exploit them, can then be used to explain the divided party victories of recent years

Table 3.6. *Election results, 1980–98 (overall party line-up after each election)*

	Democrats	Republicans	Other
US House of Representatives			
1980	243	192	
1982	269	166	
1984	253	182	
1986	258	177	
1988	260	175	
1990	267	167	1
1992	258	176	1
1994	204	230	1
1996	208	225	2
1998	223	211	1
US Senate			
1980	47	53	
1982	46	54	
1984	47	53	
1986	55	45	
1988	55	45	
1990	56	44	
1992	57	43	
1994	48	52	
1996	45	55	
1998	45	55	
State governorships			
1980	27	23	
1982	34	16	
1984	34	16	
1986	26	24	
1988	28	22	
1990	29	19	2
1992	30	18	2
1994	19	30	1
1996	17	32	1
1998	17	31	2

without resort to the concept either of realignment or of cognitive Madisonianism.[30]

Given a historical cycle of party political realignment approximately every thirty to thirty-six years, it is bound to be increasingly attractive to try to understand the years since 1968 as a consistent system of divided government and weakened parties, and to start looking for its end, and the beginning of a new system. Some feel that parties can re-engage the electorate. Kayden and Mahe feel that 'Politics appears to be becoming a more passive activity', but consider that the new technology of direct mail and massive party fund-raising may give people the feeling that 'they are engaged in more communication with the party' than ever before. Paul Herrnson's earlier claim that 'congressional elections held between 1978 and 1986 ... can be considered Republican success' must be reinforced by the Republican congressional victories of 1994 and 1996 (table 3.6). Norpoth and Kagay pointed out in the late 1980s that a plateau in self-ascribed independence was almost solely due to a drift towards the Republican Party among young voters, and could be 'a party realignment in slow motion', an assessment which, if accurate, could suggest the development of a new system in which the parties may be able to establish closer links between the party organisation, the party in office and the party in the electorate.[31]

The Republicans hope that in 2000 they can persuade the electorate to delegate control of the executive and the legislature to the Republican Party, perhaps providing the foundation of a period of Republican Party domination on traditional lines. But that is partisan speculation, and an alternative may be the continuation of the 'divided government' system of recent years. It seems clear that the American polity is used to policy-making by negotiation, and 'divided government' has not necessarily proved unproductive. A redefinition of the political culture of this system as one of healthy competition and compromise, rather than of confrontation and stalemate, could result in a system that revalued political parties without necessarily opting for single-party dominance. If this trend is real, then it may be that parties can be re-established as salient to the public, and that they may yet overcome the resistance of American ideological indi-vidualism to work again as valued intermediaries between the electorate and the officeholders. Nevertheless, there must remain some doubt that the modern party system is actually moving in this direction.

Notes

1   American Political Science Association's Committee on Political Parties, 'To-ward a more responsible two-party system', *American Political Science Review*, vol. 44 (supplement), 1950.

2   Austin Ranney, 'Toward a more responsible two-party system', *American Political Science Review*, vol. 45, 1951, pp. 488–99. For this and other point-ers I am indebted to Dean McSweeney, 'Political parties and the Constitution in the twentieth century', in *The American Constitution: The first 200 years, 1787–1987* (Joseph Smith, ed., Exeter, Exeter Studies in History, 1987), pp. 83–95.

3   Alexander Hamilton, James Madison and John Jay, *The Federalist Papers* (Clinton Rossiter, ed., New York, Mentor, 1961), pp. 34, 77–84, 456.

4   George Washington quoted in Larry J. Sabato, *The Party's Just Begun: Shaping political parties for America's future* (Glenview, IL, Scott, Foresman and Co., 1988), p. 33.

5   Xandra Kayden and Eddie Mahe, Jr, *The Party Goes On: The persistence of the two-party system in the United States* (New York, Basic Books, 1985), p. 34.

6   Richard M. Merelman, 'On culture and politics in America: a perspective from structural anthropology', *British Journal of Political Science*, vol. 19, 1989, pp. 491, 493.

7   Frank Sorauf, *Party Politics in America* (5th edn, Boston, MA, Little Brown, 1984), pp. 32–3; Beryl Frank, *The Pictorial History of the Republican Party* (Secaucus, NJ, Castle Books, 1980), p. 12.

8   I have drawn on the excellent review of America's party systems that is to be found in Alan R. Gitelson, M. Margaret Conway and Frank B. Feigert, *American Political Parties: Stability and change* (Boston, MA, Houghton Mifflin, 1984), pp. 26–35.

9   Carolyn Smith (ed.), *The 88 Vote* (New York, Capital Cities/ABC Inc., n.d. [1989?]), pp. 1, 6.

10   Stephen J. Wayne, *The Road to the White House, 1996: The politics of presidential elections* (New York, St. Martin's Press, 1996), p. 9.

11   See James W. Davis, *National Conventions in an Age of Party Reform* (Westport, CT, Greenwood, 1983), pp. 25–67.

12   Davis, *National Conventions*, pp. 27–34, believes the brokered convention system lasted to 1968; Byron E. Shafer, *Bifurcated Politics: Evolution and reform in the national party convention* (Cambridge, MA, Harvard University Press, 1988), times the movement of presidential nomination away from the party conventions as being in 1952.

13   John F. Bibby, *Politics, Parties and Elections in America* (Chicago, IL, Nelson-Hall, 1987), pp. 29–30.

14   See Walter Dean Burnham, *Critical Elections and the Mainsprings of American Politics* (New York, Norton, 1970); Walter Dean Burnham, 'The system of 1896: an analysis', in *The Evolution of American Electoral Systems* (Paul Kleppner, ed., Westport, CT, Greenwood, 1981), pp. 147–202; Frances Fox Piven and Richard A. Cloward, *Why Americans Don't Vote* (New York, Pantheon, 1989), chapters 2 and 3.

15   Bibby, *Politics, Parties and Elections*, p. 31.

16   Paul Kleppner, 'Critical realignments and electoral systems', in *The Evolution of American Electoral Systems* (Paul Kleppner, ed., Westport, CT, Greenwood, 1981), p. 17.

17   Harold W. Stanley and Richard G. Niemi, *Vital Statistics on American Politics* (Washington, DC, Congressional Quarterly Press, 1990), p. 144; 1996 results from the Voter News Service exit poll of 16,627 presidential voters, and 14,867 congressional voters.

18   Richard M. Scammon and Ben J. Wattenberg, *The Real Majority* (New York, Coward McCann, 1970); Kevin Phillips, *The Emerging Republican Majority* (New Rochelle, NY, Arlington House, 1969).

19   H. W. Stanley, W. T. Bianco and R. G. Niemi, 'Partisanship and group support over time: a multivariate analysis', *American Political Science Review*, vol. 80, 1986, pp. 969–76; James E. Campbell, *Cheap Seats: The Democratic Party's*

advantage in U.S. House elections (Columbus, OH, Ohio State University Press, 1996), pp. 162–8.

20   See, for example, James L. Sundquist, *Dynamics of the American Party System: Alignment and realignment of political parties in the United States* (revised edn, Washington, DC, Brookings, 1983).

21   Byron E. Shafer, 'We are all southern Democrats now', in *Present Discontents* (Byron E. Shafer, ed., Chatham, NJ, Chatham House, 1997), p. 174.

22   Most statistics on the 1996 vote breakdown are taken from various tables in the *New York Times*, 7 November 1996, and the 'New York Times portrait of the electorate', 10 November 1996, from the newspaper's Web page (http://www.nytimes.com), all based on data from the Voter News Service exit polls.

23   See E. C. Ladd, 'On mandates, realignments, and the 1984 presidential election', *Political Science Quarterly*, vol. 100, 1985, pp. 1–25; E. C. Ladd, 'The 1988 elections: continuation of the post-New Deal system', *Political Science Quarterly*, vol. 104, 1989, pp. 1–18.

24   J. K. White, 'The party line: interviews with Richard B. Wirthlin, William R. Hamilton, and Paul Maslin', *Party Line: The Newsletter of the Committee for Party Renewal*, vol. 19, winter 1985, pp. 15–19; J. K. White, 'Interviews with Lance V. Tarrance and Peter D. Hart', *Party Line*, vol. 19, fall 1985, pp. 11–15; E. C. Ladd, '1996 vote: the "no majority" realignment continues', *Political Science Quarterly*, vol. 112, 1997, pp. 1–28.

25   W. D. Burnam, 'Critical realignment: dead or alive?', in *The End of Realignment? Interpreting American electoral eras* (Byron E. Shafer, ed., Madison, WI, University of Wisconsin Press), pp. 101–39; W. D. Burnam, 'The 1984 election and the future of American politics', in *Election 84: Landslide without a mandate?* (E. Sandoz and C. V. Crabb, Jr, eds, New York, New American Library, 1985), pp. 204–60; see also Sidney Blumenthal, *The Permanent Campaign* (New York, Simon and Schuster, 1982).

26   John Kenneth White, *The New Politics of Old Values* (Hanover, NH, University Press of New England, 1988), pp. 76, 96.

27   Ladd, 'The 1988 elections', pp. 4–5.

28   Morris Fiorina, *Divided Government* (New York, Macmillan, 1992), p. 85.

29   See Campbell, *Cheap Seats*.

30   Byron E. Shafer and William J. M. Claggett, *The Two Majorities: The issue context of modern American politics* (Baltimore, MD, Johns Hopkins University Press, 1995).

31   Kayden and Mahe, *The Party Goes On*, p. 193; Paul S. Herrnson, *Party Campaigning in the 1980s* (Cambridge, MA, Harvard University Press, 1988), p. 125; Helmut Norpoth and Michael R. Kagay, 'Another eight years of Republican rule and still no partisan realignment?', paper presented to the 1989 Annual Conference of the American Political Science Association, p. 11.

4

The modern political system

The drive to electoral reform

Each political system in US history has been associated with changes in the political environment prompted by both internal and external forces, and the modern electoral system is no exception. The regulatory environment for elections in the present-day United States has particularly been affected by changes that were initiated as the fifth party system was decaying. These reforms concentrated in two main areas. First, the conduct of party political affairs, in particular the rules under which party organisations choose from among various contenders the one to become the party's nominated general election candidate, has changed in response to legislation and as a result of internal review. Secondly, the laws governing the financing of election campaigns have been thoroughly overhauled.

Prompted by a concern to broaden the base of public involvement in political parties and election campaigns, and to undermine the potential power of special interests in elections, these reforms have reacted together to produce an unforeseen challenge to party politics. The context has improved for candidate-centred campaigns, and the opportunities have been seized by candidates, using the range of new campaign weapons made available by advancing technology. The potential has increased for broader citizen involvement, especially in choosing candidates, but the public impression remains that special interests retain an overweening political role. The campaign finance reforms of the 1970s appeared radical, but innovative campaigners have found new ways of raising and spending funds without breaching the letter of the laws. After the 1996 election there was talk of the reformed campaign finance system being in ruins. American public opinion at the end of the twentieth century is, if anything, more sceptical of the objectivity of the electoral system and of the accountability of the government a generation after the modern party era, defined by regulatory reform, began.

The party's over

The pressure for reform was building in the 1960s. In the third quarter of the twentieth century the political debates began to spill on to the streets of the nation. Issues such as civil rights for African-Americans, the conduct of the war in South-East Asia and the position of women in society were controversies that seemed unable to fit within the limits set by the traditional political structures of the nation. Activists concerned with these issues did not neglect orthodox political channels, such as using the courts and lobbying politicians at all levels of the federal system, but they were also willing to adopt unorthodox tactics, organising demonstrations, marches and other direct action to advertise public support for their positions in the face of intransigent political authorities.

Southern African-Americans first became involved in the civil rights movement at a time when many of them were denied the vote by the corrupt manipulation of election laws. Similarly, many participants in the early days of the anti-Vietnam War movement were below the age of twenty-one, which at that time made them old enough to fight, but too young to vote. 'Movement' politics, as in the civil rights movement, the anti-Vietnam War movement, the women's movement, and others, became associated with the expression of political opinions by groups that often felt themselves disfranchised, or unheard, within the political system. In many ways the behaviour of these movements could be seen as an evolutionary extension of the normal competition between interest groups within a pluralist political system. But while the movements were stimulated by significant problems, they did not always lead to consensual resolutions.

Some citizens, quickly annexed by expedient politicians as 'the silent majority', or 'middle Americans', felt that the activists were making too many gains for their causes and for themselves. A peculiar consequence was that traditionally minded citizens felt themselves to be the unheard and unregarded, and that in their conflict over policy, both activists within movement politics and 'middle Americans' became increasingly concerned about what they each perceived as the unresponsiveness of elected politicians to 'ordinary people'. 'Silent majority' and 'movement activists' alike shared the suspicion the US political system was in thrall to those political elites who controlled the choice of candidates for office.

A fistful of dollars

Public disquiet was also roused by the extent of economic power evident in election campaigns. Campaigning was becoming increasingly expensive, and wealthy supporters were in the habit of making very large contributions to the campaigns of candidates for major office. Some felt that this too might be contributing to that perceived unresponsiveness to 'ordinary people', regardless of the fact that American election campaigns have in fact been expensive for some time. Over a century ago, in 1880, Republican James A. Garfield ran the first million-dollar presidential campaign. Expenditure has been in the millions ever since but, with the exception of occasional high-spending elections, spending rose only gradually until after the Second World War. In 1948 the Republican and Democratic campaigns together spent less than $5 million, but spending doubled by 1952, and doubled again by 1960, when the Kennedy and Nixon campaigns spent about $10 million each. When Nixon ran again, in 1968, his campaign cost $25 million, and the total spent by Nixon, his Democratic opponent Hubert Humphrey and third-party candidate George Wallace approached $44 million.[1] Campaign inflation was driven in part by new and expensive election technology, particularly the use of paid television advertising, and fed in part by the loosely regulated donations of wealthy individuals and organised interests.

Public confidence in the system was eroding, and an image developed of political decisions being made by self-serving politicians and their affluent supporters. In 1968, for example, a vigorous and often nasty contest within the Democratic Party resulted in the selection of Hubert Humphrey, a candidate who had entered none of the primary contests, as the party's presidential nominee. Even many activists saw this as evidence that political leaders were willing to ignore widespread public tumult. On the Republican side, Chicago newspaper proprietor W. Clement Stone donated $2.8 million to the Nixon campaign, thereby underwriting more than 11 per cent of the total cost of the Republican presidential election campaign. Stone followed this up with another donation in excess of $2 million to Nixon in 1972.[2] Candidates at all levels needed only a few contributions approaching this size on which to base major election campaigns.

Suspicions grew that large contributors were gaining unfair political advantage, and buying advancement for themselves and their interests. In addition, candidates were increasingly anxious about their ability to raise adequate campaign cash in such an inflationary world, and Democrats worried that they might eventually be overwhelmed by heavily backed Republicans. The 1971 passage of both the Revenue Act and the FECA initiated the modern era of campaign regulation, subsequently refined by significant amendments to the FECA passed in 1974, 1976 and 1979, as well as by judicial interpretation and the administrative rulings of the Federal Election Commission (FEC). The erosion of public confidence also stimulated politicians and legislators to initiate structural reforms aimed at re-establishing trust in the link between citizens and their representatives. The resulting financial and electoral reforms, and subsequent adaptations based on this foundation, provide the legal structure and environment within which the strategy of modern American election campaigns must be designed.

It's my party

The modern party system has shared with earlier systems in American history a concern with institutional reform. As parties change over political generations, battles can develop between established political elites wishing to maintain authority and others rising to challenge this domination. Apart from competing for domination of the party organisation, activists working within the party structures may disagree strongly on the best way to maintain or even extend its appeal to a viable coalition of supporters within the broad electorate. This competition can go on at all levels within the federalised political party structure, but national changes often set the agenda for debate.

The 1968 presidential campaign had shaken the Democratic Party to its roots. The party of the incumbent President was used to approaching elections with a sense of political advantage, but Democrat President Johnson was beleaguered in the White House, faced by failing policies in Vietnam and the inability of his 'Great Society' to fulfil expectations at home. Conservative former Democrat George Wallace launched the American Independent Party as a vehicle for his own ideas and ambitions, while those looking for a liberal alternative supported the apparently quixotic campaign of anti-war Democratic Senator Eugene McCarthy. President Johnson made an unexpectedly poor showing in the New Hampshire primary, Senator Robert Kennedy announced his candidacy, and soon afterwards Lyndon Johnson withdrew from the campaign, leaving the way open for Vice-President Hubert Humphrey to enter the lists. Tragedy overlaid this electoral chaos when Robert Kennedy was assassinated at a California primary victory celebration in June 1968, compounding the national shock that followed the assassination of civil rights leader Martin Luther King only weeks earlier.

Urban and campus unrest may have sprung from a variety of stimuli, but they all fired the feeling of national social disorder. On the one hand, the traditional leaders of the Democratic Party seemed unable to establish a bridge to the dissenting forces in their ranks and, on the other, many dissenters felt that their opinions were being ignored by the political system, especially as it became clear that, even after a vigorous primary campaign, Hubert Humphrey, a candidate who had played no substantial part in the primary elections, would be nominated. Humphrey was nominated inside the Chicago convention while outside riot police attacked the thousands of demonstrators who had assembled in the city. Television viewers across the nation saw Democrats protesting in the streets, against

Democrats in office, in a Democratic-controlled city. Chicago appeared to provide evidence that Democrats could be blamed for failed policies, for the dissent and for the inability to maintain law and order. Humphrey was never able to shake off the disadvantage of these visible fractures within the party coalition, and Richard Nixon was able to win the presidency while avoiding making firm policy commitments of his own.[3]

In an agony of self-examination the Democratic Party attempted to discover where it had gone wrong. One argument was that it had lost touch with grassroots opinion, and especially had been unable to develop to meet the policy expectations of newly active groups who were otherwise generally attracted to the Democratic Party.[4] This problem was taken up by a series of commissions charged with investigating the presidential candidate selection process. The McGovern–Fraser Commission followed immediately on the heels of the 1968 election, and promoted radical reforms, such as requiring the representation of women, young people and minorities in state delegations to the national convention, reducing very dramatically the authority of party leaders, and increasing the influence of primary elections and caucus meetings in the choice of candidates, and of the general public within these. After the spectacular defeat of George McGovern in the 1972 presidential campaign, the Mikulski Commission reintroduced a limited amount of state party authority, but while Democrat Jimmy Carter won in 1976, his appeal was firmly that of a political outsider. The Winograd Commission made a modest increase in the number of party and elected officials among national convention delegates, but it simultaneously demanded that all delegations contain men and women in equal numbers. Following Carter's loss of the White House in 1980, the Hunt Commission introduced 'super delegates' representing party leaders and elected officials in an attempt to increase the power of party regulars. Under subsequent national chairs the Democratic Party has continued to take small steps towards increasing influence for party regulars and re-asserting the authority of the presidential candidate, but none of this has fundamentally undermined the shift towards wider public involvement in the candidate selection process, and towards protected representation of minority group rights within the party, as instituted by the McGovern–Fraser Commission.

The Republicans have been affected by these changes, in some cases replicating the reforms to a limited degree at state level, in some cases subject to those state legislatures that have responded to political pressure for more public involvement by mandating a more open candidate nomination structure. On the whole, though, the Republicans initially took a less dramatic line on reform. Their rebuilding had started after the disastrous performance of Barry Goldwater in the 1964 election, and had been more directed towards a redefinition of the national party structure and its relation to state parties. In 1968 rules were introduced prohibiting discrimination in the selection of delegates, urging the encouragement of broad-based participation in party affairs, and offering to assist state parties initiating reforms. This period was very important to the long-term development of the Republicans, since those who stayed loyal in this time of adversity, including Richard Nixon and Ronald Reagan, went on to reconstruct the party, in parallel with huge investment in modern campaign skills and technology. In the last quarter of the twentieth century, Republican candidates have increasingly found national organisational advice and aid of crucial importance to their own success.

Rules changes governing party behaviour have allowed campaigners of all convictions to enter the party system to pursue their own ends. Parties have had to open their doors in order to remain relevant in the last quarter of the twentieth century, but in doing so they have become reactive, rather than proactive, organisations. According to Larry Sabato, 'the United States has the dubious distinction of hosting the most governmentally fettered parties in the democratic world.... Most states tell the parties how to elect their governmental bodies, who may or may not serve on them, where and when they must hold meetings, and/or precisely how the meetings are to be conducted.'[5] Sabato's analysis of these regulations points out how 'mistrustful and unsupportive of the parties most states are'. This has resulted in legislation which, while it enshrines the position of the two major parties in the law, generally compels parties to allow access to their organisation, meetings and primaries to any citizen wishing to take part. In other words, party organisations have little control over their 'membership'. In many respects this may not make much difference to the conduct of party politics – activists willing to give up time and effort to the constant needs of a volunteer-based organisation of any kind tend to be those most committed to its corporate aims. On the other hand, activists devoted to the causes of subgroups within a diverse organisation may also be willing to commit their time to party minutiae in order to capture the larger organisation's resources and status for their own ends. The increasing use of primary elections to choose party political candidates for offices at all levels has had a double-edged effect on political parties, on the one hand making very clear the parties' role as the major gatekeepers on the route to office, while at the same time effectively compelling them to apply only the most minimal of limits, if any at all, on public participation in the primary process.

The reforms had the avowed intent of democratising party participation and candidate selection, but one consequence has been an increased opportunity for single-issue interest groups to exercise power within a candidate selection process no longer subject to the restraining influence of party leaders. The Democratic Party, while retreating from the McGovern–Fraser reforms, nevertheless saw multiple competing groups developing within its ranks. For example, the programme for the first day of the 1990 California

Democratic Party convention lists meetings for groups under the following titles: women, African-American, Asian-Pacific, Chicano/Latino, Environmental, Rural, Seniors, Business/Professional, Disabilities, Environmental/ Rural, Filipino-American, Gay/Lesbian, Labor, Rainbow Coalition, Young Democrats.[6] The history of party political reform has indicated that long-term party insiders do run the risk of becoming isolated from demands for modernising political forms and messages. Once aware of the imperative to respond, however, these loyalists are concerned to mould the sharp conflicts between the many and various interests sheltering under the party umbrella into a seamless public presentation.

Recent presidential elections have provided striking examples of the tension between committed minorities and the leadership groups in the major political parties. In 1988 television evangelist Pat Robertson's supporters put him into second place in the Iowa caucuses, ahead of George Bush. This surprisingly strong showing provided the foundation for a substantial presence for the Christian activist voice in that year's Republican race. Republican candidate Pat Buchanan received the backing of this group in the 1992 and 1996 primary seasons. In trying to accommodate this energetic and vocal minority, Republican Party leaders suffered embarrassments at the national party conventions both in 1992, when Buchanan endorsed Bush in a bile-filled speech, and in 1996, when Buchanan supporters influenced the writing of the party platform to such a degree that the eventual Republican presidential nominee, Bob Dole, was forced to deny that he would be held responsible for delivering on these party promises even if he were to be elected.

The Democrats attempted to design a presidential nomination process that would deliver a moderate nominee acceptable to all wings of the party, and viable in all regions of the nation. The process could still provide surprises, and in 1988 an upset victory for Jesse Jackson as his loyalists turned out in numbers at Michigan caucuses was one example. But the system accomplished its aims in 1992 with the nomination of Bill Clinton from the various Democratic hopefuls, and in 1996 the incumbent Clinton worked from an early date to ensure that he faced no serious primary opposition.[7]

The influence of organised interests is not solely evident at presidential level. Dick Black, a Christian Coalition activist, won a seat in the Virginia state House of Delegates in a special election during February 1998. Organising through targeted telephone calls and a massive leafleting of local church congregations, in a low-turnout election these activists delivered the vote to a committed supporter of their cause. The intervention of interests is not always welcome. In March 1998 Tom Bordonaro (Republican) and Lois Capps (Democrat) fought a special election to represent California's twenty-second US congressional district, in a campaign influenced by hundreds of thousands of dollars of spending by anti-abortion groups, Christian activist groups and the term-limits movement, which campaigns to restrict the number of times an officeholder may stand for re-election. Special-interest support may have helped Bordonaro to an upset primary victory against a moderate Republican, but both candidates in the special election felt that constituency-relevant messages were being overshadowed by national special-interest campaigns noisy enough to demand candidate response and draw them off-message.[8]

The major actor in the electoral theatre of contemporary US politics is the candidate. The journey from contender to party nominee to office-holder is one that generally requires the capture of a party mantle, and while the chosen party route will in many cases be founded on ideological or policy convictions, it may be a purely pragmatic decision to use the most likely vehicle to success. In the contemporary political system, the candidate becomes the target of competing interests through all stages of the electoral process, including the nomination, as the candidate has to capture the party imprimatur through more or less broadly defined public competition. This competition, especially where it involves primary elections, can be expensive, lengthy and contentious. Candidates have therefore increasingly relied on their own cadre of support to take them from start to finish of the campaign. Strategies may involve appeals to traditional constituencies, or to the development of an insurgent candidacy, but in the tense relationship between candidate, party and electorate, it is characteristic that the party nominee will expect a victory to define the party in the candidate's image, rather than vice versa, at least in that constituency, and for the period of that general election campaign.

Wherein the money?

Herbert Alexander categorises the attempts to regulate campaign finance that were initiated in the 1970s into four basic forms: disclosure to the public of campaign finance activities; limiting spending on campaigns; restricting the size of campaign contributions; and introducing elements of public funding. The motivations were to curb election abuses by making the election finance system more visible, to reduce the inflationary spiral of campaign spending, to minimise potential funding inequities between candidates, and to eliminate the public fear that candidates were inordinately obligated to large-scale contributors.[9]

These aims have been fulfilled only to a very limited degree. Some provisions of the original laws have been overthrown in court, notably in the 1976 case of *Buckley* v. *Valeo*, but also in subsequent cases. Other provisions have been modified in action, by the regulatory interpretation of the FEC, by legislative amendment and by creative campaigners' discovery and increasing exploitation of loopholes. The federal law at the time of writing contains general provisions covering campaigns for Congress and the operation of the national political parties, as well as provisions particular to the presidential campaign. State elections are subject to state laws, which show immense variation, but which have developed to reflect, and on occasion to extend, aspects of the federal legal structure.

At the federal level the requirement of public disclosure of formal campaign funds, according to Larry Sabato 'the single greatest check on the excesses of campaign finance',[10] remains generally intact. Certainly campaigns do not always get their accounts in on time and the accounts are complex, so that the discovery of any mismanagement may not be made until after the election has taken place. Some critics complain that the FEC response has generally taken the form only of a modest fine or mild rebuke. On the other hand, there is a feeling among some members of Congress that the FEC puts too much of its resources into investigation and enforcement, rather than simply collecting data and making it publicly accessible, and after the Republican take-over of Congress in 1994 the FEC faced serious budget cuts and congressionally imposed term limits on senior staff appointments. In 1997, in the face of budgetary and staffing limitations, the FEC dropped 208 low-priority pending investigations into campaign finance violations. Nevertheless, there is disclosure and accounts are presented at various times during the progress of a campaign, which gives opponents, and the media, an opportunity to examine the interim returns for useful information. The FEC argues that its response to transgressions reflects properly the nature of those breaches that are discovered, and that the current structure of campaign legislation 'would [not] have succeeded without the deterrent provided by the agency's enforcement program'. The seriousness with which FEC decisions are taken is perhaps indicated by the more than 350 court cases that resulted from challenges to FEC decisions between 1980 and 1994. The FEC would claim that its authority is to some extent confirmed by its victory in 90 per cent of these cases.[11]

Certainly candidates do show an awareness of the potential damage of disclosure. Campaigns wish to avoid controversy, but in large-scale fund-raising organisations some problems inevitably emerge after the fact. The Kennedy name is charged with meaning in Democratic circles, and Senator Edward Kennedy (Massachusetts), former Representative Joseph Kennedy (Massachusetts) and Representative Patrick Kennedy (Rhode Island) have proved formidable fund-raisers. With such drawing power it is not surprising that on occasion they find themselves returning contributions. In the 1995–6 election cycle Patrick returned over $7,000, Joseph over $10,000 and the Senator gave back $63,250, as they found out that donations had come from questionable sources. In one case executives in the Oklahoma natural gas industry had engineered a scheme to donate $37,500 to the Senator, in breach of federal limits. In the words of a

Senator Edward Kennedy spokeswoman, 'Anytime that there is a hint that a contribution may have been given improperly, it is returned immediately.' In the late 1980s, many savings and loan associations (S&Ls) collapsed, at a cost to the American taxpayer estimated up to $500 billion. Members of Congress who had received campaign contributions that were S&L related, in an attempt to expunge the connection, busily returned money received from this once respectable, but now tainted, source. A similar ripple was felt towards the end of the 1996 election campaign, when allegations emerged that Democratic Party fund-raising had attracted large contributions from possibly illegal sources, most notably money channelled from major business interests in Indonesia. This was embarrassing to President Clinton and Vice-President Gore, who found themselves directly implicated in the allegations, but it also sent candidates for congressional office searching through their files to see whether any money may have come by the same tainted route, and if so to return it, without waiting to find out whether it was illegal or not.[12]

At the federal level the attempt to limit spending by congressional candidates was declared unconstitutional as part of the Supreme Court's *Buckley* v. *Valeo* decision in 1976. Federal limits on presidential campaign spending were, however, accompanied by the introduction of a major element of public funding, financed by a voluntary donation of tax dollars by individual taxpayers. The Court accepted that any candidates who chose to accept the public funding could be considered to have voluntarily entered into a contract, and therefore be bound by the government-defined spending limits, and that these limits could be avoided only by rejecting the opportunity to obtain the proffered public funds. Almost all presidential hopefuls have taken public funding and accepted the associated limits on formal campaign spending. John Connally made an unsuccessful bid for the Republican nomination in 1980, without taking public funding, raising substantial amounts from his supporters. More recently very wealthy self-financed candidates have emerged, Ross Perot in 1992 and Steve Forbes in 1996. In spite of several efforts, Congress has never extended public funding to other federal elections.

By the time of the 1996 election cycle, the National Conference of State Legislatures reported that twenty-three states had some provision for public financing of state-level political campaigns, and others had introduced varied forms of campaign finance regulation for state offices. A 1989 law passed in New Hampshire, simplifying filing procedures and eliminating filing fees for candidates who voluntarily accepted spending limits, found general acceptance in the elections of 1990. Of the 1,400 candidates competing for state and federal office only three, two candidates for the US Senate and one for the US House of Representatives, failed to accept the limitations. When Nebraska's Campaign Finance Limitation Act went into operation in 1996, spending in that state's primary elections for the

state legislature fell by 40 per cent compared with 1994. This law encourages candidates to agree to abide by a state-legislated spending limit.
If they do not agree, then state funds are made available to opponents to
go some way towards equalising the resources available to competitors for
office. In its first year the law applied to elections for the Nebraska state
legislature, the state Board of Education, the University of Nebraska Board
of Regents and the Public Service Commission. It appeared to work well
and to moderate spending without putting great pressure on tax dollars.
It is not clear whether the system works for traditionally high-spending
races. In 1998, total spending by the major party candidates for Governor
of Nebraska exceeded $1.5 million, with the Republican victor, Mike
Johanns, raising almost twice as many funds as his opponent, Democrat
Bill Hoppner. Supporters of such laws argue that they prevent incumbents
benefiting from their ability, while in office, to raise huge campaign war
chests to defend themselves against all challengers. Opponents claim that
incumbents always have advantages – of name recognition and a record
of constituency service – and that denying the opportunity to well financed
opponents to spend aggressively only serves to ensconce the incumbent
more comfortably.[13]

Legislation on contribution limits to candidates for federal office has
certainly changed the campaign environment.[14] Contributions by individuals to candidates for federal office are limited to $1,000 for each
primary and general election campaign. Individuals may also give up to
$20,000 in a calendar year to a national party committee, a category that
includes the parties' national committees as well as the parties' nationally
organised committees for US Senate and House campaigns. An alternative
route for campaign money is through independent political committees, to
which an individual may contribute $5,000 in any calendar year. There
exists an overall limit on the total contributions that an individual may
make to these campaign organisations of $25,000 in a calendar year.
Candidates and politically active committees are now faced with the imperative to collect large numbers of modest sized financial contributions
from a broad population of supporters, rather than hoping to be
bankrolled by small numbers of rich, or 'fat cat', contributors. The
committees, in their turn, can pass funds on to candidates, or to other
committees. Multi-candidate political action committees (PACs) may give
$5,000 to a federal candidate in both a primary and a general election,
and $15,000 to a national party committee. Multi-candidate committees
qualify for this preferential position in law if they collect money from at
least fifty contributors, and distribute funds to at least five federal
candidates.

National and state party committees are permitted to make modest
contributions in a similar way to PACs, but may in addition make co-
ordinated expenditures on behalf of a candidate. In the case of campaigns

for the House of Representatives, party spending on behalf of a candidate was set at $10,000 in 1974, but this figure was index-linked, and will rise to about $35,000 by 2000. The limit for Senate campaigns was $20,000 in the smallest state in 1974 figures, rising to two cents per head of the voting population in larger states. In 1994 the figures ranged from $58,600 to $1,325,415, depending on state population size.[15] The legislation has also built in a kind of institutional donation. In the recognition that much of the inflationary drive behind spiralling campaign costs for federal office was caused by the increasing use of expensive television advertising, broadcasters are obliged to charge for campaign advertising at their 'lowest unit rate', that is the preferential rate normally reserved for large-scale repeat customers, in the forty-five days before a primary election, and in the sixty-day run-up to a general election. Advertising purchased at the very lowest available rate, however, can be rescheduled by the television company at its convenience. But all time slots are sold at discount rates to bulk purchasers and, even if paying some premium to guarantee prime time exposure, campaigns will still gain the benefit of the best rate negotiated by the television station's most valued customer using that time slot.

The original aims of the 1970s reforms on disclosure, public funding, spending limits and contribution limits have not been achieved evenly at the federal level. The laws changed, and now define, the context of federal campaigns, but not always by meeting their objectives. Disclosure of fund-raising and campaign spending records has perhaps been the most successful long-term consequence. Indeed, by the end of the 1990s some observers would claim that so many loopholes and diversions had been found through which money could be raised and spent that public disclosure of the formal campaign accounts was the only visible reminder of the aims and objectives of the 1970s reformers. The public funding and associated spending limits on formal presidential election campaigns are another part of contemporary campaign practice directly attributable to the 1970s reforms, but the development of parallel campaign spending channels outside the remit of the campaign spending legislation has meant that overall spending on presidential campaigns by interested parties is effectively unlimited. In this respect the law has restructured campaign strategy, but in the long term has not limited overall expenditure on the presidential campaigns.

Campaign contribution limits have also considerably altered campaign conduct. Since candidates for federal office may spend as much as they wish, but must raise it within the confines of the legislation, a new kind of skilled campaign entrepreneur has emerged whose skills lie in attracting vast numbers of donations of $1,000 or less from individual contributors, sustaining support from PACs, convincing party committees of the invest-ment value of a particular campaign, and establishing such credibility in a candidate that any spending on the part of other interest groups will benefit the campaign. Whatever the regulatory environment, campaigners wish to gain the best advantage for themselves, and shortly after the campaign finance laws had been passed enthusiastic campaign entrepreneurs were investigating how to loosen any encumbrance that the laws represented in the pursuit of office.

Money raised under the terms of the federal legislation governing campaign funding is known as 'hard money'. There is a paper trail tracing its origins, management and disbursement. It is raised in contributions of limited size from individuals whose overall contributions are capped, or from committees whose contribution records are available to public scrutiny. In presidential elections this hard money plays a role in tandem with public funding, especially during the primary season, and in this campaign expenditure also is capped. If campaigning in the USA were wholly funded out of hard money one might be able fairly to say that many, and perhaps most, of the aims of the 1970s regulatory system were being met. The major problems with this vision are the emergence of 'soft money', and the growing role of spending by committees and organisations not directly part of the candidate campaign.

Herbert Alexander defines soft money as being 'raised from sources outside the restraints of federal law but spent on activities intended to affect, at least in part, the outcomes of federal elections'.[16] This money is not donated direct to candidate campaign committees, or to those campaign committee accounts covered by the federal law. It is not spent directly on campaigning for federal election and is therefore not subject to federal regulation. Most importantly, this means there is no limit on the size of donations, although since 1971 the FEC has required that soft money fundraising and spending activities by political parties be recorded and publicly disclosed. To a great extent this money is disbursed through state-level party organisations. The 1970s campaign reforms concentrated on candidate organisations and the combination of funding directed to individual presidential campaigns, and the opportunities within the law for committees independent of political parties to be active in election campaigns were perceived as eroding the role of parties at election time. The 1979 amendments to the FECA attempted to defend the position of political parties in an increasingly entrepreneurial campaign environment by allowing state party committees to engage in party building activities such as voter registration and turnout drives unhindered by federally imposed limits on fund-raising and spending.

The legal regulation of elections in the states is subject to change in the fifty different state legislatures, and as a result the situation is never static. This variation of campaign finance law from state to state presents opportunities for enterprising organisers to channel funds from contributors wishing to give freely to particular causes, and candidates sympathetic to those causes, to the least restrictive political environments, that is to those states where state-imposed regulation is not severe.

There has been increasing creativity in the variety of uses to which soft money is put. One study of the 1995–6 election cycle identified record spending by political parties and PACs on House and Senate races, while another commentator spoke of the presidential races accessing much of the money that 'engulfed the political system in 1996'.[17] In the first of these analyses Diana Dwyre pointed to a number of new and developing practices that have been added to the campaign spending arsenal, founded primarily on raising record amounts of soft money, including issue-advocacy advertising, party-independent spending, energetic money transfers between committees, and increased PAC and interest group spending.

A footnote to the 1976 *Buckley* v. *Valeo* decision had explained that the legislation could only apply to communications that 'in express terms advocate the election or defeat of a clearly identified candidate for federal office', and went on to pinpoint key words and phrases: 'vote for or against', 'elect', 'Smith for Congress', 'defeat'.[18] Advertisements on policy issues are not new. Policy debates in the late twentieth century on issues as varied as health care and the Strategic Defence Initiative have prompted groups to advocate their position through television advertising, but it took twenty years for this footnote to begin to find full expression in the campaign system. In the 1995–6 election cycle, party committees and interest groups both invested heavily in issue advertisements which advocated particular policies, and identified named candidates with positions on these policies, but stopped just short of calling directly for the election or defeat of those persons. Soft money can be used for these advertisements, and interest groups and other organisations can become directly involved in the funding, without channelling money through various political funds and committee accounts.

Another Supreme Court decision, this one taken in 1996, further loosened the campaign purse strings. In *Colorado Republican Federal Campaign Committee* v. *Federal Election Commission*, decided on 26 June 1996, the Court ruled that party committee spending on campaign advertising was not limited, as long as the campaign decisions were made independently of the candidate campaign.[19] Independent spending by individuals, and committees of people sharing common political opinions, wishing to influence political campaigns by supporting candidates sympathetic to their perspective has become increasingly common at election times. Such campaigning, which can include all the elements and techniques of a regular campaign, may attempt to influence the result by supporting or attacking a particular candidate, but as long as the individuals and committees underwriting the campaign effort have no links with the official candidate campaign these independent efforts are considered to be protected by the constitutional right to freedom of speech. The FEC has on occasion made efforts to restrict such expenditure, but these efforts have been struck down, even when applied to publicly funded presidential campaigns. The 1996 Court decision extends that freedom of 'independent' action to party political committees.

The changes and discoveries of 1996 have left many party and non-party campaign forces ready to raise increasing amounts of soft money to invest in advocacy advertisements. In addition, party committees have shaken off earlier limits and can now join PACs in spending unlimited amounts of hard money in 'independent' campaign advertisements for or against particular candidates. Parties have responded by shifting vast amounts of soft and hard money (entirely legally) between accounts so that it is being spent in the most efficient possible manner – hard money to places where only hard money will do, liberating soft money to play a more freewheeling role. PACs and interest groups have responded to the shifting landscape by raising and spending more freely as the options have increased.

Entrepreneurial campaigners will always seek to maximise their campaign opportunities. The combination of the failure to maintain the viability of all elements of the original campaign acts and the pressure by campaigners to find innovative ways of avoiding regulation has led some analysts to conclude that the law is loopholed to the point of virtual uselessness. E. J. Dionne, in the *Washington Post*, claimed that 'the political money system imploded in 1996', while Eliza Newlin Carney, of the *National Journal*, opined in 1996 that 'loopholes are shredding the contribution and expenditure limits that were established ... in the 1970s'. Brooks Jackson, political correspondent for CNN, considers that '1996 saw the final collapse of campaign finance regulations enacted 22 years earlier'. Campaign finance specialist Professor Anthony Corrado thought the 1996 elections 'raise serious questions about the ability of the current regulatory regime to exert any meaningful control over the flow of money in federal elections'.[20] Nevertheless, the system today results from a continuing interaction between the political actors and the forces of campaign regulation. The debate over further definitive reform is continuing but has so far been relatively unproductive, and the behaviour of the political actors will continue to be defined by, and yet try to stretch the boundaries of, the campaign finance legislation of the 1970s.

The modern political system and the voter

While the reforms of the 1970s appear to have stimulated a new and independent entrepreneurial spirit among contestants for office, this change is greeted with mixed feelings. There has been a steady growth in that proportion of the electorate identifying themselves as independent of party affiliation, and a steady decline in the strength of affiliation among those still identifying themselves with a political party. In some voters this is accompanied by a sense of something lost in the party system. In the words of one Connecticut voter, a lifelong Democrat, reconsidering his position before the 1990 elections, 'Years ago, you used to go by a political party to choose your man, but now you have to go for the guy ... who's going to rattle people, who's going to get things moving.'[21] The combination of a nostalgic, if somewhat romantic, vision of the old days, when voters could believe that voting for the party line would represent his interests, as opposed to today, when the voter feels he must choose instead an individual who will make waves, expresses well the course of electoral politics over the past quarter of a century.

There is a measure of contradiction built into this perception. The Democratic and Republican parties have become steadily more ideological in recent years, at least as measured by the behaviour of Congress. The primaries that choose candidates tend to attract voters who have strong feelings. Entrepreneurial candidates appeal to these groups of voters to gain their victories. The party political camps that form in Washington owe little to broad coalition politics, but the confrontational style that has resulted at the federal level in the 1990s has proved unappealing to many voters.[22] Paradoxically, it may be that it was more comfortable to choose by political party when they were both broader churches. It is nonetheless undeniable that political parties have historically provided many people with a helpful structure within which to make voting decisions, and that this role retains some influence even in the candidate-centred system.

Periods of high party identification in American history have coincided with periods of high turnout. Voters identifying themselves as independent of allegiance to a political party are more likely than others to express their preferences by splitting their votes between candidates of different parties, but it is also true that they are less likely to vote at all than citizens who identify closely with a political party. 'Pure' independents (those voters without any leanings towards a political party) have a lower turnout rate than independents who 'lean' to a political party, who in their turn vote at about the same rate as weak party identifiers, while strong Democrats and strong Republicans turn out in force.[23]

Self-identified 'pure' independents grew as a proportion of the electorate over the past generation, from 7.9 per cent in 1964 to 11.6 per cent in 1992. Over the same period moderate and strong party identifiers declined from 77 per cent of the electorate to 61.6 per cent.[24] Furthermore, Everett Carll Ladd believes that disengagement from party affiliation must be drawn more broadly. Parallel surveys taken in 1996 found that many respondents were inconsistent in their answers on political party. Fewer than half of the respondents consistently identified themselves as Democrats or Republicans. The other half were either self-identified independents or inconsistent in their identification. Many among the consistent party loyalists claimed nonetheless that on occasion they split their vote between candidates of different parties. Surveys taken later in the year showed that further changes in party political self-identification had taken place. Martin Wattenberg's earlier analysis had suggested that an increasing number of people felt that parties were not salient to them, a perception bolstered by Ladd's conclusion that 'a growing segment of the electorate really doesn't belong to any party and is disinclined to place much long-term faith in either party's leadership or direction'.[25]

The rhetoric of resistance to party leadership has been heard widely in late-twentieth-century America. Testifying before the Advisory Commission on Inter-Governmental Relations in 1984, Howard Callaway, Chair of the Colorado Republican Party, said, 'it [is] fashionable for the average voter to say, "I don't vote for the party, I vote for the man or woman – I am independent. I make up my own mind, no one tells me how to vote."'[26] In this period, according to Joel Silbey, 'identification with parties became the minor key in voter behavior'.[27] Everett Carll Ladd goes so far as to say that 'The public's criticism ... is that politics is too much captured by political insiders – for example, by the elected Democratic and Republican politicians in the national legislature – and in general that "the system" is too insulated from meaningful day-to-day popular control.'[28] Citizen criticism of what Ladd calls 'the political class' often argues that elected politicians are unresponsive and beholden to parties, rather than to constituents, but this may be a misperception. Officeholders are responsive, but to a range of demands made by campaign donors, interest groups, PACs and so on, as well as constituents. As political parties weaken in their role of conduit between electorate and officeholders, their ability to filter and aggregate these varied influences declines. It may be a case of what electoral scholar Gary Jacobson has called 'great individual responsiveness, equally great collective irresponsibility'.[29]

If the power of party loyalty to get voters to the polls has declined over the last generation, the public's changing image of government over that same period has done nothing to encourage hopes that America might soon enter a period of burgeoning electoral participation. In its coverage of the 1996 election, the *New York Times* published results from surveys covering the period over which the modern political system has emerged. According to this review, in 1960 about 30 per cent of respondents thought that 'government is run by a few big interests looking out for themselves'; in 1994, 79 per cent agreed with this opinion. The 70 per cent who in 1960 thought that 'the government is for the benefit of all the people' had fallen to 15 per cent by 1994. According to these results, in 1994, 66 per cent of respondents believed 'public officials don't care much what people like me think', only 20 per cent believed they could trust the government most or all of the time and 55 per cent believed that 'people like me don't have a say in what the government does'. Asked 'Do you think that quite a few of the people running the government are crooked?' 51 per cent of the 1996 respondents agreed – almost double the figure thirty years earlier.[30]

When Larry Sabato found that among the respondents to a survey '78 percent reported that they had cast a ballot days earlier in November, when in fact a paltry 37 percent had actually gone to the polls,' he deduced that '[m]ost citizens do not vote regularly, but because of political socialization by the parties, their families, and their schools, they know they *should vote*.'[31] Moreover, it would seem to be part of the political culture to believe in the power and obligation to vote, and simultaneously to deny that party affiliation guides that vote. There is no necessary antagonism between these two possible elements of a public philosophy. It could perhaps be construed as defeatist and undemocratic to admit pulling the party lever, but also defeatist and undemocratic to admit not voting at all. In any event, given the apparent inability of the parties to convince the public of their salience, and the parallel development of a cultural resistance to admitting party leadership, the potential is considerably undermined for the party to create a coalition within the electorate, by acting as negotiator between the interests in that electorate, and defining, possibly by compromise, broad policy stances that positively help the electorate to make political choices.

The modern political system and the candidate

The contemporary candidate for major political office is an independent operator, and the factor of fundamental importance which has allowed this autonomy to develop almost unrestrained has been the technological developments in media, computers and information sciences that allow campaigns rapid, powerful and direct access to voters. Creating the conditions under which a candidate will flourish in the contemporary legal, regulatory and technological environment of elections has become a sophisticated technical enterprise and a network of campaign businesses offering the necessary expertise have sprung up around the entrepreneurial candidate.

The television age has brought the opportunity for candidates to communicate direct to the electorate via a most powerful medium. As computers have become cheaper and easier to operate so have they entered every phase of campaigning. Having the financial means to undertake a campaign remains very significant, but the explosive growth of fund-raising PACs since the mid-1970s has helped provide attractive candidates with a firm financial base. It is clear that candidates with access to these modern tools of the campaign can operate with substantial independence, using modern technology and a pool of skilled operatives to grasp the opportunity to design a campaign aimed at, and responsive to, the relevant electorate. Institutional reforms made by law, such as the campaign finance legislation of the 1970s, or by changes in party rules, such as the increased reliance since the 1970s on primary elections rather than more narrowly defined party organs to choose candidates, increased the incentive for the development of candidate-centred campaign structures, based on the guidance of professional campaign consultants. While this was most noticeable at the national level, and much of the debate over reforms centred on presidential selection, there was a knock-on effect that had repercussions throughout the political system.

The picture that develops from these concerns is one of decreasingly effective political parties being shut out of campaigns run by consultants who respond to sophisticated computer analyses of public opinion polls with skilful media messages aimed at a media-consuming public, a style of operation altogether reminiscent of the way Hollywood designs and tests its products on the public. Commenting on the early stages of the 1998 race for Governor of California, a local journalist pointed to the combination of wealthy candidates financing their own campaigns, the growing awareness of the power of Latino voters, and the various candidates and issues in the campaign, contributing to an atmosphere in which those competing have 'obliterated party distinctions'. Both the early favourites in the Democratic primary distanced themselves from the party label. Even though one candidate was a sitting Democratic member of Congress she preferred to relate that in her 'bipartisan district' her support was based on 'policies I espouse, not because of the label after my name'.[32] In a three-corner race, victory went to a state-level politician running a relatively low-cost campaign, bringing hope to some that the public antagonism to the 'political class' might be waning in this most important western state. The glimmerings of that new dawn are not clear to others. In the same year in Arkansas, Republican challengers for seats in the strongly Democratic state legislature were counting on the public to say, 'It's really nice to see a fresh face. We're tired of those politicians.'[33]

Many startling strategic, pragmatic and dramatic developments in modern election campaigning have resulted from the efforts of the entrepreneurial candidates and campaigners who are working to win within this modern political system, of individualistic campaigns within a re-defined financial and party political structure.

Notes

1   Stephen J. Wayne, *The Road to the White House, 1996* (New York, St. Martin's Press, 1996), p. 29.
2   Herbert E. Alexander, *Financing Politics: Money, elections and political reform* (4th edn, Washington, DC, Congressional Quarterly Press, 1992), pp. 15, 21.

3   See Philip Davies, 'US presidential election campaigns in the Vietnam era', in *Vietnam and the Antiwar Movement: An international perspective* (ed. John Dumbrell, Aldershot, Avebury, 1989), pp. 124–36.

4   See, for example, Xandra Kayden and Eddie Mahe, Jr, *The Party Goes On: The persistence of the two-party system in the United States* (New York, Basic Books, 1985), pp. 60–74, and Alan R. Gitelson, M. Margaret Conway and Frank B. Feigert, *American Political Parties: Stability and change* (Boston, MA, Houghton Mifflin, 1984), pp. 93–7.

5   Larry Sabato, *The Party's Just Begun: Shaping political parties for America's future* (Glenview, IL, Scott Foresman/Little, Brown, 1988), p. 203.

6   'Memo of the month', *Washington Monthly*, May 1990, p. 38.

7   For coverage of the nomination campaigns of recent elections see, for example, Gerald Pomper *et al.*, *The Election of 1996: Reports and interpretations* (Chatham, NJ, Chatham House, 1997), and previous election year reviews by the same authors; Michael Nelson (ed.), *The Elections of 1996* (Washington, DC, Congressional Quarterly Press, 1997), and previous election year reviews by the same editor; William Crotty (ed.), *America's Choice: The election of 1992* (Guilford, CT, Dushkin, 1993).

8   Lou Cannon, 'Outshouting the voters', *Washington Post National Weekly Edition*, 2 March 1998, p. 14; Burt Solomon, 'Crown of thorns', *National Journal*, 14 February 1998, pp. 342–5.

9   Alexander, *Financing Politics*.

10 Larry Sabato, *Paying for Elections: The campaign finance thicket* (New York, Priority Press, 1989), p. 63.

11 Mark Murray, 'Help wanted: the FEC's familiar refrain', *National Journal*, 7 March 1998, pp. 520–1; Eliza Newlin Carney, 'The FEC versus the GOP', *National Journal*, 11 July 1998, pp. 1622–3; Federal Election Commission, *Twenty Year Report* (Washington, DC, April 1995), p. 10.

12 Eliza Newlin Carney, 'Cashing in on Camelot', *National Journal*, 21 February 1998, pp. 400–3; James A. Barnes, 'Pinning the blame', *National Journal*, 22 September 1990, p. 2262; Peter H. Stone, 'The green wave', *National Journal*, 9 November 1996, pp. 2410–14.

13 John Milne, 'Money for candidates drying up', *Boston Sunday Globe*, 29 July 1990, pp. NH1, NH5; Leslie Boellstorff, 'Spending down 40% in primary', *Omaha World-Herald*, 23 August 1996, pp. 1, 10; 'Campaign-finance law may be delayed', *Omaha World-Herald*, 16 September 1996, p. 11.

14 For a detailed overview, see, for example, Alexander, *Financing Politics*.

15 Graham P. Ramsden and Patrick D. Donnay, 'Party contributions and the competitiveness of U.S. House races in 1996', paper presented to the 1997 Annual Conference of the American Political Science Association, p. 7.

16 Herbert E. Alexander, 'Soft money', *Vox Pop*, vol. 8, no. 1, 1989, p. 1.

17 Diana Dwyre, 'Pushing the campaign finance envelope: parties and interest groups in the 1996 House and Senate elections', paper presented to the 1997 Annual Conference of the American Political Science Association; Stone, 'Green wave', p. 2410.

18 Quotations from *Buckley* v. *Valeo*, 424, U.S. I, cited in Anthony Corrado, 'Financing the 1996 elections', in *The Election of 1996* (Gerald Pomper, ed., Chatham, NJ, Chatham House, 1997), p. 146.

19 Brooks Jackson, 'Financing the 1996 campaign: the law of the jungle', in *Toward the Millennium: The elections of 1996* (Larry J. Sabato, ed., Boston, MA, Allyn and Bacon, 1997), p. 239.

20 E. J. Dionne, 'Yet a chance for reform', *Washington Post National Weekly Edition*, 9 March 1998, p. 26; Eliza Newlin Carney, 'Party time', *National Journal*, 19 October 1996, p. 2215; Corrado, 'Financing the 1996 elections', p. 136; Jackson, 'Financing the 1996 campaign', p. 256.

21 Quoted in Adam Pertman, 'Weicker image casting a long shadow', *Boston Sunday Globe*, 26 August 1990, p. 69.

22 See David C. King, 'The polarization of American parties and mistrust of government', in *Why People Don't Trust Government* (Joseph S. Nye, Jr, Philip D. Zelikow and David C. King, eds, Cambridge, MA, Harvard University Press, 1997), pp. 155–78; and Alan I. Abramowitz and Kyle L. Saunders, 'Party polarization and ideological realignment', in *The Parties Respond: Changes in American parties and campaigns* (3rd edn; L. Sandy Maisel, ed., Boulder, CO, Westview, 1998), pp. 128–43.

23 M. Margaret Conway, *Political Participation in the United States* (Washington, DC, Congressional Quarterly Press, 1985), p. 131.

24 David G. Lawrence, *The Collapse of the Democratic Presidential Majority: Re-alignment, dealignment, and electoral change from Franklin Roosevelt to Bill Clinton* (Boulder, CO, Westview, 1997), p. 141.

25 Martin P. Wattenberg, 'The hollow realignment continues: partisan change in 1988', paper presented to the 1989 Annual Conference of the American Political Science Association. See also Martin P. Wattenberg, *The Decline of American Political Parties, 1952–1988* (Cambridge, MA, Harvard University Press, 1990); Everett Carll Ladd, '1996 vote: the "no majority" realignment continues', *Political Science Quarterly*, vol. 112, no. 1, 1997, pp. 14–17.

26 Howard H. Callaway, 'Transformations in American politics and their implications for federalism', *Party Line*, vol. 18, November 1984, p. 11.

27 Joel H. Silbey, 'The rise and fall of American parties', in *The Parties Respond: Changes in American parties and campaigns* (3rd edn; L. Sandy Maisel, ed., Boulder, CO, Westview, 1998), p. 17.

28 Everett Carll Ladd, 'Of political parties great and strong', *American Enterprise*, July–August 1994, quoted in *National Journal*, 6 August 1994, p. 1884.

29 Quoted in Brooks Jackson, *Honest Graft: How special interests buy influence in Washington* (Washington, DC, Farragut, 1990), p. 322.

30 'Who stays home on election day? About half the electorate', *New York Times*, 6 November 1996, p. B13.

31 Sabato, *Party's Just Begun*, p. 20, emphasis in original.

32 *San Jose Mercury News* reporter Phil Trounstine, quoted in *National Journal*, 28 February 1998, p. 474.

33 Dan Balz, 'As California goes, so goes the…', *Washington Post National Weekly Edition*, 8 June 1998, p. 9; Lois Romano, 'Setting the stage for amateur hour', *Washington Post National Weekly Edition*, 8 June 1998, p. 12.

5

Entrepreneurial campaigns
in the present day

Opportunity knocks

Campaign planning will be affected by many influences, not least the nature of the office at stake, its place in the federal system of government and the size of the constituency involved. Most candidates will begin by confiding to trusted family members and friends, and for many offices at the community level this group may need to be expanded only modestly before it can provide all the strategic, financial and organisational assets required for a brief election campaign. However, many of the offices available in the US political system require long campaigns targeting potential voters, who are bombarded with messages from many sources regarding their political, social and personal responsibilities. Getting the campaign's message through to those citizens whose support would be most valuable to a particular candidate at the various stages of a particular race can turn out to be a complex logistical problem. While that small group of family and friends can support and advise any candidate at the start of a campaign, it is not long before candidates for most national, state-wide or major local offices look for professional help.

Well before a candidacy is declared to the public, the candidate's team of advisers will already have spent time and effort assessing the chances of establishing a credible campaign, marshalling the required initial resources, considering options for garnering continued financial support, and planning strategies for the prospective campaign. When recruiting candidates to run in the 1998 elections for the US House of Representatives, the Democratic Party concentrated on training in fund-raising and getting the vote out. In the words of Representative Martin Frost (Texas), chair of the Democratic Congressional Campaign Committee, 'We were pretty blunt. We didn't try to lure people by telling them they could do it for $400,000.' Rather it was estimated that a minimum of $1 million would be needed for a credible campaign where the constituency fell within a major media market, and $500,000 to $750,000 elsewhere.[1] Many campaigns will cost more than this. While the national committees of both major parties do all they can to give financial and other support to their candidates for federal office, they cannot underwrite all the costs, and the major responsibility is thrown back on the candidate campaign organisations.

The primary election is not a totally ubiquitous feature of American elections, but it is a stage faced by many candidates, necessitating a campaign strategy flexible enough to cover the two phases of the election: securing the party nomination, and winning the general election. The strategic problems set by the two phases differ. The primary, controlled by a mixture of party and legislative regulation, generally attracts the participation of the most politically motivated sectors of the electorate. The successful candidates in each party are then pitched into the general election, which faces the campaign organisation with the challenge of convincing a much broader electorate of the candidate's merits.

The route from nascent candidacy to officeholder is a gruelling test for any campaign team. The considerable and varied efforts expended in recent years by candidate-centred campaign organisations in charting a course through the modern political landscape have stimulated constant innovation in the discovery and exploitation of campaign resources. There are, of course, numerous candidates for minor offices whose campaign funds do not stretch to hiring professional help. 'A campaign environment in which potential models are limited in number and diversity – a small town, say, in which candidates are expected to do no more than work the county fair and distribute brochures door-to-door – discourages innovation as long as those traditional campaign practices continue to appear effective.'[2]

Over time, challengers and incumbents even for minor offices may in their turn become careful observers of successful campaigns at all levels. Large-scale, federal campaigns have the incentive and resources necessary for the expensive task of developing new campaign techniques and technologies. Low-budget, volunteer-based local campaigns are quick to learn from observing this effort, and are pleased to pick up both intangibles, such as campaign ideas and strategies, as well as tangibles, such as mailing lists and campaign software packages. There are few candidates who can afford completely to ignore the campaign industry, even if it is only to design and print the most modest campaign leaflet. Nevertheless, it is the campaigns that attract most substantial investment of resources that have seen the most innovative responses to the modern political environment, and it is to those races that we shall look for our examples.

The campaign listens: the polls and public opinion

Some of the most powerful techniques of the modern campaign are merely old campaigning methods redefined by a new technical reality. A campaign needs to project effectively the information and messages about the candidate's personality and policy positions most likely to contribute to electoral victory. In order to motivate the voters, this material must be packaged and delivered efficiently, to the most appropriate audience sectors. In order to judge to whom that information is most usefully directed, via what medium it would best be carried, and whether the message is having the intended effect, the campaign needs to collect evidence of its impact, or potential impact, on the voting groups in the electorate.

'Modern-day targeting techniques are merely a more sophisticated version of Abraham Lincoln's call to "find 'em and vote 'em".[3] Effective political polling has been developing steadily since George Gallup showed the way with his accurate predictions of the 1936 presidential election results. In spite of occasional notable errors, polling is now generally considered an effective way of tracking public opinion during the course of a campaign. Even candidates who run without the full panoply of political consultancy are likely to commission some polls on their own behalf. A major reason for this form of campaign research is to find the voters. That is, to answer such questions as who is likely to vote, what are their predispositions in the particular election, what are their opinions of the candidates' merits and what are their beliefs regarding various issues that may emerge as salient to the campaign. A very important corollary to this is whether the polling responses can be used to classify the respondents into relatively reliable voting blocs, identifiable by particular characteristics and motivated by discrete clusters of issue convictions.

Polling has increased markedly in sophistication as questioning has been refined by experience and analysis has been aided by the introduction of modern technology. The modern election age cannot be separated from the age of the computer, and polling is one area where this influence is most marked. Advances in computer technology mean that while even in the 1970s any poll data that contained a substantial amount of information could be effectively analysed only on a mainframe computer, similar manipulations, cross-tabulations and tests for statistical significance can now be carried out very quickly on a relatively inexpensive personal computer. The computer can also help design and implement the polls, by holding and sorting address lists and telephone numbers, reading and tabulating responses, and even by being programmed to assist in the conduct of telephone interviews. Computer software is available for purchase to cover all aspects of campaigning, with the result that at the cheap end of the market there now exists 'what one veteran, with a mix of wonder and pique, calls "polling out of a briefcase"'.[4] The lower-level campaigns can benefit from 'trickle-down technology'. For example, one 1996 candidate for the state legislature in Nebraska benefited from the development expenditure undertaken by Dick Lugar's failed presidential campaign. Lugar software was tweaked by a local consultancy to provide the state-level candidate with telephone contacts and appropriate follow-up letters to 14,000 households in his constituency at a cost of only $4,000, well below what the cost would have been if he had started from scratch.[5]

Many candidates, however, will want to hire a well known pollster, in part to acquire the services of someone with a reputation for accurate work, but also in order to help give the campaign credibility by association with members of the election consultancy business who bring with them a pedigree of success. Polls can have considerable influence in a campaign. In the campaign office of one 1996 gubernatorial candidate, the simple question 'How do you decide your campaign stands?' provoked consternation when a staff member, and former journalist, promptly replied, 'We follow the polls.' The other staff rapidly contradicted this position, pointing out that the polls were just to confirm which of their candidate's issues were having an impact on the public, and would do no more than influence the nuances of presenting the candidate to the voters.[6] Peggy Noonan, speech-writer for Presidents Reagan and Bush, made a powerful and relevant point, though she was discussing the influence of pollsters on incumbents: 'Everyone else has an opinion; the pollster has a fact.'[7] One might expect this to have even more impact in the fluid, opinion-riddled and volatile world of the campaign. Pollster and political consultant Frank Luntz points out one very pragmatic value to the campaign: 'Political money follows winners, or those perceived as winners. And poll results create a perception of winners and losers.'[8]

Pollsters' 'facts' are sometimes credited with greater validity than is justified, since their accuracy depends on the size of the poll, the representativeness of the sample and the stage of the campaign. Voters have become increasingly volatile in recent years and are more often delaying their voting decision, and even their concentrated attention on the election, until the late stages of the campaign. Poll results taken among the general public early in the campaign give little more than an indication of name recognition. Nevertheless, the reporting of poll results in the media has become a significant feature of the modern campaign, so that their impact on public opinion can be solid, even if their basis is not.

This is not to say that early polling is not useful. Candidates facing primary selection processes will be interested in the opinions of those most likely to participate in the primary elections, caucuses or party conventions, and these groups are more likely than the general public to be thinking over the issues well in advance of the general election. In these cases targeted polling may well be useful. For example, in Massachusetts it is a condition that to appear on the ballot for state-wide office in the autumn primary election, a candidate must first have gained the support of at least 15 per cent of the delegates at the party convention, generally held in the spring. A serious candidate must therefore be aware of opinion among those taking part in the delegate selection process and, once the delegates have been chosen, must maintain an awareness of the support that exists among those delegates. This 'delegate tracking' is crucial in elections where conventions play a part, and is just one of the specialised forms of polling that have developed.

Most general opinion polls in the United States are conducted by telephone, with a statistical correction being made to account for the tiny number of Americans who cannot be reached this way. Polls may be totally random, or randomised within set quotas or strata to ensure appropriate representation of age groups, sex, income groups and so on, or the results weighted to give an apparently fair model of the population being consulted. Bigger samples are more likely to give accurate guidance, but while good information is all important, cost factors also have to be taken into account by any campaign, and methodologies which reduce costs, while still giving good leads, are welcome. For example, tracking polls, which repeatedly call on a single group of respondents over a period of time, give a good idea of opinion movement, even if the base sample is not perfect – and at many points in the campaign the potential of opinion to shift between candidates may be more important than the precise division of that opinion in the first place.

In recent years the 'focus group' has become a valued polling tool, often used to pre-test campaign initiatives. A small number of citizens is interviewed in depth, usually in a group. Debate is invited, and evidence appropriate to the campaign is introduced. Observers hope in this way to identify those issues that play powerfully, and to gain insight into how they should construct their campaign messages. Most famous in recent elections was the 'Paramus Thirty', used by the Bush campaign in 1988. A senior team from the Bush campaign observed the reactions of thirty invited voters in Paramus, New Jersey, to messages about Democratic nominee Michael Dukakis' record on prisoners being given temporary passes to spend a few days outside jail ('furloughs'), the pollution of Boston Harbor, and the pledge of allegiance[9] (he vetoed a bill passed by the state legislature that ordered teachers to lead mandatory pledges, after he received advice from the state's Supreme Judicial Court and Attorney General that the bill was both unconstitutional and unenforceable). On being told the Republican version of these stories, the voters' support for Dukakis halved. Lee Atwater, senior Bush campaign consultant, said, 'I realized right there that we had the wherewithal to win ... and that the sky was the limit on Dukakis's negatives.' In particular, Atwater, in reference to a notorious case where a prisoner had committed rape and murder while on furlough, vowed to 'make Willie Horton [Dukakis'] running mate'.[10] Subsequently the 1988 Bush campaign concentrated on a very limited range of issues that were identified by polling and focus groups as positive for their candidate and negative for the opponent.

While polling techniques change and evolve, the ends to which the results are put are not new. The Bush attack in 1988 paralleled Dukakis' experience ten years earlier when, standing for re-election as Governor of Massachusetts, he was opposed in the Democratic primary by Edward J. King. A survey commissioned by the King campaign seven months before the primary found only 11 per cent willing to support him. However, questions on the same survey found 42 per cent of respondents saying that they could not support a candidate who opposed minimum jail sentences for those convicted of violent crimes, 36 per cent claiming they could not support a candidate who opposed the death penalty and 60 per cent stating they could not support a candidate who favoured abortion. By repeatedly reminding voters of Dukakis' liberal views on these 'hot button' issues, and doggedly refusing to be diverted from this strategy to engage in broad policy and programme debate, the King campaign engineered an upset victory by 51 per cent to 42 per cent in the primary, and went on to win the governorship.[11] Given that Andy Card, a failed Republican hopeful for the governorship of Massachusetts, was on the Bush campaign team, it is perhaps not surprising that a similar tactic, backed by polling research, would be used in the later national campaign, and more surprising that the Dukakis team were apparently not armed with counter-research strategies that would underpin a defence of their candidate against this occurrence.

In the early run-up to the 1998 elections potential candidates, political party organisations and independent bodies with an interest in investing in campaigns were using polls to identify those congressional seats most likely to produce close election results. Months before the elections Representative Martin Frost (Texas) and the Democratic congressional committee which he chaired had identified fewer than forty seats as crucial to their campaign, while the equivalent Republican committee under Representative John Linder (Georgia) was sure the campaign would be won or lost in 'a handful of districts'. The most generous estimate was of sixty-five competitive races out of the 435 seats in the US House of Representatives. Increasingly focused on the contextual information provided by polls, neither parties nor independent sources of campaign finance wish to invest large amounts of money in quixotic challenges. Candidates, however deeply committed, find fund-raising difficult for campaigns in constituencies that are perceived as difficult, and the prediction of defeat can become a self-fulfilling prophecy in a race unbalanced by early polling figures. Unwilling to face ignominious defeat at considerable personal expense, candidates become more difficult to recruit for races in many strongholds, leaving scores of congressional seats uncontested by one or other major party. As early as June 1998 almost 20 per cent of the 435 members of the US House of Representatives could already be sure of re-election unopposed by a candidate from the other major party. In this case

polling appears to have worked to reduce citizen choice in those constituencies where opposition candidates have been deterred, and to increase the
concentration of expenditure in a small number of constituencies, thereby
often marginalising local issues as the force of national campaigning
organisations is brought to bear in each constricted arena.[12]

Having obtained polling results, according to former CBS poll manager
Keating Holland, 'Reputations are made for being savvy, teasing a really
good answer to a political problem out of the data.' Furthermore, says
Holland, 'A really good pollster should be able to say not just that it looks
bad for you but *do this* and it will be better.'[13] Public opinion polls in mid-
1998 indicated that top issues with the electorate were 'improving
education and the schools' (77 per cent), 'protecting the Social Security
system' (68 per cent) and 'handling the crime problem' (68 per cent),
while issues that had occupied a good deal of government time and effort,
such as campaign finance reform efforts and underage smoking, exercised
only a minority (32 per cent and 39 per cent, respectively). These measures of public opinion feed back into the campaign, 'shaping campaign
rhetoric and television commercials around the country', and growing to
'dominate the congressional agenda'.[14] The fact that polls can have such
a direct effect on the campaign message brings to some suspicion that
candidates may become the creatures of their opinion gatherers, that they
may cease to be political leaders in the obsessive need to follow the trends
of opinion to electoral success. In the contemporary age, when office-
holding is itself seen to be part of a permanent campaign strategy,
behaviour in office can also become suspect. Discussing then Speaker Newt
Gingrich's shifting positions, *Boston Globe* journalist Chris Black concluded
that, 'He's changed because this Republican leadership is as poll-driven as
Clinton's White House.'[15]

Campaign professionals defend themselves in a number of ways. Candidates when they enter the fray come complete with a set of personal
beliefs. The aim of polling is not totally to remodel those beliefs in the
voters' image, but to help a candidate distinguish between those beliefs
held in common with the target voters and those not shared, and to
identify the issues on which voters feel strongly. Campaign decisions made
on the basis of this information will most likely lead to the selective
emphasis of elements of the candidate's beliefs, as well as selective attacks
on the opponent, in the effort to control the agenda of the campaign, but
not, say the professionals, to an unethical remodelling of the candidate.
If the candidate chooses to alter a personal position in response to public
opinion, then this may be defended as the correct stance for a potential
representative to take in a democratic system. Whether shifting or holding
fast, the campaign is forewarned by the polls that it may be necessary to
defend these positions, possibly in response to opposition attacks, and
will therefore be ready with convincing explanations of the candidate's

decisions on these contentious points, defending against charges of expediency, or emphasising principled leadership. Major shifts of position during the course of a campaign are dangerous, undermining the candidacy and giving the impression that the campaign is poorly organised and potentially untrustworthy. To retain the impression and reality of integrity and control within the campaign, 'It is critical for your campaign to determine its theme before you hit the campaign trail.'[16]

In countries with strong party systems, the theme is set by the parties. In the more fluid party political structure of the contemporary United States, the responsibility lies with the candidate and, advises Joel Bradshaw, 'As in all key elements in campaign planning, you must begin with research about your electorate.' Quite apart from contextualising the campaign strategy, this polling research may be used to attract financial and political support, and to deter potential opponents. More than two years before the presidential election of 2000, a 'trial heat' poll pitting Texas Governor George W. Bush (son of the former President) and Vice-President Al Gore against each other gave Bush a clear lead of 4 per cent. Bush strategists were hopeful that this spelled a 'big-time electoral problem' both for the Democrats and for other potential Republican candidates, by helping to accelerate the Bush campaign bandwagon.[17]

Good polling may therefore be important from the time that the field is lining up and initial decisions of style and substance are being made, through all stages of the campaign, helping to define the projected shape of the campaign, and guiding the adjustments of emphasis and message delivery right to its close. At the local level the political amateur with a social science textbook, off-the-shelf software and a personal computer can make a stab at public opinion analysis. In the larger constituencies hired specialists with team support, campaign experience and tried skills are brought in. In either case, it is not the party, or any other traditional political organisation, that is acting as the conduit for opinion – it is the technician. A growing number of campaign professionals collect and analyse the polling data, identify the powerful issues and construct the consequent advertising and media events. And with modern technology available, points out Ronald Elving, 'It is possible ... to poll on Thursday to determine what a candidate needs to do in his final days, cut a new TV commercial on Friday, beam it to stations on Friday night and have it on the air all the pre-election weekend' (national elections and most state elections being on a Tuesday).[18]

The campaign speaks: the messages and the media

Television has become the most important information resource for most Americans. Candidates for major office wishing to make an impact are not in the position of being able to ignore television news coverage, nor can they pass up the opportunity to advertise on this medium. There have been doubts expressed about the effectiveness of this form of campaigning, but recent research suggests that the overall effect of the net mix of political advertising increases turnout, and that political advertising influences voting behaviour. While this effect was modest compared with factors such as previous voting behaviour, partisan identification and feel-good issues on America's economy and international position, one researcher concluded that 'week-to-week changes in candidate support were ... substantively affected by differential amounts of television advertising', and another commented that 'television advertising matters at the margin'.[19]

To a campaigner, every margin matters in an election. An analysis of the Clinton campaign up to August 1996 showed that 99 per cent of advertising expenditure had gone into the electronic media. Even if one adds campaign events, direct mail and similar campaign activities to the advertising total, spending on the electronic media still accounts for 82 per cent of the outlay.[20] More local campaigns will find greater use for other methods of communication, but at all levels, when one candidate has decided that television is a useful campaign tool, other candidates feel pressured to follow suit. Moreover, the public has begun to expect television appearance, at least from candidates for major office; a candidate for congressional, state-wide, or even substantial local office may still use radio and print media advertising very effectively, but with no television output the campaign barely looks credible.

The use of television advertising has grown as the electronic media market has become more segmented and target audiences have become more identifiable. Audience surveys have from their beginning reported not just global figures, but have broken down results to give figures for identified groups within the total. These techniques have become increasingly sophisticated as new generations of computers have been able to amalgamate masses of survey research, census data, audience returns and other resources to identify sectors of the population with increasing clarity. Commercial advertisers have welcomed these breakdowns for their value in determining what groups most appreciate their products, and therefore in acting as a guide on how to pitch further advertising. Political advertisers are no less pleased to be able to design their messages to appeal selectively to potentially receptive segments of the global market.

In some cases the segmented market can be approached through a purpose-built media channel. On general-purpose channels, some individual television programmes will be aimed at particular viewers; indeed, in the early days of radio and television this kind of targeting was demanded by advertisers as a condition of their sponsorship. Political operatives also recognised the value of this ability to identify the viewing audience. For example, when the 1984 Reagan presidential re-election campaign became concerned about the 'gender gap' of higher support for Democratic candidate Walter Mondale among women than men, it responded with a series of advertisements on daytime television. The spots stressed the dangers of inflation and higher prices in the event of a Mondale victory, and were aimed at the large segment of US middle-aged, home-based women who watch television soap operas and light entertainment quiz games. Reagan's pollster, Richard Wirthlin, claims that while these women formed only 6 per cent of the electorate, the fact that they responded with a rapid shift towards Reagan limited the damage that gender gap could inflict on the Republican incumbent.[21]

The past twenty years has seen the development of electronic media that segment the market by channel and by geography. Locally based independent television stations, as well as franchises of the major networks, provide a popular route for regionally targeted advertising. In addition, the expansion of satellite and cable distribution of television has brought to US households the potential of many channels from a multitude of providers. Even viewers far distant from major urban media markets, if they were willing to invest a little in equipment and services, now have the potential to view scores of channels. The viewer's necessary initial investment was not negligible, and a selling point made by Ted Turner in 1978, pitching to advertisers for his Atlanta-based 'super-station', was that 'we're not wired to the ghettos'.[22] As cable and satellite development has continued, the upmarket nature of that particular audience has remained important. In 1991/2 over 70 per cent of adults with household income over $50,000 were watching cable, as opposed to fewer than 50 per cent of adults with household income lower than $30,000.[23] As early as 1987 campaigners were aware that, compared with average viewers, cable television audiences 'are more affluent, better educated, and more likely to be registered voters and politically active individuals'.[24] The proportion of American households on cable had increased to around 74 per cent by 1996, and this was clearly a market worth buying into.[25]

Two features of this media evolution were particularly important to those wishing to communicate with an audience. One was the development and expansion of specialist channels and networks: the Christian Broadcasting Network, the Fox system, MTV, the Home Shopping Channel, CNN (Cable Network News), C-SPAN (Cable-Satellite Public Affairs Network), ESPN (sports), the Weather Channel, the History Channel, the Science Fiction Channel, the Disney Channel, Nickelodeon (children and family channel), and a range of variously targeted media providers. In addition, many households received their broadcasts through local cable providers, presenting an opportunity, in addition to the use of local television stations, for highly targeted advertising based on geography as well as audience profile. Since cable franchises are allocated by local government bodies, the reception boundaries potentially correspond with political constituency boundaries, thereby providing a very efficient route to the voters. This added to the traditional form of 'broadcasting' the complementary style of 'narrow-casting'.

Advertising strategy reflects audience preference, and the audience has turned away from the national networks, towards local independent channels and cable-accessible channels, in droves. The nightly news shows of the three major national networks, which totally dominated news viewing less than a generation ago and were still the regular viewing of two-thirds of the viewing population in 1986, were watched in 1996 by fewer than half of the audience.[26] This creates new opportunities for campaigns to target voters, as these channels exist only insofar as they are successful examples of niche marketing. In 1992, while two-thirds of all campaign spending was in local markets, cable accounted for only a tiny proportion. By 1996, one commentator reported that cable spending had quadrupled since four years previously, and national campaigns as well as regional ones were finding new ways of using the segmented market to get their message across to a targeted audience in an efficient and cost-effective way.

There have been accusations that campaign advertising is often poor in content, regularly misleading and may act to alienate voters from the electoral process when especially abrasive negative advertising techniques are used.[27] The creators of these advertisements defend them as bringing important issues of personal integrity into the election debate, and John Tierney of the *New York Times* pointed out that 'negative commercials deal with issues like taxes, crime and education, and they're crammed with statistics.... A 30-second spot often addresses three different substantive issues – which is at least two more than ... in the typical two-minute television story or 500-word newspaper article.'[28] An alternative assessment was offered by Garry Trudeau, parodying the process through his *Doonesbury* cartoon strip in 1989. 'I just didn't know very much about either man,' says Doonesbury, 'But then I started watching their campaign commercials. It turns out one of the guys was a tax cheat who abused his wife and favored giving crack to furloughed sex offenders.... [And the other candidate] was a corrupt alcoholic who favored murdering babies and burning the flag.... [I voted for] the wife-beater. I thought he had the better denials.'[29] In 1996 a *Boston Globe* article on the television advertisements in the Massachusetts race for the US Senate, between John Kerry and William Weld, reflected this same view, opening, 'You can vote for the heartless liar who wants to destroy the environment, shred Medicare, attack innocent children and throw Grandma on the street. Or you can vote for the tax-happy freeloader who supports cop killers, terrorists, drug addicts, welfare cheats, gang members, unemployment and gridlock.'[30]

Only a portion of advertising is negative and personal. Campaign advertisements can be calm, serious, policy-oriented, very occasionally witty and at times scrupulously honest. Television may well be seen, as the campaign professionals claim, as a technological asset to democracy. Using the results of polls measuring voters' concerns to design and target political advertising may strike some critics as manipulative, but it may also be interpreted as the legitimate identification of important issues, the provision of relevant information to the concerned voters and the potential adjustment of political agendas to reflect worries that might otherwise have been overlooked. However, the elections of the 1990s have continued to contain plenty of examples of what one reporter called 'the negative, take-no prisoners' approach, using 'harsh, personal attacks and images that play on public anxieties and fears'.[31]

Having pinpointed potentially powerful issues, candidates are increasingly tempted to identify themselves with these issues in the most inflammatory fashion, with the intention of hitting public opinion hard. Crime and the death penalty feature regularly: in 1994 Democratic Governor Ann Richards, facing a tough re-election battle in Texas, trumpeted her pleasure that Texas had one of the largest prison systems in the world; Representative Tom Foley (Democrat – Washington), facing charges that he had lost touch with his constituents, used a tough line on crime and law enforcement in an attempt to restore his credentials; and John Ashcroft, challenging in Missouri, pointed out his readiness to use the death penalty when he had been Governor. In 1996 many Republican candidates relied on their ability in recent years to redefine 'liberal' as a pejorative term, and then to use it as a kind of general name-calling exercise. Paul Wellstone (Democrat – Minnesota) was called 'embarrassingly liberal', Bob Torricelli (Democrat – New Jersey) 'liberal to a T' and 'foolishly liberal', echoing earlier campaigns, such as that against New York Governor Mario Cuomo ('too liberal too long') and Florida Lieutenant Governor Buddy McKay ('Buddy, you're a liberal'). Democratic candidates in 1996 regularly relied on attacking their Republican opponents as clones of Republican Speaker Newt Gingrich, and of marching in lock-step to threaten Medicare, pensions, education and the environment.[32] Similar tactics are used in radio and print media, but in television advertising both the technology and the expense prompt campaigns to look for maximum impact in minimum time, a dynamic which seems to lend itself especially well to this hard-hitting style. There is a common belief among consultants that negative advertising has a rapid impact on voting intentions, but after a survey of 135 elections to the US Senate from 1988 to 1996, Gerald Pomper concluded that there was no very solid evidence of this and that, overall, 'negativism does not elect candidates, and it may actually harm their campaigns'.[33] There remains serious concern that negative advertising drives down the vote. As one New Jersey voter said,

'The nasty ads make you not want to vote at all', and some researchers claim that as many as 5 per cent of voters may stay away as a result of this style of campaigning.[34]

Harshness carries its own risks. When such vigorous tactics are used in a primary campaign, opponents from another party may gain a greater than usual advantage from this internecine warfare. All candidates have learned, perhaps most effectively from the failed 1988 presidential campaign of Michael Dukakis, that no attack should go without rapid response in kind. The counter-accusation advertisement is itself becoming a staple of the industry. When Republican candidate Dick Zimmer simulated a news broadcast in an attack advertisement against his opponent in the 1996 New Jersey race for the US Senate there appeared to be a backlash among the pundits and the public that helped Torricelli to win the race. A New Jersey newspaper called the advertisement 'a new low', and the Torricelli campaign used these assessments in a response advertisement, but it has to be said that this was in the context of a race more notable for its mutual use of negativism than for anything else. John Carroll of the *Boston Sunday Globe* identified new twists in 1996, with the 'rapid presponse, in which the president's men attack Bob Dole's positions even before he takes them', and the 'direct-response' advertisement, in which voters are prompted to telephone the opponent to complain about some particular aspect of the campaign. When Michael Huffington did this in California in his 1994 campaign for the US Senate, the volume of telephone traffic forced his opponent, Dianne Feinstein, to change the telephone number of her campaign headquarters. This tactic regardless, Feinstein fought off Huffington's challenge.[35]

The dominant opinion in the campaign industry is that the healthy pluralism of voices in American political campaigns is the best defence against distortion and untruth. Certainly the revelation of serious distortions in advertising or campaign presentation, especially if made by the press, can sometimes rebound to disadvantage the perpetrator. Nevertheless, there will be real financial costs to a candidate forced to reply to unjust attacks in the media, and there is a consequent danger that advantage may accrue to the well heeled campaign. In the recognition that voters sometimes become disturbed by the low blows hurled in negative advertisements, some newspapers have begun to review and analyse these attacks, and the 'ad watch', complete with analysis of both the style and the evidence in political television advertisements, is increasingly common in newspapers across the United States. Democrat Paul Wellstone pulled off a surprise in the 1990 election for US Senator from Minnesota against the experienced Republican incumbent Rudy Boschwitz with a 'humorous, outsider's campaign', suggesting to some commentators 'that a gentler and more original approach to campaigning could work'. The 1996 rematch presented a different scenario. Wellstone ran a campaign in which about half his advertisements were critical of his opponent, but even these would open and close with statements about Wellstone's own stand. On the other hand, almost all of Boschwitz's advertisements were unremittingly negative. Opinion polls suggested that the caustic campaign run by Boschwitz made voters more favourable towards Wellstone, who won re-election.[36]

It may indeed be the case that in some campaigns such low-key messages have worked. In these cases the incumbents had records in office on which they could be challenged, their raucous advertising could therefore be depicted as hysterical and diversionary, and the raising of such questions by the relatively neutral voices of the media, rather than the opposing campaign, gives them an added legitimacy. Nevertheless, taking such a low-key approach is not common, and other campaigns in the 1990s were not notable for their restraint. In a sample of 420 US Senate campaign advertisements aired from 1984 to 1994, researchers classified 43.4 per cent as negative. Overall, only about one-third of this sample contained specific issue information. About 40 per cent contained more vague issue information, and around a quarter of all advertisements contained no issue information at all. However, the negative advertisements were much more likely to introduce issue information to the media campaign, and this was more likely to be specific information, with almost 95 per cent of these advertisements being issue-based.[37]

Some members of the orthodox advertising industry have expressed concern. Alexander Kroll, of the New York agency Young and Rubicam, believes that 'Political advertising is so wretched that most of it wouldn't be approved by our own self-governing bodies.'[38] But for all the image of 'Madison Avenue' campaigns, few major commercial agencies choose to become involved in political advertising, preferring to avoid the controversy, not wishing to disturb current clients and favouring the steady business of product sales over the cyclical nature of campaigning. Political advertising has generated its own substantial and relatively self-enclosed business sector and while the American Association of Political Consultants does publish a code of ethics for its members, it appears to offer little to counter contemporary advertising trends.

The campaign puts it all together: political consultancy

While a campaign may lean heavily on good polling and powerful advertising, these are not the only services brought to a campaign by a successful political consultant. A political consultant may exert overall management control in a campaign, and the largest consulting firms may provide many of the services in-house, but in general, and certainly in large-scale campaigns, the campaign management is likely to subcontract for many necessary services. *The Political Pages*, an annual publication claiming to be 'the only complete A to Z directory of every product and service used by the political industry', contains thousands of entries. 'Whether you're in Maine or Alaska, Florida or Arizona', says the announcement for the 1990 edition, 'you can locate the business and individuals with political know-how in every field – fund-raising, printing, direct mail, photography, media consulting and many more.'[39] That issue claimed a distribution of 24,500, including 8,000 elected officials or candidates for office, 3,000 campaign staff, 2,000 political consultants, 6,000 national and local party leaders, and 2,000 PACs and associations. By September 1998, it was claiming to be 'the world's largest circulation annual directory of political consultants and vendors', and was accessible on-line on the World Wide Web.[40]

Campaign expertise for hire is on show monthly in the 'Marketplace' section of *Campaigns & Elections*, the journal of the campaign professional. One finds here advertisements for producers of all aspects of advertising, from bumper stickers through graphic design to full media production: for elementary leaflet distribution and sophisticated direct mail operations; for campaign computer software and hardware, computer consultants, computer database development, computer data-processing, computer financial control packages; for broad-scale fund-raising; and even for grassroots organising and collecting signatures on nomination and issue petitions. Developments in campaigning show early in these columns – as in 1994, when one provider trumpeted that 'This is The Year of Direct Mail Video', and another offered to duplicate and mail to voters 100,000 five-minute videos at $1.62 each. The September 1998 issue was devoted to 'How campaigns are using the Internet', with six special articles and numerous advertisements offering Internet services. Training seminars are offered for candidates and campaign staff covering all aspects of campaign management: 'campaign planning, plan development, targeting, vote demographic analysis, research, opposition research, direct mail ... telephone fund-raising, GOTV, targeted calling, public opinion calling'. Tapes and videos of the training sessions are for sale to those who cannot attend. Campaign training has shifted away from the political parties, as campaign consultants and other professionals of the election business have formed their own organisations, and created a market for training services. Even universities have got in on the act, offering an increasing number of programmes aimed at the budding campaign professional.[41]

As is clear from some of the products on offer, the widespread availability of inexpensive computer technology has become immensely important in the modern campaign. Computer analyses of survey responses provide accurate data very quickly to aid strategic decision-making. CD-ROMs can be purchased listing all registered voters, categorised by town, county and congressional district or state, giving data on individuals' voting frequency and previous political contributions. Cross-referenced with mapping software, databases on purchasing habits and other data available in electronic format, these voter records can be useful in a multitude of ways. Computer-generated maps can provide a visual representation of the data collected. Computers with modern word-processing software allow apparently individualised letters to be sent to citizens, contributing to the massive growth and significance of direct mail in American politics.

Direct mail is used by candidates, parties, PACs, pressure groups and others to identify supporters, to persuade waverers and, especially important under modern campaign finance rules, to raise funds. The impact of a well written letter, especially a personal one, has long been recognised, and politicians at all levels are careful to respond to constituency mail. Neither the personalisation of standard response letters nor the mass mailing of potential supporters are new inventions. But the application of modern technology to sort data, develop lists of names and addresses where the mailing is likely to produce a positive response, print person-alised letters, fold them and place them in stamped envelopes, and sort the result has vastly expanded the potential in this area. Much of the initial work on modern direct mail was done by Richard Viguerie, a consultant with conservative political convictions driven by the belief that direct mail could help unleash a conservative 'populist revolt' in the United States. Viguerie is still a force in the world of direct mail, but many candidates and political groups have gone on to develop this form of campaign message. The shift of high-cost campaigning to the television screen has not undermined the value of direct mail. In the mid-1990s, KCMS, just one of the many direct mail contractors available to candi-dates, claimed to despatch 200 million pieces of mail annually, and process twelve million responses.[42]

American homes are bombarded with 'junk mail'. Campaigns have responded with efforts to catch the householder's attention. Mass mailings that qualify for discount rates may nevertheless be stamped at the full letter rate to avoid being bunched with other junk mail. Similarly, letters may have stamps instead of machine franks on the envelope as a dis-tinguishing feature. They may be packaged to look like telegrams, with messages such as 'Urgent Tax Information Enclosed' on the envelope, to contain, on being opened, a campaign statement on the subject. The junk mail senders will say almost anything to get you to open their letters. American comedienne Rita Rudner claimed in a 1990 television sketch that on the envelopes it says 'Urgent', 'Top Secret', 'We Have Your Parents'. Once opened the contents can be another creative tour de force. Letters are not only personalised, but can appear to be hand-written, or typed but then hand-corrected. They apparently come on candidates' personal note-paper, or from the campaign hotel where the candidate has snatched a few minutes to write after a long, hard day on the campaign trail. Such artifice does not really deceive, but it can give the literature an immediacy that persuades the recipient to read on. Direct mail video relies on many of the same devices. In the words of one consultant specialising in this format, 'it's important to create a design that sparks interest and starts to tell your message the moment the video is pulled from the mailbox.'[43] Direct telephone campaigns, as well as direct mail, can be managed by computer, with the result that political messages are also becoming part of the junk telephone calls relayed into American homes. Development in the delivery of campaign messages appears continuous as computer-assisted technology provides ever more sophisticated ways of manipulating and delivering the valuable information that may lead to political power.

Opposition research has been one of the main evolutions in campaign consultancy towards the end of the twentieth century. While campaigns have since their beginnings included attacks on the opponent, it was the 1988 presidential campaign that demonstrated the usefulness of modern technology, and the power of this tool. After the Bush campaign's use of the Willie Horton case, 'aggressive dirt-digging came fully into its own. And despite cries of "foul" from the Democrats, the information about Horton, the furloughed murderer, was a matter of public record.'[44] To limit the chance of a backfire, negative advertising must be built on a solid foundation of research into the opponent. The Bush team's opposition research went well beyond their advertising strategy. They compiled a massive computer-held database on opponent Michael Dukakis, including the text of many of his speeches, covering his whole life. Actions taken and statements made by Dukakis during the campaign could be instantly compared with his lifetime political stances and personal behaviour. When inconsistencies were found these could immediately be fed back into the Bush assault, using whatever outlet was most appropriate, within the overall electioneering scheme co-ordinated by the campaign management.

Campaigns do not always have to pay good money to get their point across. Consultant Dan Hazelwood considers his profession is advantaged by 'the basic laziness of most reporters', which allows campaigns to place a story with 'a friendly member of the media ... [who will] run it as original reporting'.[45] Campaigners at all levels observe their opponents with intense circumspection. A penetrating attack, or powerful rebuttal, whether initiated in a speech, press release or advertisement, is likely to generate press and electronic media coverage, but it is clear that the underpinning information needs to be usable and accessible, and at least technically accurate. In large, high-profile races especially, campaigns turn to the professionals, driven in part by improvements in news technology that reports at speed, demanding instant candidate responses. Candidates with the research and speech-writing team that can enable them to respond quickly, appropriately and with an eminently quotable phrase are well placed in the battle for media attention.

A great deal of effort is put into calculating the issues and events that might prompt media interest, judging the form and arena that the campaign might use to stimulate this interest, and getting the words just right. Staff writers work to develop within the campaign's statements 'sound bites', brief, punchy, self-contained portions of speech, a few seconds long, which will jump out at videotape and recording editors in television and radio news rooms, and at newspaper journalists, as the perfect insert to highlight the day's campaign coverage. When skilfully done this considerably enhances the campaign's chances of having its important messages to the public voiced by the candidate, yet within the legitimising context of the news.

All campaign coverage competes with other news items, and is subject to the editorial perception of general public interest in the contest. Elections for minor office often attract only the most cursory of interest, even from local newspapers. The national networks covering national elections face the problem of fitting adequate coverage into the limited news airtime available. The result is a concentration on the horse-race aspect of elections, limited issue investigation, and sound bites, which were reduced to less than ten seconds in the run-up to the 1998 elections. As television technology provides greater choice of channels, space for campaign coverage increases, but so too does the viewers' opportunity to avoid it altogether. Any campaign will try to make sure that its message forms an attention-grabbing part of this media output, and those who can afford professional help will be likely to hire it.

According to a survey conducted in 1998, political consultants consider the 'quality of a candidate's message' to be the most important factor in winning elections, closely followed by the 'amount of money available to a candidate'. When a campaign uses negative tactics, consultants admit, it is on their advice, but they do not consider this to be the cause of public cynicism with elections. Rather, these consultants argue, the media create a negative context by concentrating reporting on bad campaign news. Only 42 per cent of these consultants had 'a great deal of confidence' in the 'wisdom of the American people', and 44 per cent felt they had 'helped elect candidates who they were eventually sorry to see serve in office'.[46] Nonetheless, consultancy grows apace. In the 1992 elections, 63.7 per cent of House candidates hired at least one consultant, up from 43.6 per cent only two years earlier. The competitiveness and financial capacity of the candidates was reflected in the use of consultants, with 75 per cent of candidates contesting open seats and over 66 per cent of incumbents using consultants, but only 16.5 per cent of challengers.[47] Consultancy offers a growing range of professional services which politicians hungry for election need to employ and for which the candidates, and inevitably their financial consultants, must raise the money.

Take the money and run

The widespread dissemination of the information and technology of campaigning in the modern political system, together with the reforms covering electoral regulation, have stimulated independent, entrepreneurial, candidate-centred campaigning, but this independence does not come cheap. Campaign finance scholar Herbert Alexander estimates that in the 1995–6 election cycle, political candidates, parties and PACs at all levels – federal, state and local – spent almost $5 billion on political campaigns.[48] Even after controlling for inflation, this total figure had almost doubled in the twelve years since the 1983–4 campaign cycle. In addition, money that was invested by organisations into issue-advocacy campaigns is not easily tracked. As long as they do not specifically urge the electorate to vote for or against a particular candidate, issue-advocacy advertisements fall outside the remit of election campaign finance even when, in the words of one Democratic consultant, they share '99 per cent of the DNA of a political ad'.[49]

The average expenditure by a major party candidate in the general election for the US House of Representatives in 1996 was $480,687, and in races for the US Senate the figure was $3,316,765 (see table 5.1). In House races especially, this figure is distorted by the large number of seats where an incumbent is so safe that no well financed opposition develops; in contrast, average expenditure rose to $628,558 in vacant House seats, where competition can be fierce. Including those candidates who lost in primary elections, and over 600 candidates representing minor parties, 2,289 people were at one time official candidates for the US House in 1996, and between them they raised $505.4 million, and spent $477.8 million. This was an 18 per cent increase in expenditure since 1993–4,

Table 5.1. *Total net disbursements by the major parties' general election candidates, 1996*

	US Senate			US House		
	No. of candidates	Total spent	Average	No. of candidates	Total spent	Average
Democrats						
Incumbents	7	$36.44m	$5,205,714	171	$97.73m	$571,520
Challengers	14	$33.75m	$2,410,714	211	$62.53m	$296,351
Open seats	13	$38.35m	$2,950,000	53	$33.29m	$628,113
Republicans						
Incumbents	13	$48.37m	$3,720,769	213	$157.23m	$738,169
Challengers	8	$23.09m	$2,886,250	174	$36.78m	$211,379
Open seats	13	$45.54m	$3,503,077	51	$32.08m	$629,020

most of which can be accounted for by a 32 per cent increase in the financial activity of Republican candidates. The 316 hopefuls from all parties who were at some time candidates for the US Senate in the 1995–6 election cycle spent a total of $287.5 million in 1996, slightly down from the 1994 total. Reported independent spending on these campaigns added another $21 million to the campaign total.[50]

Individual elections to both chambers of the federal legislature, and at other levels, can cost much more than the average, and can demand a substantial input of funds from candidates' own pockets as part of a powerful fund-raising effort. In 1996 Democrat Mark Warner spent $11.6 million challenging incumbent Republican Senator John Warner (who spent $5.6 million) in Virginia. Senator John Kerry (Democrat – Massachusetts) spent $11 million fending off the challenge of Republican William Weld ($8 million), who was looking for a change from being Governor of that state. Meanwhile, in the House, Speaker Newt Gingrich (Republican – Georgia) spent $5.6 million against a $3.3 million challenge from Democrat Michael Coles. In 1994 California Republican Michael Huffington became the biggest-spending senatorial candidate to date, with a total budget around $30 million, about $28 million of which came from his personal fortune. This followed a record-breaking House campaign two years earlier which had cost him $5 million. He failed to unseat incumbent Senator Dianne Feinstein, but claimed that he would run again in the future and, according to one observer, 'in 1995 Huffington had already begun running the first negative campaign ads in the 2000 election cycle'.[51] Subsequent life changes, including separation from his wife, diverted Huffington from immediate political ambitions. In 1998 the governorship was the big prize in California, with one candidate, Democrat Al Checchi, spending an estimated $40 million, almost all his own money, in an unsuccessful primary bid. In other 1998 races, New York Senator Alfonse D'Amato (Republican) was reported to have spent more than $7 million, and still have over $12 million on hand, as well as an active fund-raising programme in operation, four months before election day. At the same time in Illinois, Peter Fitzgerald (Republican) had already spent almost $11 million in his ultimately successful challenge for the seat of incumbent US Senator Carol Moseley-Braun. California, New York and Illinois are geographically large states with large populations, but when in 1984 Jay Rockefeller spent $12 million, most of it his own money, to become US Senator for West Virginia, he spent over $30 for every vote he received.[52]

Not all campaigns involve such high spending. Representative Matthew Martinez (Democrat) spent around $83,000 gaining a 1996 re-election in California's thirty-first district, and two years earlier it cost Michael Flanagan (Republican) only $107,000 to unseat scandal-ridden Dan Rostenkowski in Illinois. Flanagan himself was targeted in 1996, and even after spending $724,000 he was outspent two-to-one by Democrat Rod Blagojevich, who won the election. The times are unlikely to return to when Representative Natcher (Democrat) of Kentucky could achieve his eighteenth consecutive term of office in 1988 on an outlay of $8,397. By 1996 Natcher was dead, and a Republican held his old seat, in a race where the spending totalled $1.1 million. In the same year Representative Bateman (Republican) of Virginia spent $534,156 in spite of having no opponent, and Representative Salmon (Republican) of Arizona spent $456,089 in another campaign against nobody.

About $244 million was spent by presidential candidates in the 1996 primaries. After the nominations, the two major party candidates received $61.8 million each in federal campaign funds, and the Reform Party, on the basis of Ross Perot's showing in 1992, received a grant of just over $29 million, and raised about $1 million in donations. The major parties each received a further $12.4 million grant towards convention costs, to which they added $43.7 million from donations. Party political committees could co-ordinate a further $12.3 million each in spending on the presidential campaign, in addition to which the Dole and Clinton campaigns benefited from over $60 million in issue-advocacy spending. This totals about $550 million, of which a small proportion came from the national fund-raising committees of the major parties. These committees have become a major force in the whole election process and, including their contribution to the presidential election process, their total spending in the 1996 election cycle was $880 million. Anthony Corrado calculates that in 1996 the 'presidential and congressional candidates, national convention committees, and national party organizations alone spent $2.0 billion'. Quite apart from this being $650 million more than what was spent by these same bodies in 1992, it would have almost covered the total campaign expenditure of all participants at all levels of US government as recently as 1980. In 2000 there will be a campaign in which both major parties have a full presidential primary contest, probably encouraging the participation of more candidates, and greater expenditure.[53]

At the non-presidential level, a substantial proportion of campaign funds come from PACs. As discussed in chapter 4, PAC contributions were not very significant until the FECA of 1971 made them an inviting way of channelling funds to campaigns, since when there has been considerable growth in their numbers and activities. At the end of 1974, eighty-nine of the nation's 608 federally registered PACs were sponsored by corporate interests and 201 by labour organisations. By mid-1997 the total of 3,875 included 1,720 corporate-related to only 332 labour-related PACs. Other PACs were sponsored by trade, health, ideological, co-operative and membership-based groups. Total congressional campaign spending grew from about $450 million to more than $765 million between 1986 and 1996. PAC contributions kept pace at around 30 per cent of these spending figures, growing over a decade from $139.4 million to a 1998 figure of

$217.8 million. Two-thirds of these PAC contributions are given to incumbents. This imbalance is typical of the last decade, reaching its height in 1989–90, when incumbents received 79 per cent of PAC contributions. As well as making contributions to candidate campaigns, PACs may spend money on advertising or other activities in support of, or against, particular candidates. This independent PAC spending intended to influence federal campaigns was reported to amount to $10.6 million in 1996. The multimillion-dollar issue-advocacy campaigns that became so popular in 1996, some of which were sponsored by organisations that also have PACs, were not subject to federal reporting regulations.[54]

Direct party contributions and co-ordinated campaign spending were far less than payments by PACs, amounting in 1996 to $5.9 million in contributions as well as an additional $53.6 million spent by party committees on behalf of congressional candidates.[55] PACs, representing well defined business, union, issue-based and other interests, are particularly concerned to spend their cash on candidates likely to win, and donate especially generously to incumbents, already electorally advantaged by their familiarity to the electorate. In 1996, incumbent candidates in the US House of Representatives received almost 41 per cent of their campaign funds from PACs, with the proportion exceeding 46 per cent for Democrats. In a high-spending campaign system where individual contributions to federal-level campaigns are limited to $1,000, it is understandable why many candidates would like to develop good working relationships with those PACs that may wish to contribute and channel funds to the campaign effort. In states where laws have been introduced based on the national model, state-level PACs have developed to fill the same role. In less tightly regulated states, soft money can be added to other legitimate campaign contributions. At all these levels, candidates' own money can be used, and while incumbents can generally find adequate financial support to defend their offices, an increasing number of other candidates find themselves bankrolling substantial parts of their own campaigns.

Not all PACs are valued primarily for their cash. Some, such as the Veterans of Foreign Wars PAC, give only modest donations, but the endorsement of such a high-status organisation is valuable to a candidate in attracting voters. The hunt for campaign money can become tedious to those chasing and to those being chased – a seemingly endless round of poorly catered affairs with high-priced entrance. In recognition of this feeling, a fund-raising invitation circulated by Representative Sidney Yates (Democrat – Illinois) asked respondents to 'take a night off the fund-raising circuit to do whatever you wish', and to reply by ticking the box saying 'Yes, I want to stay home and enjoy my family and friends', and enclosing a suggested $300 donation. The appeal raised $20,000. A real event, especially a high-profile one, can still pull in substantial funds, and a dinner organised to raise money for Republican House and Senate candidates in 1998 brought in about $10 million.[56]

Some officeholders have discovered the value of founding their own PACs. Known as 'leadership' or 'candidate' PACs, these give politicians an opportunity to raise money in support of issues they consider significant, to aid fellow candidates with whom they have sympathy and from whom they may wish to garner future support, and to build up and train a fund-raising and campaigning organisation that might at some point be aimed at other targets. Campaign America, the leadership PAC of Senator Bob Dole, donated $377,000 to congressional candidates in 1992. It followed up with a further $563,512 in 1994 and $819,681 in 1996. After Dole's defeat in the 1996 presidential election, Campaign America became the leadership PAC for former Vice-President Dan Quayle. Vice-President Al Gore's PAC, Leadership '98, was a conduit to ethnic, geographic and ideological groups within the Democratic Party, and was a training ground for a potential presidential bid, as well as a channel for millions of dollars into candidate and party campaigns. Legislators at federal and state level may use one to construct a basis of allegiance on which to build a bid for a leadership position within the legislature. Representative David McIntosh (Republican – Indiana) was one of many members of Congress who had established a personal federal-level PAC. Aware of the value of maintaining and reinforcing his contacts in his home state, McIntosh had, in addition, a PAC established and registered under state law, raising funds for distribution to state legislative candidates. The disbursements of these PACs are modest, but they have become a significant part of the elaborate system of etiquette between American lawmakers that appears to make up in part for the absence of reliable party political structures.[57]

Some particularly creative campaigners have discovered the advantages of sponsoring charitable and educational groups, which are exempt from federal taxes, and which may, under certain circumstances, attract tax-deductible donations. To qualify for the tax breaks, these organisations are generally required not to participate in political activity or, in some cases, to take only very limited lobbying action. Nevertheless, they may advertise and pay for speaking engagements, and otherwise actively further their educational, religious or other aims. It is perhaps not surprising to find that sometimes these aims, for example engaging on one side of the debate over abortion, educating low-income communities about the citizenship value of registering and using the vote, or uniting fundamentalist Christians around the primacy of family values, run parallel to those of their political sponsors.[58]

If the campaign laws of the 1970s have helped stimulate the growth of PACs they have also, by their disclosure regulations, made this growth very visible. This visibility has, in its turn, stimulated some alarm at the growing influence of these interest-based organisations. PACs defend themselves as an important and successful conduit of public opinion, and claim that their abolition would reduce citizen participation, discourage small, individual political donations, reduce political education, reduce the accountability of campaign money, narrow the diversity of funding and cut opportunities to communicate with voters.[59] Some analysts suggest that the money would find its way into the system anyway, and is best coming through an accountable and visible route. Claims that PACs are gaining overbearing political influence are countered by the argument that in spite of their advantages they can each still donate only $5,000 to a candidate for a campaign, and that the PAC world is a pluralist one. This has to be balanced against the facts that in addition to PAC contributions and independent spending, PACs can increase their influence beyond that tracked by these figures. One method is 'bundling', soliciting and handing on contributions from persons on PAC mailing lists in the form of cheques made out directly to the candidates favoured by the organisation. The donations that result are from individuals, and therefore can be channelled to the candidate in addition to the legally limited PAC contribution, but the collection and delivery of these donations is designed to increase the visibility of the PAC in its relations to the candidate and, it is hoped, eventual officeholder. Some PACs spend considerable amounts on the recruitment and training of candidates, while others invest in issue-advocacy campaigns.

Individual PACs perform their self-ascribed civic duty with special vigour. For example, in 1995/6 EMILY's List (Early Money is Like Yeast PAC – supporting women candidates) spent $12.5 million. The National Rifle Association Political Victory Fund spent $6.6 million. Other big-spending PACs were connected with trades unions, such as the National Education Association ($5 million) and the United Auto Workers ($4 million), professional groups, such as the Association of Trial Lawyers ($5.1 million), and business interests, such as dairy farmers, auto dealers, bankers and insurance companies. Patterns of spending differ between categories of PACs. Out of 1,470 corporate PACs active in the 1995–6 election cycle, only three spent independently in favour of candidates, and only two spent independently against candidates, with $4.80 in independent spending for every $1,000 in contributions, suggesting their concern with establishing a direct relationship with the candidate. PACs based on trade, membership and health organisations spent almost $77 independently for every $1,000 given as donations, and non-connected PACs, often issue or ideology based, spent $189 independently for each $1,000 donated.

The largest independent spending in support of candidates in 1996 benefited Republican Senator Phil Gramm (Texas), to the tune of $1,179,922, and Gordon Smith, Republican candidate for the Oregon seat in the US Senate, also found $1,093,022 spent on his part. In fact, the top ten campaigns with support from independent expenditure were all

Republican. Mary Landrieu, Democratic candidate for US Senator from Louisiana, found herself subject to a barrage of $1,221,646 in independent spending against her. Seven of the top ten candidates suffering independent spending attacks were Democrats. In 1996 Democrats were opposed by $5.7 million in independent PAC spending, and benefited from $1.1 million. The respective figures for the Republicans were $3.9 million and $10.2 million. The modern campaign may be entrepreneurial, but it is clearly not ignoring party political positions.

The parties fight back

Regardless of where the public look for their political cues, it would be wrong to believe that the political parties have not responded vigorously to contemporary challenges once the dangers have been perceived. To a degree, the parties' search for relevance in the modern political system has led to them adopting many of the strategic and tactical weapons developed by political consultancy and PACs. That having been said, it is important to remember that the laws in many American states institutionalise the major parties in various functional ways. For example, stringent laws regarding access to ballots commonly discriminate in favour of the major parties. At the federal level, presidential election grants are automatically available to candidates chosen by the two major parties. Indeed, 'public policy invests the two major parties with important systemic functions while protecting their longevity',[60] but even given this apparent national commitment to the two-party system, a party not reacting to change could still be reduced to a fairly meaningless shell.

The Republican Party has been particularly energetic in its reaction to the changing environment for party political activity in the United States. Emerging from the 1964 landslide defeat of Barry Goldwater as a battered but ideologically more coherent body, the party was going through a process of rebuilding at precisely the time when legal, social and technological changes were at work, and appeared ready to explore any change for the potential opportunity that it offered. The Democratic Party on the other hand was attempting to hold together an electoral coalition forged in the 1930s, within which the ties had been loosened by demographic and policy agenda changes, and other changes in the political environment seemed at first to do little other than exacerbate these difficulties.

While the FECA appeared at first to give PACs some very substantial advantages, the amendments of the late 1970s were designed to encourage activity by national, state and local party committees in fund-raising and campaigning. The parties have seized the opportunity to become involved in 'generic' activities, such as 'party-building', voter registration and turn-out efforts, and the channelling of money into states and localities where election laws are least demanding. The Republican Party was first to recognise and exploit the opportunities in the increasingly entrepreneurial political world. Party committees adopted all the technological wizardry in the electoral marketplace to raise very substantial funds, and although the GOP got off to a flying start, the Democrats have done a great deal of catching up. Beginning in 1980 the Republican national committee also began investing in generic party advertising during the presidential campaign, and in 1984 the Democrats followed suit. Supreme Court decisions allowing party committees greater freedom to spend and the development of issue-advocacy campaigns have given the parties increasing opportunities to make themselves felt. Some of the money raised has been used to create facilities in Washington, DC, that could be useful to party candidates during campaigns. Professional advice can be obtained through party channels on advertising, direct mail and opinion polling. As well as providing services that parallel those offered by the independent business sector of the modern campaign, the parties have also eased into a brokerage role in the modern political environment, channelling campaign money, retaining a stable of consultants and generally assisting 'their competitive candidates in obtaining various resources and services by facilitating contacts and agreements between the candidates, PACs, campaign consultants, and other important electoral organizations'.[61]

To some extent this seems to be counter to a received wisdom that has parties and political consultants fighting for the same territory. As Stephen Medvic has pointed out, 'From such a vantage point, the struggle for electoral pre-eminence amounts to a zero-sum game; as consultants become increasingly indispensable, parties become expendable at exactly the same rate.' But that vision appears too simple. Both party support and the use of consultants can improve a candidate's showing in particular elections. Medvic found among a sample of 1992 congressional candidates that party support was particularly important to those challenging incumbents, but he also pointed out that 'parties and consultants are intimately linked'.[62]

Consultants are the service entrepreneurs of the US election system, and are free to take their clients where they wish, but the vast majority actually work on a relatively narrow part of the political spectrum. Most work only for candidates of one party. Some define themselves by ideological groups within the party. An increasing proportion are previous employees or volunteers with the major parties, and the political parties are emerging as the training ground of the consultancy profession. That is not to deny that a substantial proportion of consultants come to political consultancy from training and experience in the media, public relations, or some other related but non-political background. A recent survey found 89 per cent of consultants working predominantly on a one-party basis, with only 8 per cent claiming to work equally for both parties. About 54 per cent of this sample had employment ties with political parties, with Republican consultants showing an especially strong link between party employment and a career in political consultancy.[63]

Many consultants acknowledge the symbiotic relationship that they have with political parties. They recognise the role of the parties in helping them sustain their careers, and in maintaining the overall electoral campaign momentum, of which specialist consultancy is a well remunerated part. Parties are accused of too general an approach, while the consultant provides the candidate campaign with appropriate individuality. For others the interpretation of the same evidence is that parties provide a broad foundation of campaigning that may best be done by a sizeable organisation, providing a strong basis on which a candidate-based campaign can be firmly founded. According to one consultant, 'parties are good at seeing the big picture, but not very good at seeing the individual needs of the candidates. Parties can provide for common needs of candidates or needs most and/or all candidates will have. It is the job of the consultant to see the specific individual needs of a particular candidate.' Either way, the roles of party and professional consultant may be complementary and mutually supportive, even intertwined; in the words of another consultant, while political parties nationally raise funds, 'most state and national candidates have personal organizations that perform in their behalf, and use consultants liberally. Additionally, the varied national committees retain consultants and as a result your mix becomes blurred.'[64]

The contemporary campaign environment is not without its own peculiar problems. For example the FEC, apparently attempting to maximise the leeway given to parties, waited until prompted by a lawsuit before revising regulations governing the spending and disclosing of soft money. It remains to be seen whether such policing is effective or useful. That same soft money, often raised in large individual contributions, is reviled by some as a mechanism for the reintroduction of the 'fat cat' contributor, but is seen by others as having provided the basis for vastly increased party political spending, a necessary, if not sufficient, basis for the restoration of campaigns marked by intellectual and programmatic discipline. If the reinvigoration of the parties in elections is to be measured by their financial clout, the fact that the major parties' national committees spent in total $880 million in the 1995–6 election cycle is powerful testimony to their continued importance. The equivalent figure for 1980 was $207 million, and $391 million in 1988. Party committees have in the past often been more effective than has been generally recognised, both at national level and in those states where the party political context was conducive.[65] The legal interpretations allowing party committees to engage with relative freedom in underwriting independent campaign spending and advocacy spending can only strengthen this role.

Parties continue to have a role in the nomination process, but in the candidate-centred system they cannot eliminate successful insurgent candidates from taking the party's name, leading one critic to call the contemporary political party 'a taxi that rich men hire to ride into office'.[66] A strategy designed to reinvigorate parties primarily as organisational structures responding to, and replicating, the non-party political environment of recent years may be a rational response to the modern political system. According to one school of thought, it is through becoming crucial campaign resources that they will become established as stronger and more coherent policy leaders. Others wonder whether the reinvention of party committees as a species of 'super PAC' can itself have such a substantial consequence.

But the majority of people do identify with political parties, and activists and officeholders identify more strongly than most. In 1994 the Republican Party won majorities in the US House and US Senate with a campaign which had at its core the 'Contract With America', an attempt at a legislature-based platform that proved to be deeply flawed, but which stimulated more partisan loyalty in Congress than had been seen in decades. The 1996 and 1998 campaigns saw common national themes played out in constituencies across the nation, even if they were relatively simplistic Republican attacks on the now radicalised concept of 'liberalism', or Democratic attacks painting all their opponents as undermining the fabric of social security and Medicare. These developments were based on parties with increased financial clout, an active role in candidate recruitment, training and selection, co-opting, co-operating with and often leading the campaign entrepreneurs in carrying through the strategies of their contemporary leadership.

Notes

1 Quoted in Guy Gugliotta and Ceci Connolly, 'A horse race of two different colors', *Washington Post National Weekly Edition*, 29 June 1998, p. 15.

2 See Marjorie Randon Hershey, *Running for Office: The political education of campaigners* (Chatham, NJ, Chatham House, 1984), p. 79.

3 Quoted in Barbara G. Salmore and Stephen A. Salmore, *Candidates, Parties, and Campaigns* (2nd edn, Washington, DC, Congressional Quarterly Press, 1989), p. 10.

4 Ronald D. Elving, 'Proliferation of opinion data sparks debate over use', *Congressional Quarterly Weekly Report*, 19 August 1989, p. 2188.

5 Author interview with candidate, 16 September 1996.

6 Author interview with campaign staff, September 1996.

7 From Peggy Noonan, *What I Saw at the Revolution: A political life in the Reagan era* (New York, Random House, 1990), quoted in Mark Feeney, 'The care and feeding of the Gipper', *Boston Sunday Globe*, 11 February 1990, p. B43.

8 Frank Luntz, *Candidates, Consultants and Campaigning* (New York, Blackwell, 1988), p. 33.

9   Sidney Blumenthal, *Pledging Allegiance: The last campaign of the Cold War* (New York, Harper Perennial, 1991), p. 263.

10   Garrison Keillor, *We Are Still Married* (New York, Viking Penguin, 1989), p. 212; John W. Mashek, 'Ailing GOP chief regrets statements on Dukakis in 1988', *Boston Sunday Globe*, 13 January 1991, p. 1; Andrew Stephen, 'Tune in, turn on to the American way of death', *Observer*, 31 March 1991; Mark Tran, 'Hired gun who repented' (obituary), *Guardian*, 1 April 1991.

11   Philip Davies and John Kenneth White, 'The new class in Massachusetts: politics in a technocratic society', *Journal of American Studies*, vol. 19, 1985, pp. 230–1.

12   Gugliotta and Connolly, 'Horse race'; Ceci Connolly, 'Can the Democrats be the comeback kids?', *Washington Post National Weekly Edition*, 15 June 1998, p. 9; Charlie Cook, 'Why the GOP stands to keep the House', *National Journal*, 13 June 1998, pp. 1384–7.

13   Quoted in Elving, 'Proliferation of opinion data', p. 2190, emphasis in original.

14   Dan Balz and Claudia Deane, 'Bringing the classroom into the campaign', *Washington Post National Weekly Edition*, 20/27 July 1998, p. 13.

15   Quoted in *National Journal*, 25 July 1998, p. 1773.

16   Joel Bradshaw, 'Order out of chaos', *Campaigns & Elections*, September/October 1987, p. 73.

17   James A. Barnes, 'Funny numbers or telltale signs?', *National Journal*, 18 July 1998, pp. 1696–7.

18   Elving, 'Proliferation of opinion data', p. 2190.

19   Darno R. Shaw, 'Candidate appearances and television advertising in the 1988–1996 presidential elections', p. 19, and Kenneth M. Goldstein, 'Political advertising and political persuasion in the 1996 presidential campaign', p. 15, both papers presented to the 1997 Annual Conference of the American Political Science Association, Washington, DC.

20   Ruth Marcus and Ira Chinoy, 'Saving for a sunny summer day', *Washington Post National Weekly Edition*, 2/8 September 1996, pp. 11–12.

21   These details were given in a presentation by Republican consultant Richard Wirthlin to the 1987 Annual Conference of the American Political Science Association, Chicago.

22   Joseph Turow, *Breaking Up America: Advertisers and the new media world* (Chicago, University of Chicago Press, 1997), p. 37.

23   Harold W. Stanley and Richard G. Niemi, *Vital Statistics on American Politics* (4th edn, Washington, DC, Congressional Quarterly Press, 1994), p. 45.

24   John Power, 'Plug in to cable TV', *Campaigns & Elections*, September/October 1987, pp. 54, 55.

25   Patrick Novotny, 'Cable television, local media markets and the post-network trends in campaign advertisements in the 1990s', paper presented to the 1997 Annual Conference of the American Political Science Association, Washington, DC.

26   Frederic M. Biddle, 'Many drop the network news habit', *Boston Sunday Globe*, 1 October 1996, pp. 1, A18.

27   See, for example, Stephen Ansolabehere and Shanto Iyengar, *Going Negative: How political advertisements shrink and polarize the electorate* (New York, Free

Press, 1995); and Darrell M. West, *Air Wars* (2nd edn, Washington, DC, Congressional Quarterly Press, 1997).

28   John Tierney, 'Why negative ads are good for democracy', *New York Times Magazine*, 3 November 1996, p. 55.

29   Garry Trudeau, *Doonesbury*, Universal Press Syndicate, 10 December 1989.

30   Michael Grunwald, 'It's clear: ad spots tarnish reputations', *Boston Globe*, 3 November 1996, pp. 1, B4.

31   Robert Guskind, 'Hitting the hot button', *National Journal*, 4 August 1990, pp. 1888.

32   Tierney, 'Why negative ads'; Grunwald, 'It's clear'; Robin Toner, 'In final rounds, both sides whip out bare-knuckle ads', *New York Times*, 21 October 1996, pp. 1, B7; David E. Rosenbaum, 'In Minnesota race, negative ads outnumber lakes', *New York Times*, 23 October 1996, p. A21; C-SPAN review of 1994 political advertisements broadcast by the Cable and Satellite Public Affairs Network as part of its 1995 election coverage.

33   Gerald M. Pomper, 'Negative political campaigning in the United States', paper presented to the International Conference on the History and Development of Political Communications on Television, Amsterdam, 23–25 October 1997, p. 8.

34   Tierney, 'Why negative ads', p. 52.

35   John Carroll, 'Citizens! To the phones!', *Boston Sunday Globe*, 8 September 1996, p. D3.

36   John Lichfield, 'Democrats come off best in bruising battle', *Independent*, 8 November 1990, p. 12; Rosenbaum, 'In Minnesota'.

37   John F. Hale, Rick Farmer and Jeffrey C. Fox, 'Presentation of self in US Senate spot ads', paper presented to the 1995 Annual Conference of the American Political Science Association, Chicago.

38   Thomas Palmer, 'Mudslinging not for the soap sellers', *Boston Sunday Globe*, 16 September 1990, p. A3.

39   *Campaigns & Elections*, July/August 1989, p. 6.

40   *Campaigns & Elections*, September 1998, p. 47.

41   Sam Miller, 'Back to school to master campaigns', *National Journal*, 19 May 1990, pp. 1230, 1235; various advertisements taken from the pages of *Campaigns & Elections*.

42   See Richard Viguerie, *The Establishment vs. The People: Is a new populist revolt on the way?* (Chicago, IL, Regnery Gateway Inc., 1983); KCMS data from *Campaigns & Elections*, August 1994, p. 21.

43   Larry Purpuro, 'Video packaging matters', *Campaigns & Elections*, August 1994, p. 36.

44   John F. Persinos, 'Gotcha! Why opposition research is becoming more important and how it is changing campaigns', *Campaigns & Elections*, August 1994, p. 21.

45   Persinos, 'Gotcha!', pp. 21, 22.

46   Richard Morin, 'The artful dodgers', *Washington Post National Weekly Edition*, 22 June 1998, p. 34.

47   Stephen K. Medvic and Silvio Lenart, 'The influence of political consultants in the 1992 congressional elections', *Legislative Studies Quarterly*, vol. 22, 1997, pp. 61–77, quoted in James A. Thurber, 'The study of campaign

consultants: a subfield in search of theory', *PS: Political Science & Politics*, vol. 31, no. 2, June 1998, p. 146.

48 Jonathan Rauch, 'Blow it up', *National Journal*, 29 March 1997, pp. 604–5.
49 Gary Nordlinger, satellite video seminar, Annual Colloquium of the American Politics Group and the British Association for American Studies, London, 14 November 1997.
50 Statistics from the FEC press release 'Congressional fund-raising and spending up again in 1996', 14 April 1997, Washington, DC. These figures are as reported to 31 December 1996.
51 Michael Barone and Grant Ujifusa, *The Almanac of American Politics 1996* (Washington, DC, National Journal, 1995), p. 89; Clyde Wilcox, *The Latest American Revolution?* (New York, St. Martin's Press, 1995), p. 30.
52 Charlie Cook, 'Ferraro's money woes leave her vulnerable', *National Journal*, 25 July 1998, p. 1769; William Schneider, 'California's wealth of lessons', *National Journal*, 6 June 1998, p. 1330.
53 Figures from Anthony Corrado, 'Financing the 1996 elections', in *The Election of 1996* (Gerald M. Pomper, ed., Chatham, NJ, Chatham House, 1997), pp. 135–72; and Brooks Jackson, 'Financing the 1996 campaign: the law of the jungle', in *Toward the Millennium: The elections of 1996* (Larry J. Sabato, ed., Boston, MA, Allyn and Bacon, 1997), pp. 225–60.
54 Statistics from FEC press releases: 'PAC activity increases in 1995–96 election cycle', 22 April 1997; 'FEC releases semi-annual federal PAC account', 25 July 1997, Washington, DC.
55 Statistics from the FEC press release, 'FEC reports major increase in party activity for 1995–96', 19 March 1997, Washington, DC.
56 'An un-affair to remember', *National Journal*, 30 June 1990, p. 1581; Peter H. Stone, 'Dialing for dollars', *National Journal*, 6 June 1998, p. 1321.
57 M. Margaret Conway and Joanne Conner Green, 'Political action committees and the political process in the 1990s', in *Interest Group Politics* (4th edn; Allan J. Cigler and Burdett A. Loomis, eds, Washington, DC, Congressional Quarterly Press, 1995), p. 163; Peter H. Stone and James A. Barnes, 'And not a Buddhist nun on the list', *National Journal*, 7 March 1998, p. 522; Eliza Newlin Carney, 'A PAC with a twist', *National Journal*, 23 May 1998, p. 1201.
58 Richard E. Cohen and Carol Matlack, 'All-purpose loophole', *National Journal*, 9 December 1989, pp. 2980–7.
59 See, for example, FEC, *Twenty Year Report* (Washington, DC, FEC, April 1995), pp. 28–30.
60 Cornelius P. Cotter, James L. Gibson, John F. Bibby and Robert J. Huckshorn, *Party Organizations in American Politics* (Pittsburgh, PA, University of Pittsburgh Press, 1989), p. 149.
61 Paul Herrnson, *Party Campaigning in the 1980s* (Cambridge, MA, Harvard University Press, 1988), p. 123.
62 Stephen K. Medvic, 'Party support and consultant use in congressional elections', paper presented to the 1997 Annual Conference of the American Political Science Association, Washington, DC.
63 Angela Logan and Robin Kolodny, 'Political consultants and the extension of party goals', paper presented to the 1997 Annual Conference of the American Political Science Association, Washington, DC.

64 Consultant responses reported in Logan and Kolodny, 'Political consultants',
    pp. 25, 23.
65 See James Gimpel, *National Elections and the Autonomy of American State Party
    Systems* (Pittsburgh, PA, University of Pittsburgh Press, 1996).
66 David B. Wilson, 'After the primary, a switch in campaign strategy', *Boston
    Sunday Globe*, 16 September 1990.

6

State and local elections

The powers reserved to the states and the people

The federal system of US government seems subject to an almost irresistible centripetal force. The Tenth Amendment to the Constitution of the United States reserves 'The powers not delegated to the United States by the constitution, nor prohibited by it to the states, ... to the states respectively, or to the people.' Fixing the limits of this balance of power has occupied a good deal of political and legal energy ever since. Washington, DC, is the hub of the federal political structure, and elections at the federal level often dominate political discourse. The undoubted special significance of election campaigns for office in the national government should not, however, mask the considerable importance of state and local government in the United States.

Official figures for 1993 show the federal government spending $1,364,873 million. In the same year, state and local government expenditure amounted to $1,428,577 million, approximately 52 per cent of which was spent by the state governments. In some policy areas state and local governments are especially important; for example, while the federal government spent $25,878 million on education in 1993, the state and local governments spent $342,595 million, over thirteen times as much. Education is the single largest item in the state and local budget, accounting for 24 per cent of it, but other important areas of state and local government spending are public welfare (11.7 per cent, or $167,046 million), highways (4.8 per cent, $68,134 million), health and hospitals (6.6 per cent, $94,651 million), fire protection, police and corrections (5.7 per cent, $81,557 million), sanitation, sewerage, utility and (state-owned) liquor store expenditure (8.4 per cent, $119,769 million), natural resources, parks, housing and community development (3.3 per cent, $47,701 million), administration, interest, insurance and similar costs (14.5 per cent, $206,411 million). These between them account for about four-fifths of state and local government spending. A wide variety of other small budget functions swallow up the rest. In 1992, state and local

Table 6.1. *Government employment and payrolls, 1992*

Government	No. of employees	Payroll ($million)
Federal	3,047,000	9,937
State and local	15,698,000	33,183
State	4,595,000	9,828
Local	11,103,000	23,355
Counties	2,253,000	4,698
Municipalities	2,665,000	6,207
School districts	5,134,000	10,394
Townships	424,000	685
Special districts	627,000	1,370

Source: US Bureau of the Census, *Statistical Abstract of the United States: 1996* (116th edn, Washington, DC, 1996).

governments accounted for 84 per cent of all the civilian government employees in the USA, and 77 per cent of the payroll expenditure on civilian government employees (see table 6.1).[1]

To be capable of such substantial spending, these levels of government must have substantial resources. In part this comes in the form of grants from the federal government, and in 1993 intergovernmental revenue covered 28 per cent of state and local spending. In addition, states and localities generate their own revenue annually from state-wide and locally imposed individual and corporate income taxes, sales taxes and customs, property taxes, taxes on motor fuel, tobacco products, alcoholic drinks, and public utilities, motor vehicle licences, miscellaneous charges for government services and government-operated enterprises. Clearly, the complex of governments, and the officeholders, that operate this system of revenue generation and service provision have a very important place in the lives of individual citizens.

For the most part, state government structures follow the national style. Forty-nine of the states have bicameral governments, modelled on the US House and Senate, albeit different names are sometimes used for the two houses. Nebraska is the single exception, with a unicameral state legislature. Nebraska also has the distinction of being the only state where the legislature is non-partisan. In all the other states candidates for the legislature may stand as party nominees, and the legislative bodies are organised by the majority party after the election. State Governors and Lieutenant Governors reflect the executive positions taken at national level by the President and Vice-President, but many states elect other members of the executive branch too, such as state Treasurer, Attorney General and Secretary of State. Some states also hold elections for judicial positions.

The design of local government is very much the creature of the state, and varies widely across the nation. Counties, cities and other general purpose governments will usually have fairly clearly defined executive and legislative offices subject to election, although the precise design of local government structure, and the relative authority of the officeholders, will vary. There are, in addition, many specialist offices, such as County Register of Deeds, Sheriff, Attorney and Clerk of the Court, which are subject to election at the local level. Furthermore, there are almost 46,000 school districts and special districts, set up with specialist functions, such as the running of schools or the organisation and administration of drainage districts, with their own offices to be filled by election. The timing of state and local elections, and the terms of these offices, are decided by the individual states. As a result, there are fifty different, if recognisably similar, systems of government and elections in the USA. In any year, some of these offices will be up for election.

For an indication of how this affects the individual voter, one has only to examine the campaign literature, referring only to state and local offices, arriving at one household in Montgomery County, Maryland, in the run-up to a typical 1990s election. Literature arrived promoting candidates for contested elections to the offices of County Executive, district-based County Councillor, four County Council positions elected 'at large' in the county, state's Attorney for the county, Clerk of the Circuit Court, Sheriff, Register of Wills, district-based member of the Board of Education, 'at large' member of the Board of Education, state Senator, three positions of member of the state House of Delegates, state Attorney General, state Comptroller and state Governor. Three candidates for Judge-ships in the Circuit Court were standing unopposed, but there was the opportunity to vote 'yes' or 'no' as to whether the incumbent Judge of the Court of Special Appeals should remain in office. All candidates for the state and local partisan offices were registered Democrats or Republicans. The judicial and educational positions were non-partisan, though there was a clearly defined 'ticket' contesting for the Board of Education, sponsored by a teachers' organisation. One independent candidate ran a 'write-in' campaign for County Executive, distributing to potential voters sample ballots, instructions on how to write in a vote, and a pencil to do it with. Besides elections for office, the ballot requested a vote 'for' or 'against' two proposed amendments to the state constitution, one other state constitutional question and nine proposed amendments to the county charter, and campaign literature was distributed by interested parties explaining and promoting specific positions on these items.

This example would not be the same in all parts of the country. It is likely that urban dwellers would be voting for mayors, city councillors, commissioners or aldermen, rather than county officeholders, depending on their local government structure. In some states, regents of state

Table 6.2. *Local governments and elected officials, 1992*

	No. of governments	No. of officeholders
County	3,043	56,390
Municipal	19,279	135,580
Township and town	16,656	127,000
School district	14,422	88,610
Special district	31,555	84,080
Natural resources	6,228	–
Fire protection	5,260	–
Housing and community development	3,470	–
Other	16,597	–
Total	84,955	491,660

Source: Kevin J. Coleman, Thomas H. Neale and Joseph E. Cantor, *The Election Process in the United States* (Congressional Research Service Report for Congress, Washington, DC, Library of Congress, 6 July 1995), pp. 15–16.

universities would be on the ballot, or drains commissioners, parks officials or coroners. The pattern of elections taking place varies between states and localities, but in a nation where there are slightly more than two elected officials for every thousand inhabitants, there exists nationally a heritage of many and various offices to be filled.

The federal government, based in Washington, DC, includes 542 easily identified elected officeholders: the President, Vice-President, 100 Senators, 435 Representatives and five non-voting delegates to Congress. In addition, federal elected officials include the 538 members of the Electoral College, elected every four years, whose sole function is to meet once to cast their Electoral College votes for a presidential and vice-presidential team (see chapter 8). The fifty states, each with their own governments, had 7,424 legislators in 1994, but state election of executive officers and of the judiciary increases the total number of elected officials at state level to more than double this figure. But all federal and state elected officeholders still account for only 3.8 per cent of the national total of 511,039 elected offices. In 1992 the census of governments counted 491,660 elected officeholders at the local level of government in the United States, that is, elected to county, municipal, or other local governments (table 6.2).

Variations in function exist between levels of government. At the national level all elected officials are executive or legislative in function. While this is still a very important category at state level, many members of the judiciary are also elected, as are some state-wide administrative offices. At local level, county and municipal governments require general legislative and executive roles to be filled, but there are also vast numbers of specialist and narrowly defined oversight and administrative offices to be filled. Variations also exist between states. In 1992, Illinois, with 6,723 local government units serving its 11.6 million people, led the way. Hawaii, population approaching 1.2 million, relied parsimoniously on only twenty-one local government units. Townships, numbering 1,803 in Minnesota, and over a thousand in each of eight other states, were not used at all in thirty states. Four states have over 2,000 special districts each, including California, with 2,797, and Texas, with 2,266, and a further five states each host over 1,000 special districts, while Alaska gets by with only fourteen, and Louisiana with thirty.[2]

Further local flavour is added by differences in rules regarding primary elections, the partisan or non-partisan status of the offices concerned, state and local legislation on campaign finance, and so on. In this exciting diversity of electoral opportunities for voters and candidates, accurate generalisations are inevitably rare. Almost every comment on elections at this level has to be qualified by 'it varies from state to state (and then some)'. Nevertheless, power is wielded at these levels of government, policy is made, the impact on the public is immediate, and their electoral response can be swift and direct. A major attribute of the American federal system of government is the potential it affords for a diversity of state and local institutions of government, policy development and political culture, while generally preserving the political unity of the nation.

Regional political cultures

The federal system of government was especially attractive to America's founders because it offered the chance to preserve at least some of the autonomy that each of the original thirteen states felt should be exercised at state level rather than by the nation's capital. Domestic policy was to be the domain of the states and their localities, which, while often dominated by local elites, were nevertheless closer to the people, more aware of their lifestyle and under more immediate public surveillance than any national government could be. The system was designed to protect the differences between states and to maximise the responsiveness of domestic policy-makers to local concerns. Over the succeeding two centuries and more, accelerating technological changes, in which the United States has been an international leader, have often been a force for national homogenisation, speeding and simplifying transport and electronic communication across the nation. Simultaneously, and especially since the 1930s, the federal government in Washington, DC, has taken an increasingly active role in domestic policy, taking initiatives and attempting to persuade states and localities to provide services such as basic medical care for the poor with the offer of grant aid. While technological advances and federal government activism have led to the development of an increasingly national character, these changes have not dimmed the regional diversity and state and local individualism characteristic of America's past.

The original thirteen states have expanded to the current fifty, stretching from the Atlantic coast to the Pacific Ocean, and from the Arctic Circle to the tropics. Within this huge nation the policy needs of the oil workers of Alaska, the citrus growers of Florida, the tourist industry of Hawaii, the auto worker of Michigan and the microelectronics innovators of northern California are as diverse as anything that exercised the imaginations of the nation's Founding Fathers. Waves of immigration from different parts of the world have introduced ethnic variety to the United States throughout its history, but a particular feature of this has been that different periods have been dominated by discrete ethnic and racial groups. This has sometimes been a consequence of culturally supported racism, as in the importation of Afro-Caribbean slaves, or of ethnically biased legislation, as in the immigration quotas of the 1920s, designed to keep out 'undesirable' national communities, and often the consequence of overseas tragedies, such as the Irish potato famine of the nineteenth century, the wars in South-East Asia of the mid-twentieth century, and other social and economic pressures. The early immigrant communities congregated geographically, often settling in areas where the experience of the first migrants of that nationality signalled that opportunities existed. Scandinavian farmers, for example, colonised the agricultural states of the Midwest, such as Minnesota and Wisconsin. German brewers also ended up in the Midwest. Irish and Italian communities made use of opportunities in the nation's major cities, which were growing rapidly at the time these groups entered the country. Other national groups, such as Polish immigrants, were attracted to the then burgeoning areas of heavy industrial production. Geographic proximity can also be important, leading to concentrations of Asian populations on the west coast, of Latin American groups in the South and Southwest, and of Cubans in Florida. The celebration of these differences, in particular those defined by ethnic and religious heritage, has itself become almost perversely a definition of a community's 'American-ness', partly a nostalgic statement about a nation left behind, but primarily a witness to the community's place in pluralist America.[3]

This demographic web is laid over a nation where resources, natural, social and fabricated, are not evenly distributed. For example, traditional heavy industries developed around areas where raw materials could be extracted; similarly, oil extraction has prompted related business in Alaska and in southern states; the concentration of prestigious universities in Massachusetts and California has aided the development of modern research-based industries in these states; agribusiness regimes of various kinds are dependent on weather, soil and water. The characteristics of

America's regions, states and localities continue to reflect the amalgamation of interrelated ethnic, commercial, historical and geographic factors such as these, maintaining cultural, religious, social and economic diversity in the face of all homogenising pressures, and therefore creating the environments for state and local political cultures sensitive to these differences. State and local election campaigns reflect this rich variety in such terms as the issues confronted by the candidates and the ethnic representation on the ballot.

Laboratories of democracy: issues and ideology

The period of the Reagan administration generated a new and lasting interest in politics within states, with its anti-Washington rhetoric coupled with promises to return power to the state level. Initial expectations were not entirely fulfilled, but the first two years of the Reagan administration especially saw a shift away from tight federal government control over the spending of intergovernmental grants, allowing greater decision-making at the state and local levels. The number of federal grant programmes to states and localities was cut from 539 to 404 in the first two years of Reagan's term. While the number of grants gradually rose again after this clear-out, the value of such aid, taking inflation into account, fell by 19 per cent during Reagan's eight years in the White House, thereby putting pressure on state and local governments to take hard decisions on policy aims and revenue generation.[4]

During the Bush administration there was some federal government activism on the domestic front, but this was limited by the rising national debt and the rhetorical commitment of the administration to resist tax increases. Increasingly, the federal government mandated states to perform and fund functions, pressing on to the states decisions to raise funds, cut services, or face indebtedness.[5] Insofar as states gained authority, it was often the authority to decide where to make cuts and how to create alternative sources of funding for governments, an intergovernmental relationship that David Walker refers to as 'shift and shaft'. Bill Clinton came to the presidency after a period as an active Governor of a modest-sized state, but his awareness of the difficulties facing state governments could produce only limited federal-level responses. Tax increases and programme cuts initiated in his first year in office sought to tame the budget deficit, but also contributed to a nose-dive in support for the Democrats, and to the election of a Republican-dominated Congress in 1994. Thereafter the Democratic administration and the Republican congressional leadership competed with plans for deficit reduction, aimed at the reliable voters of middle America. The federal government made a noisy retreat from some areas of policy, thrusting responsibility and cost on to the states.

Welfare reform perhaps attracted most attention. President Clinton signed the Welfare Reform Bill in a televised, White House Rose Garden ceremony, in the immediate run-up to the 1996 Democratic national convention. A series of such government events were contrived in the days before the convention to put Clinton on national television in a presidential setting, apparently acting decisively to protect the nation's interests. Clinton had promised to 'end welfare as we know it'.[6] In the end, driven by a conservative Republican Congress, and by his own ambition to be seen as the President who reformed welfare, he signed the Bill at the same time as voicing the wish that it be significantly amended as soon as possible to eliminate clear injustices. The Bill removed benefits from many legal immigrants, and threatened to withdraw cash benefits entirely from individuals who remained on the welfare rolls beyond a strictly limited five-year lifetime period, regardless of the effect on children. The solutions were left to the states. From the moment the legislation was signed, and the deadlines for the withdrawal of benefits went into action, the states were handed a major fiscal and policy problem to solve, with the clock ticking.

States responded quickly and diversely. Twenty-five decided to provide one-off cash payments to help eligible families stay off the welfare rolls. For example, in Virginia a payment of about $1,100 may be given to underwrite emergency needs – but the recipient family cannot then claim any further welfare for 160 days. In some cases such targeted intervention works, and in Virginia only 17 per cent of these families returned to welfare. Seventeen states enacted their own time limits, abbreviating the federal five-year grace period. For example, in Montana a two-year limit was imposed, extendable to three years for welfare clients who perform community service. In New Jersey the state has funded fatherhood programmes, to encourage more responsibility for family support. In Massachusetts single mothers received day-care support, help to find spartan, but safe, accommodation, and training to gain language skills and qualifications. Private companies can also be involved, gaining a trained and job-hungry workforce in return for their input. State resources targeted towards these policies may be used to encourage community organisations to partner the government efforts. The success in Ottawa County, Michigan, of getting all welfare recipients into at least part-time work within a year of the Welfare Reform Bill being passed is at least in part attributed to these two factors.

Many states were not initially using the savings from falling welfare rolls to reduce taxes, but were redirecting the money to services supporting other welfare clients hopefully en route to employment. The size of the problem itself reflects state political and social cultures – while California started with 138,000 two-parent welfare families, Alabama had only fifty-two – a discrepancy explained by differences neither in overall population nor in poverty, but reflecting the abiding conservatism of the

Deep South. Not all welfare reduction can be counted as success. There had been a national 18 per cent fall in caseloads over the year to March 1998, but one government survey showed that 38 per cent of cases were forced off welfare by state rules, and were not leaving because of employment success. Chaotic poor families were suffering from the reforms, which left them and their children with little or no final level of support; some organised poor families were finding the incentives and the support a route to a more economically independent life. While many states undoubtedly worked to provide a quality service within the reformed environment, the bottom line was caseload reduction.[7]

At the same time states were beginning to take advantage of Supreme Court rulings that institutionalised the devolution of specific powers to the states. In 1997, in *Kansas* v. *Hendricks*, the Court allowed states the authority to commit sex offenders to mental hospital after they have served their sentences for criminal offences. The New York Senate responded with a bill only two days later. Other contentious issues that the Court has confirmed as within the states' remit have covered aspects of gun regulations, assisted suicide, pornography, gambling and the disposal of radioactive waste. State governments have been modernised dramatically in the last generation of the twentieth century, and state politicians are eager to take on devolution. In the words of Kansas Attorney General Carla Stovall (Republican), 'What the folks in New York want is not necessarily what the folks in Kansas want, I wouldn't want California's laws here.'[8] The varied and creative responses of states to these pressures, while not always successful, fit firmly within the Supreme Court Justice Louis Brandeis' perception of states as the 'laboratories of democracy'.

State governments have taken many policy initiatives. States have, on the basis of their own research, developed strategies designed to pinpoint areas of potential development, and have subsequently initiated programmes offering technical assistance, consultancy and even risk capital to local entrepreneurs, and retraining to the unemployed. Governors faced with public resistance to tax increases have sometimes attempted to shift opinion by extolling the public benefits of certain policies, such as education, trying to offset the antagonism to taxation by creating the image of such spending as a public investment. States have even established independent offices overseas to promote their particular business interests. The differences between state reactions express the individuality of their social and political cultures, and the experiments tried in states can have influence throughout the federal structure of American governments.

In such a structure it is perhaps natural to expect tension between the states and the federal government. It is clear that this has an effect on state-level elections. Voters expect their elected officials, even those sent to the national legislature, to have a particular interest in local, state and regional interests, using their positions to establish the common community interest, and to pursue it on all possible occasions. Washington may be the nation's political centre, and in 1800 was near to the population centre of the nation, but the geographical expansion of the nation has always been westwards, and by 1990 the centre of the nation's population was almost 1,000 miles west of the capital city.[9] It is perhaps not too surprising, therefore, that there are times when the citizens of any of America's regions may feel somewhat detached from the national government, and attached to symbols of state autonomy. Campaigns are often conducted that contain a thread of Washington-sceptical, pro-local, rhetoric, an approach that George Wallace, Jimmy Carter, Ronald Reagan, Michael Dukakis and Bill Clinton, all former Governors, showed could be used even in campaigns for the presidency.

As state governments have emerged to become significant foci of political action, they have attracted the attention of an increasing body of professional lobbyists. In any two-year period, the fifty states consider around 185,000 bills, and pass about a quarter of these. The states are increasingly the regulators of policy, whether it be business regulation (sometimes with social and environmental elements), for example in the health care, oil, or food industries, or social and lifestyle issues, such as abortion. Political lobbyists have detected steady growth in the demand for their services at state level since the early 1980s, with a considerable acceleration in the late 1990s.[10] The emergence into elections of particular issue debates can sometimes stimulate a community of voters to act, and can provoke the entry on to the political scene of pressure groups and candidates from previously quiescent voting groups. Abortion is one such policy area that exercised voters and legislators in many states after the 1989 Supreme Court decision in *Webster* v. *Reproductive Health Services of Missouri*, allowing states some discretion to introduce restrictive abortion laws, and forcing officeholders and voters to confront the issue in their state and local contests throughout the 1990s.

Within the defined political space of a state, political parties as well as issues can sometimes adopt a more clearly identifiable shape than they do at the federal level. Candidates at this level are still entrepreneurial, and parties at state level are not without severe internal division, but there are states where party rules regarding accessibility to the primary ballot, the value of official party endorsement on the ballot, the sanctions held by party leaders in state legislatures, and the relevance of party coherence in organising and dominating state policy provide a modicum of rigour to party activity. Good evidence on local party activity is not easy to obtain, but one survey of the available literature found that county- and township-level party organisations, operated by a combination of political professionals and enthusiastic amateurs, can have a powerful effect at election time. 'For example, almost 80 percent distribute campaign literature, over 60 percent organize telephone campaigns, and about 50 percent conduct registration drives.'[11]

In some states there exists a tradition of one-party dominance. Occasionally this is so complete that an activist wishing to have any effect on policy would be tempted to join the majority party, this being the only vehicle for debate. Traditionally one would have looked to the Deep South for evidence of Democratic Party dominance, and to some parts of the Northeast and Midwest for overwhelming Republican strength, but with realignment in the South weakening the Democrats' grip, and the Northeast showing less rock-ribbed Republicanism, more of the nation appears to be party-competitive. Party breakthroughs happen in unexpected places. In Massachusetts, where the state legislature has been dominated by Democrats for many years, and where the US congressional delegation was in 1996, for the first time in state's history, completely Democratic, the Governor and Lieutenant Governor were Republicans. Tennessee, home of the Democrat Vice-President Al Gore, and with a traditional Democratic majority in the state legislature, elected a Republican Governor and two Republican US Senators in the mid-1990s.

The Democrats were very strong in state elections in the 1980s and early 1990s, controlling many more legislatures than the Republicans. In 1994 the swing to the Republicans which was evident in US congressional elections also affected the states, and in the late 1990s the two parties were evenly balanced in terms of their state legislative victories, although the Republicans had control of the majority of governorships. In August 1998, thirty-nine of the ninety-nine state legislative chambers were controlled by majorities of fewer than ten seats, and most states had a party division in the control of the governorship, state house and state senate. The result was highly charged party competition of some form or other in many of the states. In the run-up to the 1998 elections, it was considered that 'in two-thirds of the state legislatures, either party can win control. There are few states where the election is not terribly significant.'[12]

Control of state-level politics has a significance apart from the obvious advantage it gives in the state's policy debates. Every ten years the seats of the US House of Representatives are redistributed between states to reflect the population shifts discovered in the decennial national census. States gaining and losing seats are then required to redesign the borders of their US congressional districts. State governors and legislatures are generally responsible for this. It is remarkable how such boundaries, redesigned in ways entirely legitimate and within the law, can nevertheless favour one party or the other in terms of results. State legislatures are careful to protect their own interests, and especially those of incumbents of their own party. As the census of 2000 approached, party control of state legislatures and governorships became increasingly significant for national as well as state reasons, especially in those states likely to lose or gain seats and therefore to be required to redraw district boundaries, and parties were identifying competitive districts in swing states for special treatment. The GOP has hoped to declare a Republican realignment for the best part of thirty years, and has seen several false dawns – in 1980 when Reagan took the presidency and Republicans took the US Senate, and in 1994 when they took both House and Senate. With 1998 gubernatorial victories in Texas, Michigan, New York, Pennsylvania, Florida, Illinois and Ohio, the Republicans hoped that their electoral successes would be consolidated after the census by friendly state legislatures to provide a firm foundation for power in the twenty-first century. The Democrats, looking forward to maintaining their competitive position over the coming generation, were equally aware of the importance of state-level victories, especially in the key state of California. The redrawing of district boundaries was rarely, if ever, discussed in these campaigns, but it was never off the parties' agendas.

Laboratories of democracy: the candidates

The local base of American politics and the increased political authority wielded at state level have made state executive office both more attractive and more risk-laden. The governorship is one position where executive skills can be shown over a very broad range of policies involving a very substantial budget. Credentials established at this level are not easily dismissed. The presidential contests of recent years have included a number of former governors: Carter (Democrat – Georgia), Reagan (Republican – California) and Clinton (Democrat – Arkansas) got to the White House; Wallace (Democrat – Alabama), Romney (Republican – Michigan), Brown (Democrat – California), Shapp (Democrat – Pennsylvania), DuPont (Republican – Delaware), Babbitt (Democrat – Arkansas), Dukakis (Democrat – Massachusetts) and Alexander (Republican – Tennessee) did not. Early muscle-flexing for the 2000 presidential contest included Republican Governor of Texas George Bush and a field of half a dozen other state governors. The office of Governor is clearly an established launching pad for the ultimate prize of American politics.

The 1990s saw some politicians moving out of the federal government to compete for state office, with Pete Wilson (Republican) serving most of the decade as Governor of California after leaving the US Senate, and former US Senators Lawton Chiles (Democrat – Florida) and Lowell Weicker (Republican turned independent – Connecticut) spending respectively two terms and one term in the Governors' mansions of their states. In 1998 the majority of gubernatorial candidates were state politicians looking for elevation, but once again some federal officeholders were taking part, with US Representatives Jane Harman (Democrat – California), Barbara B. Kennelly (Democrat – Connecticut) and Glenn Poshard (Democrat – Illinois) challenging for their states' governships.

Lowell Weicker's term as Connecticut Party incumbent of the state governorship also showed the potential of states and local governments to enable some minor party activity. Many states make it very difficult for minor parties to gain access to the ballot but, in spite of this, small numbers of minor party representatives and independents sit in some state legislatures. US Representative Bernie Sanders, who sits in Congress as an independent, began his political career as Socialist Mayor of Burlington, Vermont. As well as the Weicker term in Connecticut, the 1990s have seen Alaska and Maine elect independent governors, and in 1998 former wrestler Jess 'The Body' Ventura (Reform Party) took 37 per cent of the vote in Minnesota to win the governorship in a three-way race.

State governorship offers the challenge and potential, and comes with risks. Governors are clearly identifiable political leaders whose fortunes are therefore tied closely to the perceived success or failure of their administrations. They can influence redistricting in the wake of census years, and can construct state-based political machines to make themselves foci of political power in nationally significant networks. They are also executives of governments with huge budgets. The median revenue collected by a state government in 1994 was over $11 billion. The smallest state budget exceeded $2 billion, and the largest were $115 billion in California and $82 billion in New York.[13] In the 1998 elections, when thirty-six state governorships were up for election, the general health of state economies made the management of these budgets especially attractive. According to a leading state legislator, 'Indiana has a $2 billion surplus, California has a $4.5 billion surplus. What do you do with that money? That's the issue that will tip the 1998 election.'[14] Earlier in the 1990s a weak economy, especially in regions such as New England, together with public antagonism to the tax increases imposed in some states, had quite a different effect, prompting a substantial turnover as some governors gave up the struggle for re-election and others were removed from office at the elections. The governors are the most visible leaders of state policy, and the voters hold them responsible for economic and social policy successes and failures.[15]

The state and local political scene acts as an incubator of political talent. Not all candidates for high office go through an apprenticeship at local or state level, but many do. Among those entering the US Congress for the first time in 1997, for example, was Senator Max Cleland (Democrat) of Georgia, who had spent two terms in the state Senate and thirteen years as Georgia's Secretary of State. Senator Mary Landrieu (Democrat) of Louisiana had formerly spent six years in the state legislature and eight years as state Treasurer. Senator Gordon Smith (Republican) of Oregon had been President of the state Senate. On the way to a seat in the US House of Representatives Kay Granger (Republican) of Texas had formerly been a member of Fort Worth city council, and had risen to be the first woman elected Mayor of that city. Bill Jenkins (Republican – Tennessee) had nearly thirty years of state-level political experience, as a state Representative, Speaker of the state House, Commissioner of the state Conservation Department, policy adviser to the Governor, and as an elected circuit court judge. Steven Rothman (Democrat – New Jersey) had served two terms as Mayor of Englewood and three years as a judge in Bergen County. Similar career patterns can be found throughout the nation.

One interesting consequence of this is the ripple effect that moves through a state on the resignation of a senior politician. In 1984 Senator Paul Tsongas of Massachusetts suddenly announced his resignation for health reasons. Among those who announced their availability for the office were two incumbent US congressmen, the state's Lieutenant Governor, the state Secretary and a former state Representative. Not all of these stayed in the race, but one US congressional seat was vacated, and two state Senators entered that election. The vacillations of the other US congressman prompted a challenge to him from a former state Senator and an incumbent state Representative. Meanwhile, one of the state Senate seats vacated in the reshuffle was occupied by another incumbent state Representative. With the lower-level races drawing candidates with town, county, or other local experience, the network of apprenticeship is shown in action from top to bottom. A similar effect was seen in 1998, when, on Friday 13 March, Representative Joseph P. Kennedy II suddenly announced his decision to withdraw from the election for the congressional seat he had held for twelve years. Among those who reportedly spent the next few days considering whether to enter the hustings were two state Senators and three city councillors from two different cities. State Representatives were considering a run for the potential vacancies that might be created in the state Senate, and others were eyeing the lower-level opportunities that might open up. Other potential candidates had formerly been in office as state Senators, state Representatives, and as Mayor.[16]

Many candidates for office at all levels come from backgrounds that have not included previous election to office. For example, among those in the wings for Joseph Kennedy's seat were a company managing director and a millionaire businessman with no previous elected experience, and there have been high-profile and sometimes successful campaigns in recent years by wealthy candidates with no previous political experience. The electorate may be convinced by a candidate's skills as an entrepreneur, administrator, lawyer, or whatever. But credentials established through local and state political involvement can be very useful. Fully half of the fourteen US Senators newly elected in 1996 had served in their state legislatures. Five of the rest had served in appointed, advisory, or executive branch roles in state and local politics, and of the other two, one had formerly served as assistant to his state's US Senator, and the other had spent a period as an administrator in the Veterans' Administration. Eight of them had moved from state politics to the US House of Representatives on their way to US Senate.

The importance of establishing these kinds of credentials are perhaps indicated by the willingness of Patrick J. Kennedy, son of Senator Edward Kennedy (Democrat – Massachusetts), to spend $80,000 in 1988, winning a seat in the Rhode Island legislature. Kennedy, a twenty-one-year-old student at the time of his election, received a $300 salary for the post, but used it as a stepping stone to the US House. In 1994, after spending $1,070,000 on his campaign, he became the youngest member of the US Congress, where he has proved a powerful fund-raiser, and a strong ally of Democratic Leader Richard Gephardt.[17]

State and local elections can also be the training ground of less privileged candidates. Between 1970 and the early 1990s the number of African-American elected officials in the United States increased from 1,469 to over 12,000. Most of this growth was in local office-holding. Over the same period the number of African-American county officials grew by almost nineteen times, from 92 to 1,715, and at municipal level African-American representation grew to over seven times the 1970 level, from 623 office-holders to 4,566 (see tables 6.3 and 6.4). There is reasonable criticism that the concentration of this growth at the local level indicates increasing public unwillingness to vote for African-American candidates the more senior the post. Certainly neither major party has yet put an African-American candidate on its presidential ticket, although there was much talk of General Colin Powell, former chairman of the Joint Chiefs of Staff, as a Republican challenger, until he announced that he would not be entering the race. The one African-American US Senator in the 1990s was Carolyn Moseley Braun, of Illinois, who served one term in the Senate, from 1992 to 1998, after serving three years as Cook County Recorder of Deeds and ten years in the Illinois House of Representatives. In 1996 America elected its first ever Asian-American Governor outside Hawaii, when Gary Locke, formerly King County executive, became Governor of Washington.

In the US House of Representatives, African-American officeholders are primarily, though no longer wholly, confined to Democrats in constituencies with predominantly African-American electorates. Georgia Democrats Sanford Bishop and Cynthia McKinney, both first elected in 1992, gained re-election in 1996 and again in 1998 even after their constituencies had been redrawn to include a majority white electorate, and Julia Carson (Democrat – Indiana) was in 1996 elected to a seat where the population is two-thirds white. There is a single African-American Republican congressman, first elected in 1994, J. C. Watts, Jr, of Oklahoma. All of these

Table 6.3. *Race and sex of local elected officials, 1992: numbers and percentage of those reporting*

Government	Female	African-American	Hispanic	American Indian, Eskimo, Aleut	Asian, Pacific Islander
County	12,525 (22.3%)	1,715 (3.1%)	906 (1.7%)	147 (0.3%)	80 (0.1%)
Municipal	26,825 (22.1%)	4,566 (3.8%)	1,701 (1.4%)	776 (0.6%)	97 (0.1%)
Township	27,702 (26.7%)	369 (0.4%)	216 (0.2%)	86 (0.1%)	16 (0.0%)
School district	24,730 (31.2%)	4,222 (5.4%)	2,466 (3.1%)	564 (0.7%)	184 (0.2%)
Special district	8,749 (13.7%)	670 (1.1%)	570 (0.9%)	227 (0.4%)	137 (0.2%)
Total	100,531 (23.7%)	11,542 (2.7%)	5,859 (1.4%)	1,800 (0.4%)	514 (0.1%)

Source: US Bureau of the Census, *Statistical Abstract of the United States: 1996* (116th edn. Washington, DC, 1996). p. 283. This source lists the total number of offices at 493,830. There was no reporting of sex in a total of 69,044 cases, and no reporting of race/ethnicity in 74,069 cases. The percentages are calculated on the basis of cases reported only.

Table 6.4. *Race and sex of state and federal elected officials, 1993–5*

Office	Female	African-American	Hispanic	Asian, Pacific Islander
State-wide elected executive office and state legislature	1,619	522 (1993)	182 (1994)	
US Senate	8	1	0	2
US House	47	40	17	4

Source: US Bureau of the Census, *Statistical Abstract of the United States: 1996* (116th edn, Washington, DC, 1996), pp. 279, 283, 284. All figures are for 1995 except where noted.

had served first in state or local office. Watts was elected to the Oklahoma state corporate commission in 1990, becoming its chairman in 1992. Carson spent four years in the Indiana state House, fourteen in the Indiana state Senate, and six as trustee of Center Township. McKinney and Bishop each spent four years in the Georgia state House of Representatives, with Bishop also serving two years in the Georgia state Senate.

African-Americans are not the only underrepresented group among America's officeholders, and, as social and political restrictions loosen, and latent ambition grows, groups such as Hispanics and women have found opportunity to train for the rigours of campaigning and office-holding at the local and state level. Of the nation's local government officeholders in 1992, 2.7 per cent were African-Americans, 1.4 per cent Hispanic, and 23.7 per cent were women (table 6.3). Compared with their respective representation in the 1992 voting-age population of 11.3 per cent African-American, 7.9 per cent Hispanic, and 52.3 per cent female, all these groups are clearly still underrepresented. The proportions of African-Americans and Hispanics in the voting-age population still shows some growth. By 1994 African-Americans made up 11.5 per cent, but the major growth is in Hispanic voting strength, up to 9.2 per cent by 1994. The impact is already being felt in constituencies where these groups are concentrated enough to have a bloc impact. In 1996 immigration, foreign policy and welfare issues prompted Hispanics to vote in numbers never seen before. With projections by the National Academy of Science suggesting that by the middle of the twenty-first century about one-quarter of the US population will be Hispanic, 14 per cent African-American and 8 per cent Asian-American, the long-term impact on policies and elections could be profound.[18] Even given the remaining barriers to political advancement, the numbers show a steady growth in representation in recent years, and the myriad of elections for local and state offices offer some opportunity to develop a political career structure. Regulatory changes such as the imposition in some states of term limits may serve to increase the opportunities available for entry to the political system.

Laboratories of democracy: the regulations

The regulatory machinery that the fifty states apply to elections shows as much variation as almost any other aspect of the federal political structure. States, and on occasion localities, have a large degree of independent authority to regulate many aspects of the campaigning and elections process. State and local parties, where they are strong and autonomous, may add their own level of electoral regulation to that imposed by governments. State and local variations in the regulations of campaign financing have been mentioned in chapter 4, but there are few areas of campaigns and elections totally immune from this complex of influence. Furthermore, the rules change over time as opinions shift with alterations in personnel and the balance of power within the many bodies that can influence the process. The resulting variations and permutations help to give every state and local election its own character. This brief discussion is therefore limited to a few examples.

One of the key electoral regulations to have affected the states in recent years is term limits. The self-styled term-limits movement emerged strongly in the 1990s, primarily as a reaction to the very high levels of electoral success achieved by those members of Congress who stood for re-election. Some critics believed that this led to a Congress that was unresponsive the public and lacking new blood. One proposed answer was to limit the number of consecutive terms that legislators could serve in office. The principle already pertained to the presidency and to many governorships, but the legislatures had previously escaped this sanction. The Republican Contract With America, the manifesto of the 1994 congressional races, promised that Congress would vote on the issue, but the change was not approved, and a subsequent Supreme Court decision has made such a move moot. The legislation passed by some states to limit congressional terms has been found unconstitutional by the US Supreme Court, which, in a five-to-four decision, opined that the legitimate state regulation of congressional election procedures cannot go so far as to impose 'substantive qualification rendering a class of political candidates ineligible for ballot position', and that this could be achieved only by constitutional amendment. The drive for a Term Limits Amendment to the US Constitution has not so far been successful.[19] Congressional term limits remain a heated topic. Some who entered the US House of Representatives in the early 1990s pledging to restrict their stay to three terms have prevaricated on whether to stand down as their six-year deadline approaches, and the executive director of US Term Limits has responded with a commitment to 'make sure [that for each of these Representatives] every man, woman and child in his district knows he broke his pledge'.[20] Supporters of term limits have put large sums behind their philosophy. When both candidates in a 1998 special election in New Mexico agreed to the principle of term limits, but one considered four to six terms more appropriate than three, Americans for Limited Terms spent $247,000 promoting her opponent.[21]

While state legislation could not impose term limits on the US Congress, it could do so on state officeholders, and the attention shifted to the state level. By 1998, eighteen states, with between them about one-third of the nation's state legislators, had passed term limits, with total terms of six or eight years being commonplace limits. Given that most of this regulation was passed in the late 1980s and early 1990s, its effect was not becoming apparent until the mid to late 1990s. In Arkansas a 1992 term limits law contributed most to the fact that half of the 1998 elections to the Arkansas state House were for open seats. In Michigan two-thirds of the legislature turned over in 1998, and one-third of Oregon's House retired in that year. California, first affected in the 1996 elections, had another twenty-seven state Representatives and Senators reach their deadline in 1998. A total of around 200 state legislators across the country in that year were being forced from their seats by term limits, an effect that would get bigger in later years as more of the recent legislation came into effect, for example when the state legislation in Florida and Ohio takes effect in 2000.[22]

Supporters of term limits claim that they prevent entrenched interests retaining authority, and they create more opportunity to enter politics, to the inevitable advantage of previously underrepresented groups. Opponents stress the loss of accumulated expertise, and the loss of the guiding authority of skilled leadership, when the leaders are inevitably near the end of their limited terms. They point to the California state assembly, where the stability of fourteen years with Willie Brown as Speaker has been replaced, though not wholly because of term limits, by a political version of musical chairs in which there have been five Speakers in less than five years. They also claim that there is a temptation for officeholders to become more self-interested. In the words of North Carolina legislator Daniel Terry Blue, 'If you know that you can serve in a place only six or eight years, you'll come in and you'll start immediately thinking about the next place you can move to, rather than spending time to develop real expertise where you are.'[23] Certainly there will be an increased turnover in state legislatures, and perhaps some increased competition, as term-limited Representatives look for a move to Senate, or legislatures look to the executive or judicial opportunities. In undertaking this experiment the states are fulfilling very well their role as laboratories for democracy.

State and local regulation affects even the most elementary aspects of voting, such as the layout of the ballot, the technology used for recording and tabulating the votes, and the opening hours of the polling places. The ballot, for example, may be organised to emphasise the party political allegiances of the candidates, with the offices listed at the side of the ballot, and the candidates for each office ranged across the ballot in party columns. To vote the party ticket, one merely has to follow one column of candidates. On the ballots of twenty-one states a voter may vote a 'straight ticket' for all the candidates of one party – a voting option on the ballot is included to cast a single vote for 'all the candidates of the X party'. Alternatively the ballot may be organised to stress the offices being contested, presenting each office and set of candidates to the voter as separate sets of choices. Generally offices appear on a ballot in an order dictated by some sense of putting the 'most important' offices first, for example nationwide, followed by state-wide, followed by local offices, but this too can be varied. Forty-six of the fifty states allow voters to write in the name of candidates who do not appear on the printed ballot. Nevada includes the option of voting that none of the candidates are suitable for the post.

Most elections in the United States are run on the 'first past the post' system, whereby the leading vote catcher wins the contest, but this is not universal. In some states, especially in the South, a runoff primary is required between the leading primary election candidates if no one re-ceives more than 50 per cent of the vote at the first attempt. In Arizona the term of office of Republican Governor Ev Mecham, elected by a minority vote in 1986, proved such an embarrassment that a law was passed requiring a runoff general election should no candidate receive an absolute majority of the vote cast. When a very tightly fought election in 1990 resulted in no candidate receiving more than 50 per cent of the vote, this law was triggered and, since the law as drafted did not include any description of the format or timing of the runoff, prompted some rapid electoral ad libbing in the state. For two decades Louisiana uniquely held open 'primary' elections, in which an absolute majority cancelled the requirement for a subsequent 'general' election, and the vast majority of the state's congressional elections were decided in advance of the Novem-ber national general election, but a Supreme Court decision in 1998 required that Louisiana change its practice to observe the national election day set by the US Congress.[24] Apparently unique among all of the nation's electoral levels, Cambridge, Massachusetts, uses proportional representa-tion to choose its city councillors.

Ballot layout can itself be affected by the technology of the vote. Fewer than 10 per cent of voters in America use paper ballots. For most of the century the most common technology was some variation of the voting machine, first used in New York state in the 1890s. These large machines present the voter with a layout much as it would be on a printed page, but the votes are placed by pressing the relevant small levers on the face of the machine. About 28 per cent of voters still used this method in 1992. More recently computer-readable voting systems have become more popular. For the most part these systems rely on the voter to punch holes in computer-readable cards (about 39 per cent of voters), although there are computer systems that use technology to scan paper ballots (16 per cent), and that can offer the use of other electronic methods (4 per cent). Around 10 per cent of voters lived in counties using mixtures of these methods, and 3 per cent were continuing to use paper ballots.[25] Poll opening hours vary from state to state, and some states delegate the authority, within specified parameters, to local government. Starting times vary from 6 a.m. to 'not later than 11 a.m.', and closing times from 6 p.m. to 8 p.m. In twenty-seven states voters may take time off work to vote – usually about two hours, and sometimes subject to prior notice – and eighteen states treat election day as a state holiday.

All of these variations can have an effect on the election. Faced with long ballots voters often suffer 'ballot fatigue', that is participation in the election drops off as voters are required to work their way through a ballot, so the order in which offices are presented on the ballot, and the readability of the design used, will affect the drop-off, and therefore the real voting turnout, for some races. Highly technological voting methods may discourage some voters, but they may also introduce new problems in tallying the vote. For example, it is claimed that on occasion some punch card systems may fail to record votes, as the cards do not always punch out cleanly enough to be read. The close victory, by 0.8 per cent of the vote, of Florida Senator Connie Mack over Democrat Buddy McKay was followed by questions as to whether the design of the ballot and the operation of the voting equipment had any effect on the result.[26] Regulation of absentee ballots varies between states, and in those states, such as California and Oregon, where any qualified voter can use an absentee ballot, they have formed an increasing proportion of the vote in recent years, sometimes swinging the results, and certainly affecting the candidates' campaign methods to include the provision of absentee ballots to large numbers of targeted voters. In a recent special election for the US Senate, Oregon experimented by using exclusively postal votes, and was rewarded with an unusually high 'turnout'.

State parties and lawmakers between them act as gatekeepers to the ballot. Candidates generally have to obtain a number of signatures to appear on the ballot, with the local law determining how many signatures, and whose signatures count. The major parties are given preferential treatment in many states, getting on the ballot on the production of a modest-sized petition, while minor party or independent candidates may have to obtain the petition support of thousands of the state's registered voters to claim a place in the general election. The primary elections, caucuses and conventions that precede general elections are at least nominally organised by the state party organisations, within regulatory limits set by state law. While in many states access to the ballot may be a relatively simple operation, this combination of regulation can make the route fairly complex even within the confines of the major parties. Most states used closed primaries, where voting is restricted to those who have declared a party affiliation. Depending on the state, this declaration either may be made on the day of the primary, or must be at some specified time before. In other states the voter may receive the ballots for all the party primaries, but will choose to use just one in the polling booth. A small but increasing number of states list all candidates on one primary ballot, imposing different regulations as to how the general election candidates will emerge from this format. Party endorsement of particular candidates in the primary, perhaps through the use of a prior state party convention to assess the support of party loyalists, increases the potential to establish a close relationship between the party organisation and party members in office. The advocates of stronger party systems would like to see a greater freedom for state-level parties to regulate access to the ballot, at least that access associated with the party label, and to endorse favoured candidates within the primaries, but apart from the general favouritism that state election regulations show towards the major parties, there appears to be little sympathy among the general public for such a shift.

The degree of variation that can exist in election regulation between states and localities is set in sharp relief by the case of Buford, Texas, forty miles east of El Paso, and with a population of around fifty people. Incorporated as a municipality in 1962 to avoid annexation and regulation by any neighbouring town, Buford's local economy included a proliferation of sex businesses. In the drive for economic success in this niche market, the citizens of Buford omitted to hold any elections. In 1998 El Paso County claimed that without an elected government, Buford could not claim to be a municipality. The citizens of Buford hired a lawyer to defend their local interests, and prepared to find out how to run an election.[27]

Laboratories of democracy: representation and campaigns

Within the federal system it is certainly true that campaigns at the state and local level may at times be inexpensive, issue-based, highly focused, ideological and keenly party political. But localism is no guarantee of any of these features. Negative advertising and personal attacks can be part of almost any campaign, candidate-centred appeals can at times be even more strongly made at the local level, where many voters feel that 'politics' should not be allowed to get in the way of the efficient management of government, and while some local campaigns are indeed inexpensive, important state-wide, city-wide, and even state legislative races can involve massive investment in the campaign.

A number of states have economies as large as those of some nations, and the contest for leadership in these states can be particularly fierce. In the 1990s, gubernatorial elections for California, for example, were vigorously fought and expensive to run. Republican Pete Wilson held the governorship from 1990 to 1998, after an initial race in which the Republicans were reported to have spent $7 million on mailings to motivate absentee voters as well as telephone banks and getting other voters to the polls. When Wilson left the office in 1998 the Democratic candidates were estimated to have spent in excess of $60 million on the primary campaigns, with the winner then facing a further expensive race against well financed Republican opposition. In the key state of Texas, Republican George W. Bush spent $14 million in 1994 defeating incumbent Governor Ann Richards (Democrat), whose losing campaign cost $17 million. In 1998 Bush spent $23 million, having raised more than $24 million, in his successful bid for re-election. He took 69 per cent of the vote against a relatively weak opponent. The Texas Governor's brother, Jeb Bush, running his second campaign to be Governor of Florida, had raised $6.7 million by June 1998, in spite of that state's $500 limit on individual contributions. Tensions in the 1998 battle for the governorship of Massachusetts were exhibited in another form, according to the *Boston Globe*, which reported Republicans coming near to fist fights in the contest to endorse their gubernatorial candidate.[28]

Other state executive races can also be expensive. In 1994 elections in Massachusetts, Joseph D. Malone spent over $2 million in the race for state Secretary, and Scott Harshbarger spent $1.5 million being elected Attorney General.[29] Races for state legislative seats can also be fierce, but the costs vary widely between states, from a few hundred dollars to campaign budgets in the hundreds of thousands of dollars – as high as those for federal office. In Iowa the 1996 elections gave the Republicans an opportunity to take control of the state Senate, and the GOP raised over $400,000 to put into key races in addition to candidate funds. In neighbouring Nebraska, state Senator Floyd Vrtiska, running a low-key campaign against modest opposition, spent over $9,000 on his primary campaign, and had in excess of $11,000 on hand months ahead of the general election. These may be considered small expenditures, but victory in Nebraska brings remuneration of just $12,000 annually, plus a per diem allowance, and the dearth of candidates willing to take on the strain and expense of campaigning for such a reward left one-third of seats uncontested in 1996. Lack of competition elsewhere may be down to other reasons. A *New York Times* editorial accused the New York state legislature of drawing district boundaries that protect incumbents of both parties, local party leaders of avoiding races in which their candidates stand any chance of losing, and the creation of 'nonaggression pacts ... to assure that both sides can coast back into office without opposition'.[30]

Not all races are so cut and dried. The redesign of Miami's mayoral office to include strong executive powers, and a salary of $97,500, brought a considerable field of contenders into the race. An initial election reduced the field to two, with the winner decided by a run-off election, in November 1997. But Circuit Judge Thomas Wilson decided that the apparent victory, for Xavier Suarez, was flawed by 'a pattern of fraudulent, intentional and criminal conduct', especially in the falsification of some of the 5,000 absentee ballots, some of which were cast for electors who were dead. The Circuit Court ordered a new election. The Appeals Court decided that the absentee ballots were invalid, and apparent runner-up, Joe Carollo, should be declared Mayor. Months after election day, the decision was still before the courts. Boston's city council elections have not ended up in court recently, but they attract considerable effort and expenditure. In March 1998 Council President James M. Kelly held $110,670 in his campaign account, and Daniel Conley's campaign fund showed a balance of $81,850, while Maura Henigan, whose campaign was based mainly on loans from herself, had a deficit of $67,820.[31]

Elections for the various offices at state and local level encourage the airing of quite specific issues. In 1996 Janine Headen attracted 22 per cent of the vote, on a 10.1 per cent turnout, but was defeated in her fifth attempt for election to the School Board of Council Bluffs, Iowa, but was ready to run again 'until the parents of this community are satisfied the kids are being prepared educationally'. The candidates for re-election to Pottawattamie, Iowa, County Board cited their success in helping attract a proposed $100 million soybean processing plant to occupy vacant industrial land in the community. Their opponents claimed that the lack of communication between the Board and county citizens justified removing the incumbents from their $20,000 salary positions. University of Nebraska regents are not salaried, but the 1996 election saw an ill-tempered contest, including comments on the need for family and religious values of decades past, and accusations that the challenger had 'extremist views' and that the incumbent was an 'administrative lap dog' who misused her position to obtain forty-three tickets to a major football game. Challenging for Douglas County, Nebraska, Register of Deeds, a $58,101 salaried post responsible for keeping a record of real-estate transactions, the candidates stressed leadership qualities, improvement of computer facilities and public service. Candidates for the Papio-Missouri River Natural Resources District Board discussed water quality, flood control and the use of the $17 million annual budget. Citing controversial Nebraska Supreme Court decisions overturning term limits, and granting retrials in some murder cases, Citizens for Responsible Judges announced a plan to raise and spend $80,000 opposing the re-election of Judge David Lanphier.[32]

Campaigning at this level is affected by modernising technology, but still contains much of traditional style. Even in a campaign expected to spend $1 million, Shannon O'Brien, running for Massachusetts state Secretary in 1998, spent hours on her home telephone, asking her supporters to run fund-raising events. 'A picnic, a union-hall bash, a clambake, a kaffeeklatsch: Whatever it is and wherever it is ... she will get there.'[33] Fifteen months before the election, O'Brien had already covered 70,000 miles attending campaign events. Phil Keisling conducted a door-to-door campaign for a place in the Oregon House of Representatives. 'I would knock on 12,000 [doors] by the time I had finished, and at each I would give roughly the same pitch. "The speech" lasted about 90 seconds – a length, I had discovered, just short of where the natural courtesy of most voters would give way to impatient foot-tapping.' An efficient connection with the voter can be even more important. When the unchallenged incumbent in Massachusetts' thirteenth Suffolk state legislative district suddenly withdrew his candidacy after nominations had closed, even though his was the only name that would appear on the ballot, half a dozen hopefuls launched write-in/sticker campaigns. In order to vote for any of these candidates, voters have to lift a window on the voting machine, and either write-in or affix a sticker with the name of the candidate. As one candidate pointed out, 'It's not just convincing people to vote for me, it's teaching them how to vote for me.' There were echoes of the grassroots campaign effort after the 1996 Nebraska primary elections. Tom Skutt, Jr, Republican candidate for the State Public Service Commission, was confined to home on election night with a sore throat, blamed on setting up campaign signs in the rain. Nancy Jean Read, an Omaha school district van driver, and candidate for the Omaha public power district, attributed her primary election success to asking 'friends, family, people at work to tell people to vote. It was all word of mouth.'[34]

There remains at large in the United States a nostalgic faith in the potential for democracy to work. On occasion this belief can be manipulated cynically by candidates and incumbents who pepper their constituents with vacuous references to the flag, the Constitution or some such, relying on the response of citizen loyalty to these powerful national icons masking the unwillingness of the candidate to take a lead on meaningful policies. At other times this fluid, but deep, belief in democracy acts as the bedrock of the voters' commitment to 'independence' from political parties. It is also used as the foundation of a call by former Presidents Carter and Ford, co-founders of the Center for National Independence in Politics, for voters to shake off the effect of expensive modern media campaigns, and instead to find 'Democracy through education'.[35] New developments in local democracy are also provided by technological changes. Santa Monica, California, opened a computer network in 1989, enabling citizens to comment direct on city council affairs via the electronic mail network. While such commentary does not have the authority carried by a town meeting vote, its potential to aid the exercise of popular control is clear. As use of the Internet becomes more widespread, governments are investing in connections and Web pages and the public are becoming more involved; it is therefore increasing in significance as an instrument of democracy.[36]

Many Americans see the town meeting, a democratic hangover from colonial times still used in some states, as the nearest thing to 'true' democracy still operating in the United States. The town of Cornish, New Hampshire, was incorporated in 1768. It is still run by a town meeting, which is generally attended by almost half of the community's residents. In 1988 the meeting voted to raise $300 to pay the annual bill for town trash removal; it heard that the township health chairman had spent $1.67 in the year, minimising expenditure by not claiming her own expenses; it decided against spending $45,181 to set up its own police department, but for $8,500 to computerise the town treasurer's operations; by deciding to organise volunteer citizens to paint the town hall, rather than paying a contractor, it reduced the bill from nearly $7,000 to just over $700; it established citizen working parties to examine issues of moment in the town; it elected five fence viewers, presumably to keep a watch on the maintenance of the town's fences. In this simplest of electoral assemblies the roles of citizen, voter, legislator and executive appear to mould into a seamless whole.[37]

Laboratories of democracy: direct impact

James Morone refers to an ambivalence 'at the heart of American politics', on the one hand a 'fear [of] public power as a threat to liberty', on the other 'an alternative faith in direct, communal democracy. Even after the loose collection of agrarian colonies had evolved into a dense industrial society, the urge remained: The people would, somehow, put aside their government and rule themselves directly.'[38] While the town meeting represents a hangover from colonial direct democracy, some states have introduced other forms of direct democracy, the most common being initiative, referendum and recall elections.[39] The initiative and referendum, available in the mid-1990s in some form in twenty-eight states plus the District of Columbia, give voters an opportunity to comment directly on legislative measures, while the recall, offered in seventeen states, is designed to ensure that legislators remain responsive to their constituents' issue positions. Introduced as part of Populist and Progressive reforms about a hundred years ago, these electoral forms are found most often in the Plains, Mountain and western states, where the originating political philosophies held most sway.[40]

Initiatives take a number of forms. In eighteen states voters can propose amendments to the state constitution by collecting enough signatures on petitions to place the proposal on the ballot. Fourteen states and the District of Columbia allow citizens to place proposals enacting or amending state laws direct on to the ballot. Four states restrict such legislative initiatives to an indirect process, in which the proposal is referred to the state legislature before appearing on the ballot for popular approval. Eight states allow both direct and indirect forms of initiative. Referendums appear on the ballot in those states where there is a process to allow public judgement on enacted legislation. In twenty-one states these items can get on the ballot either as a result of citizen petition, or by decision of the state legislature. Two states use citizen petition only, while three put such matters on the ballot solely as a result of state legislative action. Recall elections are also stimulated by public petition, but in this case the subsequent public vote is solely on the question of whether a particular officeholder should be removed from that position before the term expires. Seventeen states and the District of Columbia allow the recall to be applied to at least some offices (see table 6.5).

Each state sets criteria for the submission of public petitions. Typically they set requirements as regards the number of signatures required – usually a percentage of the total number of voters, based on recent election turnouts. Citizen initiatives may need as few as 3 per cent of the number of voters in the last state-wide election. Recall petitions can require as many as 40 per cent to sign the petition. Signatures on state-wide petitions may be required to show support from a breadth of counties in the state. States may prescribe the policy areas that can be subjected to initiative. Passage of an initiative generally leads directly to legislation, though particular cases may always be subject to legal challenge. Even in states that do not allow for public direct involvement in legislation, voters are still aware of the power of referendums, since all states save one (Delaware) require public approval of state constitutional amendments, and some state constitutions require other matters, especially fiscal and taxation issues, to be put on the ballot for approval.

The recall is the least used of these mechanisms, but there have been some famous recent recall elections. Dennis Kucinih became the youngest Mayor of Cleveland, Ohio, in 1977, but his inability to cope with that city's financial crisis led to a recall attempt. In spite of surviving that by a narrow margin, Kucinih soon left the Mayor's office and his repeated attempts to gain election to another office failed until he entered the US House of Representatives in 1996. Dianne Feinstein, then Mayor of San Francisco, was subjected to a recall election. She survived easily, and may even have gained momentum on her career rise the US Senate. Successful

Table 6.5. *States using referendums, initiatives and recall*

	Constitutional amendment by initiative petition	Statute by initiative petition	Referendum by citizen petition	Referendum submitted by state legislature	Recall
Alaska		×	×	×	×
Arizona	×	×	×	×	×
Arkansas	×	×	×	×	
California	×	×	×	×	×
Colorado	×	×			×
Delaware				×	
DC		×	×		×
Florida	×				
Georgia					×
Idaho		×	×	×	×
Illinois	×	×			×
Kansas					×
Kentucky			×	×	
Louisiana					×
Maine		×	×	×	
Maryland			×	×	
Massachusetts	×	×	×	×	
Michigan	×	×	×	×	×
Mississippi	×				
Missouri	×	×	×	×	
Montana	×	×	×	×	×
Nebraska	×	×	×	×	×
Nevada	×	×	×	×	
New Mexico			×	×	
North Dakota	×	×	×	×	×
Ohio	×	×	×	×	
Oklahoma	×	×	×	×	
Oregon	×	×	×	×	×
Rhode Island					×
South Dakota	×	×	×	×	×
Utah		×	×	×	
Washington		×	×	×	×
Wisconsin					×
Wyoming		×	×		

Source: Kevin J. Coleman, Thomas H. Neale and Joseph E. Cantor, *The Election Process in the United States* (Congressional Research Service Report for Congress, 6 July 1995).

recalls are rare, and localised, and each case is likely to be highly charged. Sheriff Dan Scheiderheinz of Merrick County, Nebraska, was recalled by a vote of 1,579 to 1,379 in May 1996, after thirty-four years in office. Complaints about the Sheriff Department's poor response to calls from the outlying areas of the county, but in particular public disquiet about the handling of a murder enquiry in 1994, prompted this recall.[41]

Though these instruments of public access had existed for some time, the passage in 1978 of California's tax-cutting Proposition 13, followed two years later by the similarly hard-hitting Proposition 2½ in Massachusetts, focused national attention on the power of voters to affect policy directly. The California tax revolt, led by Howard Jarvis and Paul Gann, was a powerful act in a nation where the public's sympathy for substantial social policy spending was being eroded by their antipathy to the necessary levels of taxation. It had a dramatic nationwide effect as citizens in other states followed the California example with initiative petitions of their own. The revolt rolled across the states, becoming a significant part of the 1980 'sagebrush rebellion', as Senator Laxalt called it, that swept Ronald Reagan to the White House and gave him a Republican majority in the Senate.

While the initiative fell into relative disuse in many states until the last decade, in California it has been a constant feature of state and local politics. Sophisticated campaign advertising techniques were developed in the service of initiative politics and were used later in candidate campaigns. All sorts of issues have appeared on the ballot in the various states, including such matters as the regulation of professions and businesses, anti-smoking legislation, vehicle insurance rates, the use of nuclear power and gun control. The interested parties, especially those whose business interests may be affected, are increasingly willing to spend large sums to protect those interests, campaigning on critical ballot questions and promoting favourable questions of their own.

On 5 November 1996, 106 initiatives were on various state ballots. Term limits initiatives were on the ballot in fourteen states, and won a majority of the vote in ten of these. Five states saw the passage of campaign finance reform for state and local elections. The voters in five states refused to allow or expand gambling, while Michigan and three other states approved such changes. Colorado, Massachusetts and Washington passed restrictions on various forms of hunting and trapping. Tax limits were passed in Florida, Nevada, California and South Dakota, but failed in Idaho, Oregon and Nebraska. Many initiatives may affect business, for example by proposing regulations on products, industries or professions. These attract vast investments of campaign funds from the relevant interests. One major political consultancy advertised its effectiveness after the 1996 election, pointing out that its work had successfully helped clients to defeat propositions that aimed: to ease lawsuits for securities fraud; to regulate health maintenance organisations; to tax the health industries; and to introduce other 'anti-business' initiatives.[42] In California and Arizona measures were passed permitting the medical use of marijuana for pain relief. But the most controversial was California's Proposition 209, which banned the use of affirmative action on the basis of race, sex, colour, ethnicity or national origin. It was portrayed by its opponents as threatening to wipe away in a matter of months thirty years of gains from affirmative action policies, and by August 1997 its impact was clear in the fall in the proportion of African-American and Hispanic students enrolling in the graduate schools of California's universities. There was more controversy in California when Proposition 227, abolishing bilingual education, passed with 60 per cent of the vote in June 1998. The state schools system immediately faced the task of replacing bilingual programmes with provision for just one year of intensive English education to over 1.4 million California school students not proficient in English.

Other 1998 propositions included attempts to limit trades unions' authority to spend money on political activities, in California, Colorado, Nevada and Oregon. In Alaska there was a vote on a billboard ban. The size of hog farms reached the Colorado ballot. Michigan faced a choice on an assisted suicide law. In Oregon, where initiative access is among the most liberal, eighty-one initiatives were filed, and ten reached the ballot, covering issues including the use of marijuana for pain relief, mandatory jail terms and environment funding for Oregon's parks and streams. As this activity has grown, it has attracted huge funding. In California alone official returns show that over $141 million was spent on twenty-seven initiative races in the 1996 election cycle. The advertising budgets of these candidateless campaigns can be very high, especially where the interests of major organisations, business, or labour are involved. Americans for Tax Reform contributed almost $500,000 to underwrite a direct mailing in support of California's anti-union Proposition 226. Citizens for a Sound Economy planned a $2 million spend on television advertisements in the same campaign. In addition, the collection of signatures is itself costly. Union organisations were spending at similar levels on the other side. Just getting the signatures to qualify for the ballot can be expensive. Consultancy firms will collect the signatures, charging a per capita fee. In states where the petitions requirements are high, employing commercial help may be the only way of overcoming the logistical problems of collection. Faced with a late entry petition, to legalise particular forms of gambling at Indian reservations, signature collectors were given the incentive of $1.50 per name, and the 403,269 valid signatures were exceeded in less than thirty days. When gaming interests urgently needed signatures for a Florida petition in 1994, the rate went up to $2.50 a name.

Ballot questions provide a perfect opportunity for single-issue advocates to have an impact on politics. The critics claim that the single-issue approach encouraged by the initiative subverts the effectiveness of representative government by taking matters out of the hands of state and local legislators, imposing inflexible parameters on government, distorting the policy agenda, and increasing the potential power of highly financed, corporate-backed campaigns. A system which encourages issue decisions to be made without reference to broad public policy consequences contains the seeds of irresponsibility, a perspective exemplified by the fact that 1,316 state initiatives were circulated officially in the election cycles of 1992, 1994 an 1996. They also point out that the wording of ballot questions, and the nature of the campaigns, often leaves voters confused about the effect their votes are likely to have, and that while some initiatives prompt a high level of voting, in many cases propositions are passed on very small and unrepresentative turnouts.

On the other hand, many activists and some observers have welcomed this reinvigoration of state and local direct democracy. Voter turnout increases when populations concerned about issues become interested in vigorously contested ballot questions. The political agenda clearly can be shifted, expanded, or limited by citizens acting in concert in this way. Candidates for state office find themselves forced to take a stand on issues high on the public agenda, and the figures can be interpreted differently. Richie Ross, a consultant based in Sacramento, California, points out that in that state the decade to 1998 had seen about 300 initiatives submitted, just eighty-five of which qualified to get on the ballot, and only a handful of which were approved. Certainly this increasingly fashionable electoral form is a very particular contribution of the states to the American federal system. There is no provision for anything similar at the federal level, and it would need a constitutional amendment for that to change.[43]

Notes

1   US Bureau of the Census, *Statistical Abstract of the United States: 1996* (116th edn, Washington, DC, 1996), p. 298.
2   *Statistical Abstract 1996*, p. 319.
3   See, for example, Gillian Peele, 'Social groupings in the USA', R. A. Burchell, 'Recent patterns and policies in US immigration', and P. J. Davies 'Demographic movements within the USA', all in *The USA and Canada, 1998* (London, Europa, 1998).
4   See David B. Walker, 'American federalism in the 1990s', in *Political Issues in America Today: The 1990s revisited* (Philip John Davies and Fredric A. Waldstein, eds, Manchester, Manchester University Press, 1996), pp. 131–57.
5   For a discussion of state reactions to the fiscal pressures of the Bush years, see Steven D. Gold (ed.), *The Fiscal Crisis of the States* (Washington, DC, Georgetown University Press, 1995).
6   See, for example, Marilyn Werber Serafini, 'Not a game for kids', *National Journal*, 21 September 1996, pp. 2011–14.

7 Judith Haveman, 'Putting dad in the picture', *Washington Post National Weekly Edition*, 15 June 1998, p. 29; Barbara Vobejda and Judith Havemann, 'Losing welfare as a punishment', *Washington Post National Weekly Edition*, 30 March 1998, pp. 29–30; Judith Havemann and Barbara Vobejda, 'The two faces of welfare feform', *Washington Post National Weekly Edition*, 5 January 1998, pp. 30–1; Jon Jeter 'The first welfare reform victory', *Washington Post National Weekly Edition*, 29 September 1997, p. 32; Judith Havemann, 'It's crunch time for welfare reform', *Washington Post National Weekly Edition*, 22 September 1997, p. 29; Barbara Vobejda and Judith Havemann, 'And now comes the hard part', *Washington Post National Weekly Edition*, 1 September 1997, p. 29; Barbara Vobejda and Judith Havemann, 'When one size doesn't have to fit all', *Washington Post National Weekly Edition*, 7 July 1997, pp. 30–1.

8 Ceci Connolly, 'Seizing power while the seizing is good', *Washington Post National Weekly Edition*, 7 July 1997, p. 30.

9 The Bureau of the Census has two ways of measuring the centre of US population. In 1990 the median centre was placed in Lawrence County, Indiana, while the mean centre was two states further west, and had crossed the Mississippi River into Missouri. See *Statistical Abstract 1996*, p. 27.

10 Louis Jacobson, 'Capital gains', *National Journal*, 8 November 1997, pp. 2248–50.

11 Gregg W. Smith, 'Taking stock of local party organizations', *Vox Pop*, vol. 9, no. 2, 1990, p. 7; see also James Gimpel, *National Elections and the Autonomy of American State Party Systems* (Pittsburgh, University of Pittsburgh Press, 1996).

12 Professor Alan Rosenthal, quoted in William Schneider, 'Where the sun's setting on comity', *National Journal*, 15 August 1998, p. 1950.

13 *Statistical Abstract 1996*, p. 306.

14 Indiana state Representative Paul S. Mannweiler, president-elect of the National Conference of State Legislators, quoted in Schneider, 'Where the sun's setting', p. 1950.

15 For examples of strongly contested gubernatorial races, see Michael Aron, *Governor's Race: A TV reporter's chronicle of the 1993 Florio/Whitman campaign* (New Brunswisk, NJ, Rutgers University Press, 1994); Gerald C. Lubenow (ed.), *California Votes: The 1990 governor's race* (Berkeley, CA, IGS Press, 1991); Gerald C. Lubenow (ed.), *California Votes: The 1994 governor's race* (Berkeley, CA, IGS Press, 1995); David A. Leuthold, *Campaign Missouri 1992* (Columbia, MO, University of Missouri Press, 1994), especially chapter 2.

16 Geeta Anand, 'Hopefuls begin jockeying for position', *Boston Globe*, 14 March 1998, p. A8.

17 Tom Gannon, 'After tough first year in R. I. House, Patrick Kennedy is looking ahead', *Boston Sunday Globe*, 12 November 1989, p. 84; Michael Barone and Grant Ujifusa, *The Almanac of American Politics, 1996* (Washington, DC, National Journal, 1995), p. 1189–90.

18 Philip John Davies, 'Ethnicity, race and 1990s US politics', *Politics Review*, vol. 7, no. 4, April 1998, pp. 29–33.

19 *U.S. Term Limits* v. *Thornton*, 93–1456 – see 'Term limits ruling gives new hope for access', *Ballot Access News*, 11 June 1995, pp. 1–2.

20 Paul Jacob quoted in Annys Shin, 'Term limits groups turn up the heat', *National Journal*, 7 March 1998, p. 518.

21 Craig Crawford, 'Pledging the limit', *National Journal*, 20 June 1998, p. 1468.
22 Luis Romano, 'Setting the stage for amateur hour', *Washington Post National Weekly Edition*, 8 June 1998, pp. 11–12.
23 Quoted in Schneider, 'Where the sun's setting'.
24 *Foster v. Love*, 96–670 – see 'States cannot change November election date for federal offices', *Party Developments*, vol. 4, no. 4, February 1998, p. 24.
25 Statistics from *The Election Data Book* (Lanham, MD, Bernan Press, 1993), quoted in Coleman, Neale and Cantor, *The Election Process*, p. 69.
26 David Beiler, 'Shortfall in the sunshine state', *Campaigns and Elections*, August 1989, pp. 40–1.
27 '"Sin city" wages legal battle', *Guardian*, 1 August 1998, p. 14.
28 Sue Ann Pressley, 'Who's afraid of the Big Bad Bush?', *Washington Post National Weekly Edition*, 9 February 1998, p. 12; Craig Crawford, 'Thanks, Dad!', *National Journal*, 28 February 1998, p. 475; Liz Schwefler, 'Raising money by the Bush(el)', *Capital Eye*, vol. 6, no. 1, p. 6; Terry M. Neal, 'A kinder, gentler "Jeb" Bush', *Washington Post National Weekly Edition*, 8 June 1998, p. 10; 'Republicans are fighting mad over selection of state delegates', *Boston Globe*, 8 March 1998.
29 Don Aucoin, 'Beacon Hill's glass dome', *Boston Globe Magazine*, 2 November 1997, p. 24.
30 Jim Smiley, 'GOP seeks control of Iowa senate', *Omaha World-Herald*, 13 September 1996, p. 15; Paul Hammel, 'Number of legislative hopefuls slips', *Sunday World-Herald*, 15 September 1996, p. 4B; Paul Hammel, 'Stalder, Vrtiska strategies differ in district 1 race', *Omaha World-Herald*, 20 September 1996, p. 18; 'New York's upcoming non-elections', *New York Times*, 15 September 1996, section 4, p. 14.
31 'Dead absentees voted in Miami', *Party Developments*, vol. 3, no. 5, April 1998, pp. 6–7; 'Kelly's greenbacks separate him from the rest of the city council', *Boston Globe*, 8 March 1998.
32 All the following are from the *Omaha World-Herald*: Gary Newman, 'Bluffs board incumbents re-elected', 11 September 1996, p. 15; Gary Newman, 'Former board member, new candidate, challenge Pottawattamie supervisors', 11 September 1996, p. 18; R. Ruggles, 'NU board of regents race pairs consultant and lawyer', 10 September 1996, p. 12; Cindy Gonzalez, 'Ms. Barrett, Takechi to vie for register of deeds post', 15 May 1996, p. 8; Julie Anderson, 'NRD board candidates stress water issues and experience', 20 September 1996, p. 18; Leslie Boellstroff, 'Nelson decries campaign to oust high-court judge', 6 September 1996, p. 15
33 Aucoin, 'Beacon Hill's glass dome', pp. 27, 31.
34 Phil Keisling, 'Thrills, spills, and bills', *Washington Monthly*, October 1990, pp. 12, 14; Michael Jonas, 'House hopefuls take the plunge', *Boston Globe*, 20 October 1996, p. 10; David Hendee, 'Mrs. Boyle, Skutt, picked for PSC race', and Toni Heinzl, '6 advance on ballot for OPPD', *Omaha World-Herald*, 15 May 1996, pp. 8, 9.
35 From a 1990 fund-raising letter, and *Voter's Self-Defense Manual*, issued by the Center for National Independence in Politics, Tucson, Arizona.
36 John Markoff, '"Talking" on the computer redefines human contact', *New York Times National Edition*, 13 May 1990, p. 1.

37   Paul Angiolillo, Jr, 'A license for Yankee ingenuity', *Boston Sunday Globe*, 25 June 1989, p. 79.

38   James A. Morone, *The Democratic Wish: Popular participation and the limits of American government* (New York, Basic Books, 1990), quoted in *National Journal*, 1 December 1990.

39   For an overview, see Thomas E. Cronin, *Direct Democracy: The politics of initiative, referendum, and recall* (Cambridge, MA, Harvard University Press, 1989).

40   Coleman, Neale and Cantor, *The Election Process*, pp. 55–9.

41   Paul Hammel, 'Merrick County sheriff ousted', *Omaha World-Herald*, 15 May 1996, p. 7.

42   Advertisement by Goddard, Causen/First Tuesday, back cover, *National Journal*, 9 November 1996.

43   Jack W. Germond and Jules Witcover, 'California's at it again', *National Journal*, 16 May 1998, p. 1144; Peter H. Stone, 'Going after union dues', *National Journal*, 18 April 1998, p. 883; David S. Broder, 'Taking the initiative on petitions: signature for a price', *Washington Post National Weekly Edition*, 20 April 1988, p. 11; Rene Sanchez and William Booth, 'Across the country, bilingual education is facing new tests', *Washington Post National Weekly Edition*, 8 June 1998, p. 9; David S. Broder, 'The battle over the ballot', *Washington Post National Weekly Edition*, 10 August 1998, pp. 12–13.

7

Congressional elections

'We interact with the people who are angry'[1]

In their answers to a survey undertaken in spring 1998, members of Congress predicted that 72 per cent of the American public distrust government. Non-elected members of the federal government, appointees and senior bureaucrats predicted the level of distrust to be 62–63 per cent. A simultaneous public opinion poll, in answer to the question 'Would you say you basically trust the federal government in Washington or not?' found 57 per cent saying 'No', 39 per cent 'Yes' and 4 per cent undecided.[2] Representative David Skaggs (Democrat – Colorado) makes a telling comment that elected officeholders may hear more from their agitated constituents than from their satisfied ones, but this is unlikely to be the only cause of the difference. The congressional estimate would have been pretty accurate earlier in the 1990s, when public trust in government rarely moved out of the 20–30 per cent range, and while more of the 1998 public expressed trust than the officeholders had expected, a figure below two-fifths of the electorate is relatively high for any survey since the early 1970s, and is hardly a ringing endorsement. Through the last generation of the twentieth century well under half of the American public have trusted their government.

There is apparent in this survey a disconnection between the public and their elected Congress. While 64 per cent of congressional respondents expressed a 'great deal' of trust in the wisdom of the choice made on election day by the public who had elected them, only 31 per cent of members of Congress thought the public knew enough about the issues faced in government to form wise opinions on what should be done. A majority of these federal officeholders believed the public to be anti-government, while 57 per cent of the public were assessed by the survey as in favour of government activism. A very high 83 per cent of Republicans in Congress described themselves as anti-government, and many had no doubt been part of that group for whom 'criticizing government is a popular campaign theme', which was in part blamed by some for the bedrock of public distrust over the past quarter century. Their faith in this campaigning approach will have been strengthened by the fact that a public increasingly sceptical of politicians and of 'politics as usual', in the 1990s, put the Republicans in control of Congress in succeeding elections after over half a century of Democratic dominance.

The perceived public scepticism in responding to election campaigns appears magnified to an almost ideological 'anti-government' position among Republican members of Congress. This may be a natural consequence of political activism and the electoral process, in which those who hold political positions more strongly rise to office. Alternatively officeholders may be misinterpreting the wish of their electorate to see government challenged, and transforming it into a more aggressively anti-government stand. Or there may be a straightforward difference between the rhetoric of congressional position-taking and the reality of congressional policy-making. One presidential appointee to federal office commented perceptively, 'You know, while my father thought everyone in government was a crook, he never objected to getting his Social Security check.'[3] Polling in 1998 may have caught the broad essence of this complex relationship between public and government. While broad-brush mistrust of the government was lower than officials expected, nevertheless 60 per cent of the public polled felt criticism of the federal government to be justified. Given the range of federal government actions it might seem reasonable that most people would find something to criticise, without necessarily being 'anti-government'. A Congress that interprets subtle and selective public criticism of government less perceptively, as blanket anti-government feeling, is in danger of adopting rhetoric and actions that feed greater public distrust.

While public trust in Congress and federal government grew in the late 1990s, other measurements suggest that Senators and Representatives cannot take this improvement in their standing for granted. A survey of the perception of the relative honesty of twenty different professions found a quarter of the public rating politicians as 'not at all honest' and only 1 per cent thinking them 'completely honest'. Politicians came bottom of this list, behind the classic comparison group, used-car sales people, who were rated 'not at all honest' by only one-sixth of respondents.[4] The term limits movement of the late twentieth century has expressed some of the frustration of a population that often appears to feel that government is not responding effectively to contemporary challenges. A 1998 poll by Opinion Dynamics, for the Fox television network, may have tapped into this when it found that 41 per cent of respondents would like to see new people in government, as opposed to 35 per cent more willing to rely on experienced personnel (24 per cent no opinion). And when Opinion Dynamics asked, 'Do you think the average congressional representative deserves to be re-elected, or would we be better off throwing them all out and starting over with new people?', 48 per cent of responses were for throwing out, and only 29 per cent for re-election of this 'average congressional representative'.[5]

Large-scale replacement of congressional membership is, nevertheless, rare. The last quarter of the twentieth century has been a time of continued expression of a deteriorated relationship between the electorate and the elected, and Congress has been a major focus of attention. Campaigners in the late 1970s adopted from the movie *Network* the slogan used by the late Peter Finch, whose character becomes one of the oppressed and unheard, asking them to join him in shouting for all in authority to hear, 'We're mad as hell, and we're not going to take it any more'. But while 'mad as hell' voters have consistently informed pollsters of their declined trust in government, they have not reacted by throwing out the incumbents wholesale.

Throughout the second half of the twentieth century on average over 90 per cent of US Representatives presenting themselves for re-election have achieved it. Only in four elections has the re-election rate fallen below 90 per cent: 1964 (87 per cent), and 1966, 1974 and 1992 (each 88 per cent). In 1986, 1988 and 1990 the re-election rates were as high as 96 and 98 per cent. US Senators are less safely ensconced in office, but their median re-election rate for the second half of the twentieth century has still been in the low 80 per cent range, and as high as 97 per cent in the 1990 election, and 92 per cent in 1994 and 1996.[6]

After the 1990 election one cartoonist lampooned the American electorate with a sketch of a voter yelling into a megaphone, but the megaphone, labelled '36% national turnout', was turned the wrong way around, and the slogan, 'We're mad as hell and we're not going to take it any more', was coming out not loud and clear, but instead miniaturised.[7] A number of factors may help account for this apparent anomaly. A major force is the familiarity of the incumbent, who will build a record for constituency service. A poll that found respondents equally divided on their approval/disapproval of Congress also found voters giving 70 per cent approval rates to their own Representative in the US House, a full 24 per cent higher than the same group's support for Congress as a whole.[8] While there may be some confusion in the public perception of Congress, it is also important that opinion be properly assessed. The electorate makes a distinction between approval of the way institutions are behaving, assessment of the role of individual officeholders, trust in groups of persons, and justifiable criticism of policy and policy-makers. Voters are also affected by the hot issues of the moment, the noise of which can drown out the complexities of debate. Those in the business of elections do not always serve this public subtlety well by developing game plans that ride on emotive issues, adopt broad-brush attack styles that obscure rational, detailed debate, and accentuate the negative.

There has certainly been change in Congress in recent years. Change does not come just through defeating incumbents. In the 1980s and 1990s the US House has seen on average over 10 per cent of its complement retiring at each election, with particularly large-scale retirements in 1992 and 1998. In the Senate the average retirement rate over the same period has approached 20 per cent, with a particularly large tranche in 1996. Some of those retiring may have done so in the face of increasingly hard races. In any case open seats, without the encumbrance of voter loyalty to a known public figure, are easier ground for challengers, and campaigns in these seats tend to be competitive and heavily funded. Having dominated for decades, the Democrats found themselves in the 1990s with Republicans in charge of both chambers of the US Congress. Public trust in government may remain low, but there is no doubt that party power in Congress has been restructured by the electorate.

Congressional structure and electoral input

In a political system that prides itself on its multiple points of access and its pluralist representation of the public interest, the US Congress perhaps most clearly expresses these ideas in institutional form. The executive may appear to be the dynamic centre of US government and will indeed, if properly led, set both the tenor of administration and the parameters of all major political actions, but the legislative keystone is the Congress, where ideas are developed into bills by Representatives, Senators, and their staff, and then sometimes passed into law. Both experience and research led L. Sandy Maisel, a politics professor and one-time congressional primary candidate in Maine, to claim that 'in a real sense, the aura of Washington, the sense of history, the call of patriotism draws many into the political arena', but parallel with this rose-tinted perspective is the wish to be effective, and it is equally significant that feeding Maisel's developing political ambition was the firm belief that congressional 'members alone are at the center of the real action'.[9]

The 100 Senators, 435 Representatives and five delegates elected to the US Congress are, nominally at least, in Washington, DC, on behalf of their constituents. They also represent a national balance of power between the two major political parties. After the 1998 elections the Republican Party held control of both House and Senate, although the House, very unusually, included a Representative from neither of the main parties, as Bernard Sanders, an independent with declared socialist beliefs, was re-elected from Vermont. Democratic dominance in both chambers was consistent over some sixty years, and from the mid-1950s to the mid-1990s that party controlled both chambers with the exception only of the first six years of the Reagan administration (1980–6) when the

Republicans held control of the Senate. Democratic congressional power was, however, eroding and 1994 saw an upset victory for the Republicans, who took control of both chambers.[10] At the time some observers viewed this as a referendum on the first two years of the Clinton presidential administration, but while Clinton fought and won a re-election campaign in 1996, the Democrats made gains in the House, lost further ground in the Senate, but could not regain control of either. The 1998 elections saw the Republicans retain control of Congress, and that party had its longest continuous period of congressional authority since the 1920s. Nonetheless, the 1998 results were disappointing to the Republicans, since their majority in the House was reduced, as the presidential party gained seats in this mid-term election – an event almost without precedent in US electoral history. The result was so surprising as to precipitate the resignation of Republican Speaker Newt Gingrich (Georgia). Another southern Republican, Bob Livingston of Louisiana, took over as Speaker, but within weeks he resigned after revelations about his private life. Dennis Hastert (Illinois) was then chosen as Speaker.

Senators, two from each state regardless of its size, are elected for a six-year term, with one-third of the whole body being up for election in alternate years. In the case of a senatorial seat becoming vacant by the death or other ill-timed departure, the practice is general for the state Governor to appoint an incumbent to serve until the next biennial election day comes around, when an election to serve out any remainder of the term is held. Representatives' constituency boundaries are not so firmly fixed, except that they cannot cross state boundaries. The 435 seats are distributed between states according to population size after each decennial census, boundaries then being decided by the state legislatures, subject to the criteria that, within the state at least, the constituencies should be of equal population size. While there is variation caused by the proviso of fitting whole numbers of seats within the state boundaries, the average size nationwide of a Representative's constituency is projected at about 630,000 by the year 2000. The five delegates elected to the House of Representatives are from American Samoa, the American Virgin Islands, the District of Columbia, Guam and Puerto Rico. While they can take part in debates and sit on congressional committees, they have no vote on the floor of the House. All members of the House of Representatives are subject to election every two years, with special elections being held if a seat becomes vacant between normal election times.

While the geographical and party constituencies served by members of Congress are obvious, albeit with the proviso that the parties' ideologies are broad and their sanctions weak, these alone do not define the universe of those to whom Senators and Representatives offer service. The business of Congress is done primarily within the confines of its various specialised committees and subcommittees. The spring 1998 edition of *The Capital*

Source lists twenty committees of Senate, twenty committees of the House of Representatives, and four joint committees. These cover such areas of interest as agriculture, the budget, foreign relations, veterans' affairs, national security, science, small business and taxation.[11] Each of these committees operates through a complex of subcommittees. The Republican leadership has cut back sharply on the number of subcommittees, and in the late 1990s there were typically about ninety subcommittees in the House and about seventy in the Senate.[12]

All members of Congress are appointed to several of these committees and subcommittees, often competing to join those committees whose area of interest would complement the concerns of the citizens who have elected the member. For example, a rural Representative might naturally seek to sit on the Agriculture Committee, or committees with a high profile where the connection might serve to improve the member's name recognition and career prospects. The committees and subcommittees of Congress hold hearings where members can investigate problems seriously, listen calmly to evidence, promote specific positions on issues of concern, attack institutions, individuals, sacred cows and bêtes noires, and generally grandstand to their hearts' content. While there is a clear hierarchy, and the former Republican Speaker of the House, Newt Gingrich, asserted the leadership authority of his office especially strongly, the operation of Congress is nevertheless distributed broadly between these committees, and the fact that the legislation of the United States is written within these committees makes them very powerful bodies indeed.

This identification of distributed power also means that any person or institution nationwide can identify precisely which committee, and probably even which members of a particular committee, are the politicians with the most influence on legislation directly affecting their own livelihood and beliefs. Lewis Anthony Dexter is just one of the pluralist analysts who has claimed that this gives interest groups within the electorate an enormous potential to target any specific issue-based displeasure with great precision. Issue-based interest groups, the argument goes, can identify any dilatory committees, committee members and committee leaders, then, by working with and contributing to opposition campaigns within the relevant members' home constituencies, can punish the miscreants directly at the polls.[13] In truth, such a plan is not easily put together as a broad-based grassroots operation. Nevertheless, the committee structure does offer a clear opportunity to identify useful points of contact which institutions and their lobbyists have found an enormous aid in the pursuit of their own interests. Communities of interest have developed between congressional committees, government agencies and the private sector around the legislative briefs of the committees, and these communities of interest form a powerful and tenacious part of the constituency served by Representatives and Senators.

Investing in Congress

The structure of Congress provides interest groups and lobbyists with multiple, identifiable and efficient points of access. The committee and subcommittee assignments of legislators gives an immediate indication of those who will be dealing with legislation relevant to any particular interest group. Analysis of the legislative voting records of Representatives and Senators allows groups to identify clearly those legislators most likely to be favourable and those unfavourable to their particular interest. Such information is used carefully in targeting officeholders for special consideration at election time.

Interests have, on occasion, targeted for electoral attack specific US Representatives and Senators unsympathetic to their cause, but it has been much more general for major business, labour and other interest groups, through their PACs, to support the incumbent members. Major players on the political scene value an investment in the friendship, or at least the predictability, of a known personality with increasing seniority in the congressional system above the gamble on a political challenger who, even if victorious, is as yet untried, and would be too junior to carry much weight in the institution. Sitting candidates generally get re-elected, and therefore interest groups usually want to have access to them. To get support, a challenger must have a good chance of victory, as well as a sympathetic policy stance, and even then PAC money is scarce for challengers. In 1996 challengers in competitive races only received 3 per cent of all corporate PAC donations.[14] Campaign contributions are a method of ensuring access to incumbent politicians, and money is not generally wasted on lost causes. Ideological impact can be achieved through other financial channels. Contributions of hard and soft money to national and state party organisation, independently financed issue-advocacy campaigns, and parallel political routes can be used in an attempt to influence the electoral agenda, and to alter the landscape over which elections are fought.

PAC contributions from corporate, trade, membership and health-related organisations are considerably higher than those from labour union sources, and one might therefore expect funds to tend towards Republican candidates more likely to be ideologically friendly to these political investors, but the tendency to invest in the officeholder goes a long way to explaining the balance of distribution of PAC moneys. Over the three election campaigns between 1987 and 1992, when the Democrats were in control of the US Senate, PAC contributions ran 54.4 per cent in their favour. In the US House, Democratic control was rewarded between 1985 and 1994 with 66 per cent of all PAC funds donated in House races over that period. Republican-supporting groups and individuals counterbalanced the pragmatic advantage of funding channelled to Democratic officeholders in part by putting substantial funds into the national party, with the Republican national committees outspending the Democrats consistently in every election over the last quarter of the twentieth century, and by a total of $633 million in the decade 1986–96 alone.[15]

In 1994, when Democratic congressional control slipped, PAC contributions to US Senate candidates split 50:50 between candidates of the two major parties. After Republican control of the Senate had been established, the 1996 election saw a dramatic swing, with 65 per cent of PAC contributions going to Republican candidates for the US Senate. In 1994 PAC contributions to US House candidates favoured the Democrats 67:33. After the turnover of control in 1994 the next election saw PAC money distributed evenly between the parties' candidates, and 1998 appeared to show more money from PACs moving towards Republican candidates. With the advent of Republican control of both chambers of Congress in 1994, the Republican tendency to cater for corporate, business, trade and industrial interests was no longer countered by a pragmatic pressure to contribute to Democratic candidates on the grounds that they would likely be the controlling party in Congress. Without the participation of labour PACs, who made 93 per cent of their 1996 congressional candidate donations to Democrats, the balance of donations would have been overwhelmingly to Republicans, with every other category of PAC favouring them.[16]

The reporting requirements of modern election law make the close bonds between PACs and incumbents easy to identify. In the two-year election cycle up to 1996, House incumbents received $117.7 million from PACs, while challengers were given $21.7 million. The discrepancy in the Senate was not quite as severe, with $28.7 million going to incumbents and $7.4 million to challengers.[17] PAC contributions to Democratic House incumbents in the 1996 elections accounted for almost 48 per cent of their campaign chests, and Republican House incumbents received 37 per cent of their funds from PACs. Democratic and Republican challengers in the House respectively received less than 23 per cent and just over 10 per cent of their campaign funds from PAC sources. In the Senate the proportion of campaign funds raised from PACs is lower, but still the proportion of incumbent funding raised in this way is double that for challengers.[18]

Much of this money may come from PACs representing local constituency interests, for example an industry or labour union with an important presence in the state or district of the incumbent. But increasingly members are relying for their contributions on out-of-district sources, whether PAC or individual. Officeholders may be targeted for donations on the basis of their policy stands on legislation relevant to donors. Donors are particularly aware of those legislators serving on congressional committees whose legislative remit impinges on areas significant to the interest group. Congressional committee chairs, who have particular leadership roles in legislation and congressional oversight, benefit especially from this attention. A sample of nine Republican Representatives who ran for election in 1994 (when they were leading Republicans in a Democratic Congress) and again in 1996 (when they were running for the first time for re-election as Republican committee chairs) received a total increase in PAC contributions of $1,711,961 over that two-year period, a boost of 78 per cent. Over the same period the PAC contributions to nine former Democratic committee chairs, now running for election as minority members, rose by only 5 per cent.[19]

Even minor members on significant committees attract serious financial attention. Bill Brewster, US congressman for Oklahoma's third district from 1990 to 1996, already had a track record as a state legislator before his first congressional race, and 37 per cent of his campaign funds came from PACs. After one term in the House, PACs provided 62 per cent of his campaign war chest. On re-election Brewster was appointed to the most prestigious and powerful Ways and Means Committee, with effective control over the design of the nation's tax code. The money flowed in, with 71 per cent of his campaign funds coming from PACs for the 1994 race. The oil and gas industry has large concerns in Oklahoma, but the $145,000 donated to Brewster by the industry's interest groups saw themselves, in the words of Jean Mastres of Occidental Petroleum, as 'concerned constituents, if you will, not just concerned constituents of Oklahoma but constituents of the energy industry'. Representative Brewster, a Democrat, but a conservative on taxation and on many reforms, steadfastly opposed tax increases on tobacco, and resisted health care reforms. The tobacco industry donated $17,000 to Brewster, and health care interests put $139,000 into his campaigns. This 'financial constituency' increasingly moves the focus of the officeholder from local interests towards national forces. The presence of the federal government in Washington, DC, gives an incumbent access to a national network of PAC and other contributors that many officeholders utilise efficiently.[20]

During the one hundred and fourth Congress (1995–7), the Center for Responsive Politics tracked PAC contributions against the legislative voting records of the members receiving funds.[21] The report points to the congruence between policy positions and contributions received. Agribusiness interests feature, protecting government subsidies for their products. Support for the sugar industry is estimated to add 50 cents a pound to the consumer cost. The sixty-one US Senators who voted to maintain this aid received an average of $13,500 each from relevant PACs in the six years to 1996. The thirty-five who voted to eliminate the programme received an average of $1,500 from the same PACs. A federal subsidy programme for peanuts, estimated to cost consumers 33 cents on a jar of peanut butter, was supported by 212 US House members, in receipt of an average $1,542 contribution from peanut PACs in 1995–6, and opposed by 209, who had received an average of $150. The chair of the House Agriculture

Committee, a central character in this kind of decision, received $23,000 from these PACs.

The close relationship between moneyed interests, incumbents' campaign war chests, and legislative interests feeds a cynical view of the national legislature, as in Philip M. Stern's words, 'the best Congress money can buy'.[22] But despite the large sums involved there is little clear evidence of direct causal links between donations and elected members' legislative voting behaviour. If officeholders maintain a particular policy position which attracts the attention and support of relevant interests, this is hardly surprising. Big-spending interest groups do not always get their way, and while the aggregate sums are large, they are made up of many small donations. Even a PAC's maximum of $5,000 per candidate per election donation forms a modest part of the average winning campaign chest. Donors claim that they are, at most, ensuring themselves access to a congressional incumbent should an issue arise on which they would like to make sure that their opinion was being heard.

Major legislative issues do attract public scrutiny, but special interests are concerned with the detail of legislation, especially with specially written loopholes or subsidies. Some of these are applied generically to classes of business or industry. Others are more specific, often bringing together constituency and interest group influence, for example the tax provision attached to one act of Congress, limited to a 'corporation incorporated on June 13, 1917, which has its principal place of business in Bartlesville, Oklahoma'.[23] This roundabout identification pinpoints Phillips Petroleum, one of many beneficiaries of the 1986 Tax Reform Act, which was estimated to contain $16.2 billion in corporate tax benefits of this kind.

A number of analysts are convinced that causal connections exist between donations, fund-raising and subsequent legislative decision-making. John R. Wright argues that lobbying does influence votes, and contributions ensure ease of access for lobbyists, thereby establishing a prima facie, albeit indirect, connection.[24] Observers have also increasingly been leaning to the conclusion that PAC money rewards congressional voting sympathetic to the PAC position, and while it does not affect the votes of unsympathetic members, it helps mobilise the existing biases within Congress into action when necessary, especially at the critically important committee level and on issues where public visibility is low.[25] Interviewed in 1990, one member of the House Ways and Means Committee put it in the following way: 'We don't trade votes, but what happens is we gravitate towards people who can help us financially. I've noticed it myself.... We become friends, and then we trust them on the issue.'[26]

Interest groups can legitimately claim to represent a broad range of citizen concerns, and their operation in the political marketplace is often portrayed as legitimate competitive advocacy, a route towards a fairly bargained balance of civic rights and obligations. Labour groups are often interested in broad areas of civil rights, issue-based groups promote particular visions of personal liberties shared by substantial citizen minorities, and the promotion of business can be as good for employees as for owners and shareholders. Nevertheless, there remains the concern that those unable or unwilling to invest in access may in the end be disadvantaged. The words and career of former US Senate Majority Leader, and in 1996 Republican presidential candidate, Bob Dole put this into sharp relief. Dole's responses over the years to questions on political finance have sometimes expressed disdain for the connection: 'PACs give to incumbents ... because access to an officeholder is more important than a member's party, ideology, or even voting record on the issues, and I never knew you had to buy access.'[27] Furthermore, in Dole's words again, 'there aren't any Poor PACs or Food Stamp PACs or Nutrition PACs or Medicare PACs'.[28] Dole's Senate campaigns in Kansas inevitably cost millions of dollars over the years. One report claims that between 1979 and 1994 Dole's campaigns and his leadership PAC received $381,000 from the Ernest and Julio Gallo Winery, $245,000 from Koch Industries (oil), $217,800 from Archer, Daniels Midland (agribusiness) and substantial amounts in repeated contributions from other major interests.[29]

It can be argued that the interests exemplified by Dole's list of 'missing PACs', shared by large sectors of the population, will be heard by Senators and Representatives anyway, responsive as they are to the ballot booth as well as to the contributor. But some of the affected populations do not have a high turnout, and their disaffection therefore holds little electoral threat for the members. Research suggests that non-moneyed interests might be little heard, for example finding 'little evidence that committee members respond to the interests of unemployed workers except insofar as those interests might be represented in the activities of well-financed and well-organized labor unions'. In addition, the researchers challenged the pluralist belief that strongly held public opinion can effectively countervail well organised and well financed minority opinions, concluding that, at least on occasion, 'members are more responsive to organized business interests within their districts than to unorganized voters even when voters have strong preferences and the issue at stake is salient'.[30]

Home advantage

If there is some doubt about what the major donors are expecting, or likely, to receive for their money in the long term, there is little doubt as regards the immediate value of the money to officeholders in financing professional, year-round political campaigns. It may be that an operation of this nature is essential in the face of a serious challenge, but even before any challenge has emerged the raising of a substantial campaign war chest by an incumbent serves a purpose. Charles Peters pointed to just one such example in his June 1990 *Washington Monthly* column:

> I have in my hands a press release from the office of Rep. Toby Moffett that points with pride to an article in a Meriden, Connecticut Record Journal headlined, 'Moffett Leads in 5th District Fund Raising.' Why, you may wonder, would a congressman think it politically wise to brag that he has the most money? The reason – and this helps explain why incumbents are obsessed with fundraising – is that this kind of headline intimidates. It either frightens away potential opponents or discourages their potential supporters.[31]

Financial and other campaign preparations may be made considerably in advance of the election, and the earlier a major campaign fund is amassed the more intimidating it can appear to potential challengers. Some sixty US Representatives who already knew in June 1998 that they would be facing no major party opposition that year nevertheless had raised campaign funds totalling $22 million. Several experienced incumbents had more than $1 million on hand, but financial power was not restricted to the senior members. Peter Deutsch (Democrat – Florida) raised $841,774, and Thomas Davis (Republican – Virginia) $816,729. The money may be used in general campaigning, for promoting name recognition and GOTV efforts, but having been left unopposed in 1998, these candidates have developed the foundation of a fund that can be maintained to deter potential challengers in the future.[32]

While adequate campaign funds are essential, and some incumbents appear to believe that nothing succeeds like excess, money alone does not win. Political consultant Dick Morris, who has achieved a level of notoriety for his work with Republicans and Democrats, including long-standing links with Bill Clinton, points out that the price of candidate participation is a high minimum expenditure. You have to pay to play, and visibility and credibility depend on a minimum layout to communicate with the constituency. But he claims that entry cost expenditure levels alone are not determinant.[33] If anything, high spending is more valuable to those few challengers who are able to raise substantial funds, since they face incumbents, who hold the associated advantages.

Sitting members have more weapons at their disposal than being in an advantageous position from which to raise money. Campaign spending can put a candidate's name before the public in the run-up to an election, but an effective incumbent can act in ways to increase name recognition among voters throughout the term of office. Furthermore, much of this can be done as part of the daily business of office-holding. In his classic study *Congress: The electoral connection*, David Mayhew sought to 'conjure up a vision of United States congressmen as single-minded seekers of reelection', a vision that he thinks 'fits political reality rather well', and for which he finds a fair degree of evidence in the day-to-day behaviour of the members.[34] Incumbents find it valuable to take every opportunity to represent themselves to their voters as the friend and individual protector of the constituency generally, as well as of its individual citizens. Much of this legislator–voter relationship is subsumed under the general rubric of 'constituency service'.

The loosely structured nature of Congress does allow some opportunity to deliver political goods to the constituency. Members co-operate to provide each other with opportunities to spend taxpayers' money on worthy projects in each other's districts. Any facilities coming to the constituency at federal expense will likely be opened with some pomp and circumstance, and will be claimed during the next election campaign as being the result of the incumbent's personal efforts, skill and prestige in Congress. The budget package approved by the US Senate in October 1998 included fifty-two pages of '"locality-specific, special-interest, pork-barrel spending projects," including $1.1 million for manure handling and disposal in Mississippi and $100,000 for Vidalia onion research in Georgia'. Incumbents often take advantage of important legislation to add clauses bringing federal expenditure to their own constituencies, and it is considered an act of congressional courtesy to allow colleagues this opportunity to take home the bacon. Bills that become heavily ornamented with highly directed expenditure of this kind are sometimes called 'Christmas tree bills'. Newt Gingrich, faced in 1998 with complaints about the self-serving nature of this behaviour, dismissed the critics as 'perfectionists'.[35]

Insofar as such resources are available for distribution it is certainly true that some members have more success than others, and this influence is generally closely associated with the member's ability to gain assignment to the choice committees of Congress, and his or her seniority on that committee. Therefore the issue of seniority may itself become an election asset. An incumbent attacked for being old and out of touch can, as long as there is some evidence of federal largesse in the constituency that can be produced, respond that those taking this point of view are threatening the community with the replacement of a well placed, powerful friend by a junior, untried Senator or Representative who will take years to be in a position to benefit the constituency so directly.

As well as service to the constituency as a whole, congressional office-holders also value their direct links with individual constituents, presenting themselves as the ombudsmen of the federal government, and inviting citizens to bring direct to the congressional office any problems they have that relate in any way to the government. While much of this constituency service is of genuine benefit to the individuals and the communities involved, it is less clear that it results in a coherently organised national legislature. It does seem, though, to benefit the members of that legislature:

> Congressmen ... earn electoral credits by establishing various federal pro-
> grams.... The legislation is drafted in very general terms, so some agency
> ... must translate a vague policy mandate into a functioning program, a
> process that necessitates the promulgation of numerous rules and regula-
> tions and ... the trampling of numerous toes ... aggrieved and/or hopeful
> constituents petition their congressman to intervene in the complex ...
> decision process of the bureaucracy ... the congressman lends a sympathetic
> ear, piously denounces the evils of bureaucracy, intervenes in the latter's
> decisions, and rides a grateful electorate to ever more impressive electoral
> showings. Congressmen take credit coming and going.[36]

Generous congressional staffing allowances allow congressional members to offer personal services to their constituents. The number of
employees in Congress attached to individual members and to committees
numbered almost 15,000 in the early 1990s, having grown by about 200
per cent between 1960 and 1980, since when there has been relative
stability.[37] A proportion of these staff, together with unpaid interns, both
in the Washington office and in constituency offices, pursue constituency
service casework designed at least in part to maintain and improve the
incumbent's name recognition among the voters.

The value to the incumbent of constituency service is in its electoral
impact. But not every constituent needs to approach a member of Congress for service, nor do all constituents have an intimate knowledge of
the facilities brought to the locality by the member. Therefore the service
that is done must be mined for its electoral potential. Skilful Senators and
Representatives keep in close contact with their constituents through press
releases to and interviews with local newspapers, through personal mail
responding to constituents' concerns, and through mass mailings of newsletters to all constituents. Personal homepages on the World Wide Web
are a 1990s addition to this communications arsenal. Much of this can
be done at government expense. News releases and public appearances are
generally managed by the members' government-salaried staff. Letters
responding to constituents' mail are, reasonably enough, carried at government expense as part of the members' 'franking privilege'. This access
to the US mail has also subsidised the delivery of regular mass mailings
to constituents, which have become a feature in recent years.

It is important that members of Congress, based in Washington, DC,
avoid appearing to become divorced from constituency concerns, and
sympathetic and rapid response to and analysis of constituent mail have
always been considered important aspects of tending the fences back
home. The addition of accessible computer technology in recent years has
meant that congressional offices have been able to upgrade this effort,

maintaining a substantial file of response letters covering standard questions that can be personalised and returned very quickly, analysing incoming letters to warn the office of themes that are emerging, and developing and maintaining a database of personal information on constituents that may be of use in directing appeals for electoral support and campaign contributions, especially when combined with membership lists acquired from sources such as professional associations and interest groups. Rules covering the franking privilege caution that it is not to be used for patently political purposes and warn, for example, against 'excessive use of personally phrased references', which 'for the most part shouldn't appear more than eight times a page', but a 1990 survey of about 200 congressional newsletters found few so parsimonious, with Representative Dennis Hastert (Republican – Illinois) managing forty-eight references to himself in four pages, and Representative Newt Gingrich reaching fifty-four.[38] While much of this mail is part and parcel of the necessary constituent service provided by incumbents, a significant proportion is designed to maximise constituents' ability to recognise and respond positively to the incumbent's name come election time.

In a political system where party affiliation is only a limited guide to people's voting behaviour, the officeholders have to establish alternative touchstones of loyalty, and the direct relationship with the constituency, given the name 'home style' by political scientist Richard Fenno, is a crucial part of this establishment of a continuing link between incumbent and constituency.[39] Some activists believe that issues must be given a constituency angle if they are to be significant in a congressional election, and the higher political mortality rate suffered by Senators in most election years is often put down to their failure to maintain their close links with the constituency as efficiently as their colleagues in the House. Senate seats, elected state-wide, generally provide incumbents with a larger, more varied constituency, where an electoral majority is likely to contain a more diverse range of interests than a House constituency. Senate terms of office, six years as opposed to the two-year terms in the House, also give more time for the incumbent and the voters to drift apart, and for suspicions to arise that the Senator is ceasing to be a home product, and becoming too engrossed in Washington.

In an effort to undermine any such doubts, publicity generated by the congressional offices will highlight their member's role in defending and advancing constituency interests, and in promoting general issue stands that are likely to attract a positive public response among constituents. Some of this effort is entirely ersatz; for example, in 1990, Representative Chester Atkins submitted twenty-one separate resolutions to the House congratulating each police force of the twenty-one communities within his Massachusetts constituency.[40] Members use similar devices to 'stroke' some constituent group. Helpful publicity will also result from the usefulness of the member's congressional committee assignments to the constituency. Courtesy between members within Congress ensures that even junior incumbents have occasional opportunities to chair congressional committee hearings, with resultant beneficial publicity, especially if the topics being discussed have a direct bearing on constituency affairs or, as is sometimes the case, the hearings are being held 'on the road', and in a member's home constituency, rather than, as usual, in Washington. Representatives and Senators generally do work hard on the behalf of their constituencies. Such efforts are part of the obligation and the fulfilment of their jobs. But the electoral dynamic impels them not to allow their work, and their vocal commitment to their constituencies, to go unnoticed, so every effort is made to bring the Representatives' and Senators' records home in a way that is meaningful to the voters.

Turnover

One of the main benefits of incumbency is the opportunity afforded by the position to raise and spend very substantial campaign funds, thereby frightening off a serious challenge, or forcing any challenger to raise and spend a similarly large war chest from a less advantageous position. Therefore the incumbency advantage is also blamed for helping to fuel the acceleration of congressional campaign spending in recent years. There seems to be a fine line between a member's constituency loyalty and a sense on the part of many incumbents of the imperative to maintain a very healthy campaign fund, driving officeholders increasingly to solicit large proportions of this fund from outside the geographical boundaries of the constituency. This creates a potential divorce between the constituency that provides the votes and the constituency that provides the funds, raising the question as to which constituency the incumbent serves.

Even some incumbents have complained that fund-raising has such a grip on officeholders that the business of Congress is disrupted. Senator Robert C. Byrd (Democrat – West Virginia) complained in May 1990 that 'Right now, because of the outrageous cost of running for a seat in this body, we are not full-time Senators.... Every Member here has a part-time job as a fund raiser.' Democratic Senator Thomas Daschle of South Dakota estimated that 'For two years prior to an election, any Senate candidate spends 30–70 per cent of his political time raising money.... In the last year, they spend at least 50 per cent of all their time raising money if they have a close contest.'[41]

It has been an increasing problem in recent years to recruit effective candidates willing to challenge incumbents. The commitment demanded is huge. Money must be raised and the months of campaigning are long and hard, filled with 16-hour working days. For many candidates just

Table 7.1. *Turnover in the US Senate, 1988–98 (thirty-three to thirty-five seats contested each year)*

	No. seeking re-election	Defeated in primary	Vacancies after retirements and primary	Incumbents defeated at general election	No. (%) of 'new faces' in Senate
1998	29	0	5	3	8 (8)
1996	20	1	14	1	15 (15)
1994	26	0	8	2	10 (10)
1992	28	1	8	4	12 (12)
1990	32	0	3	1	4 (4)
1988	27	0	6	4	19 (10)

Source: Calculated from Harold W. Stanley and Richard G. Niemi, *Vital Statistics on American Politics, 1997–1998* (6th edn, Washington, DC, Congressional Quarterly Press, 1998), pp. 47–8, and *National Journal*, 7 November 1998, pp. 2610, 2662.

gaining local name recognition is difficult and the incumbents they face are generally well known and veteran campaigners. There is, nevertheless, change over time. Incumbency may regularly protect in excess of 90 per cent of congressional officeholders standing for re-election, but natural mortality opens up seats irregularly, and retirement leads to regular opportunities for change.

As can be seen from tables 7.1 and 7.2, there is a steady turnover in both chambers of Congress that belies the high incumbency retention rates. Post-election analysis of members of Congress not returning to their seats in 1994 and 1996 showed a substantial proportion propelled by their ambition into elections for the US Senate, or for their state governorships (table 7.3). Other retirements can be explained by a spectrum of reasons. Ageing officeholders may retire because they no longer wish to feel the

Table 7.2. *Average percentage turnover at each US House election, by decade, 1970–96*

	Total turnover	Deaths	Retired/ resigned	Nomination defeat	Election defeat
1990s	21.9	0.5	13.4	1.9	6.0
1980s	12.2	1.0	7.2	0.6	3.2
1970s	18.8	1.0	11.2	1.4	5.2

Source: Harold W. Stanley and Richard G. Niemi, *Vital Statistics on American Politics, 1997–1998* (6th edn, Washington, DC, Congressional Quarterly Press, 1998), p. 43.

Table 7.3. *US House members not returning to Congress, 1994, 1996 and 1998*

Elected to Senate	Lost race for Senate	Elected Governor	Lost race for Governor	Other retire-ment	Defeated in re-election attempt
17	19	2	10	82	69

Source: Immediate post-election analyses in *National Journal*, 9 November 1996, pp. 2422–3, 12 November 1994, pp. 2650–1, and 7 November 1998, p. 2605.

pressure of the job. Others move on to pursue different opportunities in the private sector. The prospect of a particularly vigorous election challenge may precipitate the decision by some incumbents to leave office.

This steady turnover gives the opportunity for change. In the Senate after the 1996 election, forty-five of the hundred seats were occupied by persons whose first term in office started in the 1990s. At the same time, in California, the state with the largest complement of seats in the US House, twenty-six of those fifty-two US Representatives first entered the House in the 1990s. A shift of voting preferences at congressional level over the past decade has been evident in the gains made by the Republican Party in the 1990s.

'Unsafe at any margin'

A sitting member has a record of behaviour in office. While the office-generated mailings and press releases will emphasise all that appears positive about this record, any lapses in political or personal judgement will give a prospective challenger the opportunity to attack. A long record may be portrayed by the incumbent as indicating a mature and successful career, especially with increasing congressional seniority. On the other hand such longevity allows the opponent the opportunity to investigate the track record for any evidence of political or personal indiscretion, inconsistency, poor decision-making, lack of concern with constituency affairs, and other potential failures. Such probing may be particularly problematical for an officeholder with a long career, since the environment of political decision-making does alter over time, and decisions made or positions taken years before do not necessarily appear as reasonable as they once did.

Opponents have little compunction in portraying incumbents as inconsistent, undecided or misguided, even when these behaviours might reasonably be explained in terms of changing political expectations over time, and election campaigns give few opportunities for calm or reasonable explanations in the face of attack. Insofar as citizens vote retrospectively, they do so in response to their assessment of the officeholder's performance in office. It is this retrospective element in the voting decision that means that a record in office may be a liability as well as a benefit. This encourages opponents to seek out and emphasise any negative aspects of the incumbent's record, and incumbents have to be ready to strike back hard against any such campaign attacks.[42]

The perceived lack of competitiveness in congressional seats has been blamed in part for the growth of hard-hitting, personalised campaigning. A challenger faced with such odds, the argument goes, has to exploit to the maximum any chink in the political armour of the incumbent, attempting to inflate any identified personal or political error of judgement to the level of scandal in order to subvert the institutional advantages of office. And while open seats, left vacant by retirement or death, usually offer a more competitive race than that of incumbent against challenger, the number of such openings is small enough that both candidates are likely to run as hard-hitting a race as they would have done against a sitting member. Party campaign committees, not immune to the difficulties suffered by their challengers, have on occasion attempted to open up incumbents to attack by exploiting contentious issues between elections. It has become the received wisdom that incumbents subject to such attacks must respond quickly and hard. During a formal campaign, when such attacks are most likely, and when an effective response may depend on the purchase of substantial advertising time, this can be another expensive contingency for which to plan. Regardless of the regularly high incumbency re-election rates, even a few unpredicted defeats in the nation are enough to keep congressional incumbents feeling 'unsafe at any margin'.[43]

Individual constituency campaigns and local factors have real significance, but there can be no doubt that congressional campaigns have become increasingly nationalised in the latter part of the twentieth century. Voters do associate each of the major parties with different positions, and different expectations of success, on such issues as management of the economy, social and education policy, defence and foreign affairs. Groups within the electorate tend to vote for a candidate from that party perceived as most successful in the policy areas most important to the voting group. Occasionally, short-term issues can become of particular significance to some voting groups. In the 1998 congressional elections those voters who considered social policies, such as education, to be most important leaned firmly towards Democratic candidates. Those voters who considered President Clinton's sexual encounters with Monica Lewinsky to be an important indicator of the failure of the President's moral and constitutional leadership role leaned strongly towards Republican candidates.

Broad national policy concerns have set the context for congressional elections, especially with the growth of national media. Cable, satellite,

Internet and other developments have expanded media outlets in the USA, but the mainstream electronic media, especially network television, continue to provide a nationalised delivery system for news. Local media outlets are important, but they compete with instant coverage of national events. As computer-based media networks grow in significance, room is created for the exploration of a myriad of topics, but, equally, people throughout the nation can be in direct touch with national debates. This experience of policy through a pluralist media structure may act to increase the influence of national political topics.

The parties too have been involved in this trend. They are competing for market share. In such a competition the more one can limit the variables, the better. In recent years the parties have taken an increasingly active role at national level in recruiting and training candidates, and in raising, distributing and spending campaign funds. While most campaign money is still raised by individual candidate campaigns, national party committees have moved towards careful targeting of their own financial efforts towards important marginal campaigns (see chapter 3). The growth of soft money used by parties has increased the potential of this spending, and has increased the influence of the party committees who create the advertisements that are financed from this source. For example, in October 1998 the national Republican senatorial committee was reported to be spending $7 million on a late issue-advertising campaign in such states as Kentucky, Nevada and North Carolina.[44]

In 1994 the incumbent President, Bill Clinton, had suffered a major congressional rebuff with the failure of his flagship health legislation. Clinton, elected in 1992 with the support of only 43 per cent of the population, was seen as a liability to his party, and Republican candidates nationwide attacked opponents by labelling them as Clinton allies. In addition, then Republican House Minority Leader Newt Gingrich coaxed his fellow Republican candidates into support of a statement of policy stands and intentions they called the 'Contract With America'.[45] While this played a modest part in the campaign of most candidates, the sweeping Republican successes of that year put Gingrich and his Contract into a very strong position with regard to defining the political agenda.

In 1996 the campaigns were influenced by other national pressures. In the first place, being a presidential election year, the race at the head of the ballot was a strong guiding element for all political debate.[46] The Democratic Party spent many millions of soft money dollars on an issue-advocacy campaign on behalf of the President, which helped define the issues of all that year's campaigns. Individual campaigns by candidates of both major parties showed similarities of theme. Newt Gingrich, then Speaker of the House, had real political skills, but a confrontational style that was not widely popular. The Democrats saw an identifiable target in Gingrich, and this time they consistently portrayed their opponents as clones of this bête noir. From the other side, the leading Republican political consultants advised their candidates to attack their opponents as dangerously 'liberal', and made the attack on 'liberals' into a theme in races across the nation. Interest group money also began to take on an increased role in defining the electoral debate, with the American Federation of Labor–Congress of Industrial Organizations (AFL-CIO) undertaking a multimillion dollar campaign of issue-advocacy advertisements highlighting the benefits of Democrat policy positions placed in marginal Republican constituencies.

By 1998 the number of groups, and the amount of money, invested into issue-advocacy campaigns had increased dramatically. One report claimed that twenty-nine groups spent $150 million this way in 1996. But in 1998, even without the draw of a presidential race, sixty-seven groups were reported as spending $330 million. One candidate complained that he sometimes felt like a spectator in his own campaign.[47] Issues surrounding the presidency came to the fore in this election, as the special prosecutor appointed to investigate allegations against President Clinton published his report claiming that there existed grounds for impeachment, in particular with reference to the conduct of the President's relationship with a White House volunteer and employee, Monica Lewinsky.[48] In the later stages of the campaign the Republicans attempted to capitalise on the public reaction to this affair by running a number of nationally produced advertisements, at a cost of $10 million, in fifty-six targeted constituencies.

With the South realigning in the last years of the century, to reflect a more national pattern of party competition, there is no longer any region of the country where the political debate is run on the basis of distinctive political assumptions, thereby allowing more scope for issues to be promoted nationwide. Not all nationalised campaigns work to the advantage of the investor. The issue-advocacy advertisements funded by the labour unions in 1996 had only a modest electoral effect. The Republican campaign on the Clinton–Lewinsky affair might even have provoked a public backlash, as the President's party gained House seats in a mid-term election for the first time since 1934. Within the contemporary American political scene the effects of national media coverage, federal campaign consultancies, issue campaigns funded by interest groups, and the growing use of soft money in issue-advocacy campaigns by the political parties all influence the campaign debate towards shared national issues.

Congressional competition at the millennium

The beginning of the twenty-first century will see the redrawing of many House constituency boundaries as the 2000 census results are fed into the political system. The shift in population since 1990 is expected to result in a reallocation of around ten or more seats, between a total of perhaps twenty states which have gained or lost population to a relevant degree. Burgeoning states in the South and West, such as California, Florida and Texas, are likely to gain. At most risk of loss are states with slow growth or decline, mostly industrial states of the East and Midwest, but also the some less successful southern states. But the real losers are those House incumbents who will find their constituencies redistricted out of existence, or at least suffer the problem of shifting constituency boundaries disrupting the stability of their relationship with the electorate. The potential gainers are candidates ready to fight for the newly created open seats, or to challenge incumbents made less secure by new boundaries. Faced with such changes to the campaign playing field, some congressional office-holders, becoming tired with the strains of office and the rough and tumble of campaigns, might be more tempted than usual to retire from public life, contributing to the natural turnover in Congress. Other office-holders will see the need, as in any period of electoral challenge, to redouble the efforts to strengthen their positions.

While few members of the US Senate or House of Representatives feel completely confident about their impregnability, the potential electoral disruptions of the early years of the twenty-first century should be weathered by most who wish to stay in office. Officeholders are in a good position, if they remain wary, to adapt to changes in electoral rules and to shifts in constituency opinion. But the career of even the most high-profile politician may be subject to sharp turns. Newt Gingrich, then the highly visible Republican minority whip, in 1990 held on to his seat by only 972 votes against an under-financed Democratic opponent, as a result of what seemed to be voter reaction to Gingrich's preoccupation with his national ambitions. Having led his party to a startling victory in 1994, Gingrich found his own re-election a great deal easier. But his confrontational style as Speaker of the House made support for him fragile, and the equally startling Democratic victories of 1998 destroyed Gingrich's status as a great Republican strategist, and led to his resignation as Speaker, and his announcement that he would be leaving the US House altogether.

A number of factors may combine to make Congress a more competitive institution in the twenty-first century. Although the anti-incumbency mood of the 1990 electorate did not cause sweeping changes, it did serve to reduce the comfortable majorities held by many incumbents. The share of incumbents re-elected with at least 60 per cent of the vote dropped from 88 per cent in 1988 to about 68 per cent in 1992 and 1994.[49] Public disquiet with the role and behaviour of Congress has not noticeably declined, but attempts to apply term limits to federal legislators have failed in Congress, and state attempts to impose these limits on the US Congress have fallen to challenge in the Supreme Court on constitutional grounds. The shift of the 1990s has been in favour of the Republicans, and that party is hoping to consolidate these gains in 2000 and beyond, in a way that they have not succeeded in doing in the 1990s. This notwithstanding, relatively small party majorities in Congress at the end of the twentieth century give both parties the incentive to campaign with the prospect of gaining or maintaining legislative dominance.

Notes

1   Representative David Skaggs (Democrat – Colorado), quoted in Alexis Simendinger, 'Of the people, for the people', *National Journal*, 18 April 1998, pp. 850–5.
2   Survey conducted by the Pew Research Center for the People and the Press in association with *National Journal*, reported in Simendinger, 'Of the people, for the people'.
3   Victor H. Reis, Assistant Secretary for Defense Programs, quoted in Simendinger, 'Of the people, for the people'.
4   Richard Morris, 'So what else is new?', *Washington Post National Weekly Edition*, 2 March 1998, p. 35.
5   'The elections', *National Journal*, 1 August 1998, p. 1832.
6   Gary C. Jacobson, *The Politics of Congressional Elections* (4th edn, New York, Longman, 1998), pp. 21–2; Paul S. Herrnson, *Congressional Elections: Campaigning at home and in Washington* (2nd edn, Washington, DC, Congressional Quarterly Press, 1998), pp. 18–19; Harold W. Stanley and Richard G. Niemi, *Vital Statistics on American Politics, 1997–1998* (6th edn, Washington, DC, Congressional Quarterly Press, 1998), pp. 47–8.
7   Summers cartoon from the *Orlando Sentinel*, republished in *National Journal*, 22 December 1990, p. 3102.
8   Dan Balz and Claudia Deane, 'Bringing the classroom into the campaign', *Washington Post National Weekly Edition*, 20/27 July 1998, p. 13.
9   L. Sandy Maisel, *From Obscurity to Oblivion: Running in the congressional primary* (Knoxville, TN, University of Tennessee Press, 1982), pp. 15–16.
10 Clyde Wilcox, *The Latest American Revolution: The 1994 elections and their implications for governance* (New York, St. Martin's Press, 1995).
11 *The Capital Source: The who's who, what, where in Washington* (Washington, DC, National Journal, 1998), pp. 23–4.
12 Stanley and Niemi, *Vital Statistics*, pp. 200–1.
13 See, for example, Lewis Anthony Dexter, *Sociology and Politics of Congress* (Chicago, IL, Rand McNally, 1960).
14 Paul Herrnson, 'Interest groups, PACs, and campaigns', in *The Interest Group Connection* (Paul S. Herrnson, Ronald G. Shaiko and Clyde Wilcox, eds, Chatham, NJ, Chatham House, 1998), pp. 48–9.
15 Calculated from FEC press release, 'FEC reports major increase in party activity for 1995–96', 19 March 1997.

16 Calculated from FEC press release, 'PAC activity increases in 1995–96 election cycle', 22 April 1997.

17 Stanley and Niemi, *Vital Statistics*, p. 103.

18 Stanley and Niemi, *Vital Statistics*, p. 89.

19 Candice J. Nelson, 'The money chase: partisanship, committee leadership change, and PAC contributions in the House of Representatives', in *The Interest Group Connection* (Paul S. Herrnson, Ronald G. Shaiko and Clyde Wilcox, eds, Chatham, NJ, Chatham House, 1998), p. 56.

20 Robert Dreyfuss, 'How money votes: an Oklahoma story', *American Prospect*, no. 19, Fall 1994, pp. 42–57.

21 Nancy Watzman, James Youngclaus and Jennifer Schechter, *Cashing In: A guide to money, votes, and public policy in the 104th Congress* (Washington, DC, Center for Responsive Politics, 1997).

22 Philip M. Stern, *The Best Congress Money Can Buy* (New York, Pantheon, 1988). See also, for example, Dan Clawson, Alan Neustadtl and Mark Weller, *Dollars and Votes: How business campaign contributions subvert democracy* (Philadelphia, PA, Temple University Press, 1998), and Brooks Jackson, *Honest Graft: How special interests buy influence in Washington* (revised edn, Washington, DC, Farragut Publishing Co., 1990).

23 Clawson, Neustadtl and Weller, *Dollars and Votes*, p. 67.

24 John R. Wright, 'Contributions, lobbying, and committee voting in the U.S. House of Representatives', *American Political Science Review*, vol. 84, 1990, pp. 417–38.

25 Janet Grenzke, 'PAC money and congressional voting', *Vox Pop*, vol. 8, no. 1, 1989, p. 8; Richard L. Hall and Frank W. Wayman, 'Buying time: moneyed interests and the mobilization of bias in congressional committees', *American Political Science Review*, vol. 84, 1990, pp. 797–820; Jean Reith Schroedel, 'Campaign contributions and legislative outcomes', *Western Political Quarterly*, vol. 39, 1986, pp. 371–89.

26 Carol Matlack, James A. Barnes and Richard E. Cohen, 'Quid without a quo?', *National Journal*, 16 June 1990, p. 1479.

27 *Congressional Record*, 10 April 1989, pp. S3537–8, quoted in Charles Lewis, *The Buying of the President* (New York, Avon Books, 1996), p. 114.

28 Quoted in Elizabeth Drew, *Politics and Money* (New York, Collier/Macmillan, 1983), p. 96.

29 Lewis, *Buying of the President*, p. 131.

30 Hall and Wayman, 'Buying time', pp. 814, 797.

31 Charles Peters, 'Tilting at windmills', *Washington Monthly*, June 1990, p. 6.

32 Peter H. Stone, 'Fat and happy', *National Journal*, 6 June 1998, p. 1321.

33 Interview, BBC2 *Newsnight*, 2 November 1998.

34 David R. Mayhew, *Congress: The electoral connection* (New Haven, CT, Yale University Press, 1974), pp. 5–6.

35 Senator John McCain, quoted in Richard E. Cohen, 'An autumn of discontent', *National Journal*, 24 October 1998, p. 2505.

36 Morris P. Fiorina, *Congress: Keystone of the Washington establishment* (New Haven, CT, Yale University Press, 1977), p. 48. See also Bruce Cain, John Ferejohn and Morris Fiorina, *The Personal Vote: Constituency service and electoral independence* (Cambridge, MA, Harvard University Press, 1987).

37   Stanley and Niemi, *Vital Statistics*, p. 199.

38   Weston Kosova, 'Congress's mail prostitution ring', *Washington Monthly*, September 1990, p. 34.

39   See Richard F. Fenno, *Home Style: House members in their districts* (Boston, MA, Little, Brown, 1978); and Richard F. Fenno, *Senators on the Campaign Trail: The politics of representation* (Norman, OK, University of Oklahoma Press, 1996).

40   Renee Loth, 'Praise the cops – all of the cops', *Boston Sunday Globe*, 17 May 1990.

41   Carol Matlack, James A. Barnes and Richard E. Cohen, 'Senatorial curtsy', *National Journal*, 16 June 1990, pp. 1462, 1463.

42   See Morris Fiorina, *Retrospective Voting in National Elections* (New Haven, CT, Yale University Press, 1981).

43   Thomas E. Mann, *Unsafe at Any Margin: Interpreting congressional elections* (Washington, DC, American Enterprise Institute, 1978).

44   'Hands out, GOP is dialing for dollars', *National Journal*, 24 October 1998, p. 2575.

45   Clyde Wilcox, *The Latest American Revolution?* (New York, St. Martin's Press, 1995), pp. 48–56.

46   See, for example, James E. Campbell, *The Presidential Pulse of Congressional Elections* (Lexington, KY, University of Kentucky Press, 1993).

47   Jonathan Rauch, 'Drop that ad, or we shoot', *National Journal*, 24 October 1998, p. 2483.

48   See, for example, the *New York Times*, 12 September 1998, for the full text of the Starr report, and immediate reaction.

49   Jacobson, *Politics of Congressional Elections*, p. 26.

8

Presidential elections

Leading the ticket

Political foresight is often limited, even for those with imaginative genius. In an interview given shortly before his death, the late Orson Welles, a liberal Democrat, told of being asked to consider running for election as US Senator from California. He claimed that on thinking this over he felt that the drive needed to be a successful Senator could be maintained only by an ambition ultimately to occupy the White House. This, he then considered, effectively put him out of the running, since he could not imagine any circumstances under which the electorate would choose a divorced ex-movie actor as President of the United States. By the time Welles was giving the interview, Ronald Reagan had been elected to the presidency.

Reagan's career move notwithstanding, Welles' diffidence was not without foundation. Social and cultural barriers, both unstated and tangible, have always blocked the route to the White House. Divorce figured among the difficulties subverting the ambition of both Republican Nelson Rockefeller and Democrat Adlai Stevenson to occupy the presidency. Al E. Smith, Democratic candidate in 1928, found his Roman Catholic faith was reason enough for some potential support to fade away, and John F. Kennedy, also a Catholic, had to develop a campaign strategy in 1960 that tackled this issue head on. While there are times when these barriers seem absolute, such limitations have collapsed in the past, and will no doubt continue to do so. At the time of writing neither major party has nominated a woman, or a non-white citizen, as its candidate for the nation's highest office. Minor parties have nominated women, African-Americans and Hispanic candidates on presidential tickets. The Democratic Party broke new ground by nominating Geraldine Ferraro as its candidate for the vice-presidency in 1984, Jesse Jackson made vigorous challenges for the Democratic presidential nomination in the 1980s and remained a powerful presence in the 1990s, and Colin Powell was seriously mooted as Republican candidate in 1996 before he announced his unwillingness to run. At the turn of the millennium, there is a feeling that more barriers may be about to fall.

Celebrity, on the other hand, is no barrier to presidential election. While most Presidents have served in some political office before entering the White House, a number have also been successful in other careers. For many that parallel career is in the law, and President Taft, whose first love was the law, was probably happier in his eventual role as Chief Justice of the Supreme Court than he ever had been as President. Woodrow Wilson was an educator, and his first presidency was that of Princeton University. Herbert Hoover was an engineer and mining company executive of international renown, and Lyndon Johnson built up a powerful corporate interest in Texas-based media outlets while also developing his political career. Jimmy Carter managed skilfully the growth of family agribusiness interests in Georgia, and George Bush, while pursuing an active career as a politician and diplomat, had a firm foundation in the family's oil business. President Eisenhower stepped from military to political leadership, following the pattern of such Presidents as Andrew Jackson, William Henry Harrison and Zachary Taylor.

While the US entertainment business produced its first President in the 1980s, it has for many years had its share of participants with firmly held political beliefs across the political spectrum, some of whom have taken up successful political careers, for example 1940s Democratic Congresswoman Helen Gehegan to 1990s Republican Congressman Sonny Bono. Since the entertainment industry can produce substantial profits for the successful, those with the ambition to participate politically in either a lead or supporting role have the advantage of close access to people with funds.

Personal wealth is not a prerequisite for a presidential candidate, but the 'log cabin to White House' image is more powerful rhetoric than historical reality. While the parents of Lincoln and Garfield may have brought up their young families in log cabins, even most nineteenth-century Presidents enjoyed more palatial surroundings.[1] It is nevertheless fair to say that presidential candidates have come from backgrounds covering a wide spectrum of social status. For some scions of financial and political dynasties, such as Franklin Roosevelt, John F. Kennedy and George Walker Bush, the economic and political advantages stemming from their backgrounds have helped them on their way to electoral success, but other Presidents, such as Richard Nixon, Ronald Reagan, Gerald Ford and Bill Clinton, were born into families of very modest means, and forged business and political careers that attracted financial and electoral support from others en route to the White House.

Candidates and Presidents from unorthodox backgrounds can benefit from underestimation of their skills. Ronald Reagan was consistently underestimated by his opponents in campaigns and in office, but in hindsight Senator Edward Kennedy assessed Reagan as 'a successful candidate and an effective President above all else because he stood for a set of ideas. He stated them in 1980 ... and he wrote most of them not only into public law but into the national consciousness.'[2] Bill Clinton became known as 'the Comeback Kid' after repeatedly committing political and personal mistakes that subverted his public support to a degree that convinced his opponents he must be finished, only to act skilfully, and build on any luck coming his way, to regain the political, if not the moral, high ground.[3]

The making of Presidents

Successful campaigners learn essential lessons from the experience and study of previous campaigns. Nonetheless, in a system with so many offices, covering such a variety of functions, at all the different levels of the federal system, in a political environment that changes over time, virtually all campaigns can lay some claim to a certain uniqueness, at least for those personally involved. The campaign for the presidency, a nation-wide race for the highest office available, is the ultimate in special cases.

For all major party presidential hopefuls, the campaign process starts with a pre-nomination period that lasts for months, sometimes years in advance of the election. The first target is to establish a campaign organisation that has the potential to capture the party's nomination to run for the presidency. Hopefuls and their immediate teams of supporters assess the chances of a bid for the party nomination. They forge alliances and line up support within their political party. They discuss strategy and put initial resources into place to support a potential campaign. If the results of this intelligence-gathering are disappointing, even a hopeful who has invested considerable time, effort and expense may take the campaign no further.

Candidates who continue in the race are at this stage competing against others within their own party, Democrat against Democrat, Republican against Republican, to become that party's officially nominated candidate in the presidential election. In pursuit of this ambition they must campaign for support in the presidential primaries and caucuses that take place across the nation. Presidential primaries and caucuses for each political party are held in every state of the USA, the District of Columbia, some other regions controlled by the USA, and for political party supporters living abroad. Each state or other unit decides the timing and processes of its primary or caucus. By tradition this season of primaries and caucuses opens formally with the New Hampshire primary and the Iowa caucuses, around early February of election year, and runs through to the final state contests in June. The season of primaries and caucuses provides a hard test for any campaign organisation, and the field of candidates tends to reduce as the weaker campaigns run out of resources.

Delegates are selected by these many primaries and caucuses, to be sent to the parties' national conventions, which take place in late July or early

August. Delegates are usually clearly identifiable by their loyalty to a particular candidate. The delegates from all the states vote to nominate the party's candidate. A simple majority vote is needed. In recent years successful candidates have commonly established clear majority support among the delegates before the end of the primary/caucus season, but still the convention vote formalises the result, and provides the parties with their officially nominated candidates for presidential election.

The major party nominees for President and Vice-President launch the general election campaign in their acceptance speeches to the party national conventions. Then the nominees are once again campaigning across the USA, but this time competing as official party nominees – Democrat against Republican – for the votes of the general electorate. At the November election the voters cast their ballots to make their choice between the party nominees for President, a process made more complicated than it appears by the Founding Fathers' constitutional provisions for an Electoral College. In fact the November election chooses teams of Electors from each state. These Electors in their turn meet in their own states to vote for the President and Vice-President, and these votes are sent to Washington, DC, to be counted. An absolute majority of Electoral College votes is needed for election, and if an absolute majority is not forthcoming other constitutional procedures are engaged. In the twentieth century this became little more than an arcane and decorative part of the process, but it need not always be so, and the tradition that Electors from each state vote en bloc for the popular vote winners in their state contributes a dynamic element of political geography into presidential campaign strategy. Once elected, the President is inaugurated into office in the January following the election.

A presidential campaign relies on many of the same resources as any other attempt to win office in the United States. At the core is the entrepreneurial candidate and a small group of supporters, probably a mixture of personal friends and professional colleagues, and possibly including the battle-hardened veterans of previous campaigns for other offices. This group, supplemented by professional campaign staff and volunteer helpers, will attempt to discover a strategy to project their candidate into office. The strategy must cover the intra-party battle for nomination as well as the subsequent inter-party race for election. Money must be raised and spent effectively, but within the limits of the law; good communications with the electorate must be guaranteed by the most effective possible use of the media; voter support must be tested, tracked and categorised, to identify and attempt to expand the candidate's potential coalition of support in the electorate to the point of victory.

While all these elements are familiar to the seasoned campaigner, when the targeted office is the presidency every feature of the campaign acquires extra elements of complexity. The nomination race involves the campaign finding a way through a maze of caucuses, primaries and conventions in all parts of the nation, opening in the winter snows at the start of election year and culminating in a national party convention at the height of summer. The apparent simplicity of a national general election is complicated by the continued existence of the Electoral College. The superficial similarity with other campaigns is further diminished by the existence of campaign finance laws unique to the presidential election. Furthermore, the development and operation of a campaign strategy to cope with this challenge has to be done under the observation of the national and international media, some elements of which have the potential to become major players in the action.

The pre-nomination campaign: financial foundations

The redesign of election finance law in the 1970s perhaps affected presidential elections more than any other. The FECA, as amended, introduced federal grants to candidates for the presidency, funded by income tax payers who chose, by ticking a box on their tax return, to direct one dollar of their annual tax payment to the presidential election campaign fund (increased to three dollars in 1994). The Act also introduced overall limits on campaign spending. The Supreme Court's decision in *Buckley* v. *Valeo*, while finding the government's unilateral introduction of spending limits on all federal election campaigns unconstitutional, took the stance that the arrangement for presidential elections fell within constitutional limits.[4] Since presidential candidates were being invited to enter a contract with the government, acceptance of the available grants could be made conditional on compliance with the spending limits, as any candidates who objected to the limits could, if they wished, take the alternative route of refusing the proffered grants and associated spending limits and instead rely on a totally independent fund-raising effort unfettered by contractual obligations. The overall spending limit for pre-nomination campaigns set in 1974 was $10 million, but this is adjusted annually in line with the changing cost of living. In 1996 the limit for the pre-nomination campaign had reached $30.91 million. In addition, campaigns are free to raise extra funds to cover fund-raising expenses (limited to $6.18 million in 1996), and the legal and administrative costs incurred in complying with the bureaucratic demands of financial regulation, exempt from the spending limits.[5]

Eligibility for pre-nomination aid is restricted to those candidates who raise, in each of twenty different states, a minimum of $5,000 in contributions of up to $250 each from individual supporters, producing a total of at least $100,000 nationwide. Candidates, having established their eligibility, receive aid from the government's presidential election campaign fund. This matches equally each individual contribution up to $250, and the first $250 of each contribution of a larger amount. Since individuals may legally make contributions up to the limit of $1,000 per person, the precise proportion of funds added to each candidate's campaign chest by the federal government varies according to the proportion of funds raised from the public in small contributions.

In 1996 three presidential candidates, Democratic incumbent Bill Clinton and Republicans Bob Dole and Steve Forbes, were the highest spenders. Clinton and Dole each received about $13.5 million dollars in federal matching funds, close to the maximum $15.5 million federal aid available in that election year.[6] Forbes decided to run without the encumbrance of finance limits, and therefore did not attempt to qualify for federal matching funds, and financed most his campaign with $37.5 million from his own fortune. Republican Bob Dornan did not raise enough funds to qualify for matching funds, and another Republican, Morry Taylor, ran a self-financed campaign with $6.5 million of his own money. Among the other major party hopefuls qualifying for federal matching funds the contribution went from a high of 40 per cent of Pat Buchanan's expenditure to 20 per cent of Alan Keyes among Republicans, and down to 17 per cent for fringe Democrat Lyndon Larouche. To some extent this reflects how much contributions of $250 or less make of the total funds raised. If large donations make up the bulk of individual contributions, the federal matching funds will be a smaller proportion of the overall fund. The differences between candidate fund-raising patterns can be very marked. In the 1992 primary season, 83 per cent of contributions to Republican George Bush came in amounts of $750–$1,000, while Pat Buchanan, his opponent for the Republican nomination, received 82 per cent of his contributions in amounts of less than $250. In the same year's Democratic race, Bob Kerrey and Bill Clinton led in raising money through larger donations, with 43 and 42 per cent respectively coming from $750–$1,000 donations, while Paul Tsongas and Tom Harkin picked up 60 and 73 per cent of their contributions in amounts of $250 or less. Democrat Jerry Brown raised 100 per cent of his money in small donations as a matter of principle.[7]

Figures reporting receipts of ten major party candidates who received matching funds during the 1996 primary season aggregate to show that these candidates received over forty-six cents from the government for every dollar raised from individuals, and that federal matching funds made up about 32 per cent of their overall primary campaign disbursements in that election. These matching funds are not restricted to candidates for the Democratic and Republican parties, and in 1996 John Hagelin (Natural Law Party) received $358,883, amounting to 32 per cent of his primary campaign spending. Harry Browne (Libertarian) raised virtually all of his million-dollar campaign fund from individual contributions, while Ross

Perot and Dick Lamm fought out the Reform Party nomination without qualifying for federal matching funds – Perot underwriting his campaign with $8 million from his own pocket, and outspending Lamm by a factor of 200:1.

The matching funds come with a complex of attached conditions, and before the 1990s only one major candidate, John Connally bidding for the Republican nomination in 1980, had chosen to run without taking the available government support. In 1992 Texan billionaire Ross Perot ran a self-financed independent campaign for the presidency. While this did not involve any equivalent of the primary season for party nomination it may have been the model that inspired the 1996 self-financed campaigns by Republican multimillionaire hopefuls Steve Forbes and Morry Taylor. Their strategy was different from that of Connally, since his campaign plan was still based on raising money, whereas the 1996 freelancers relied almost exclusively on their own deep pockets.

The FECA imposes limits on spending state by state, ranging in 1996 from $618,200 for small states such as Vermont to $11,273,990 for California, as well as a national limit. Some flexibility of spending strategy is allowed, and the state limits total to a figure well in excess of the overall national limit, but there is no limit on flexibility for candidates who are free of federal funds. This flexibility is especially valuable in relatively small states that have huge media impact because they come early in the presidential primary season, in particular Iowa (limit $1,046,984) and New Hampshire ($618,200). A decent showing in these states is essential to a successful campaign, and candidates in receipt of matching funds must find ways of working within the limits, for example by campaigning from locations across the borders of neighbouring states.

In 1996 eleven candidates qualified for and accepted federal matching funds during the primaries, and between them received over $55.94 million from this source. Of this total, $41.56 million (74 per cent) went to the Republicans, since Bill Clinton faced only token opposition for the Democratic nomination. One can expect the demand on this fund to be much greater in a year when both parties have a truly competitive nomination contest. The eligibility qualifications for matching funds have not been adjusted since they were set in 1974. Given the rate of inflation over the subsequent years this has effectively made it easier (at least, cheaper in real terms) to qualify for federal funds, and may have acted to increase the demand on federal funds in relative terms.

When an incumbent runs for re-election effectively unchallenged, there is a substantial campaigning advantage that may have repercussions for the general election, since the incumbent, challenged or not, may still raise funds, attract matching dollars and spend to the legal limit during the primary season. Hence, while the official 1996 Bill Clinton campaign spent the maximum allowed, almost $40 million, against no effective opposition in the primaries, eleven candidates within the Republican Party spent over $182 million competing against each other through a long and battering primary season. In such a case it is not difficult to predict which nominee enters the general election with a campaigning advantage.

Notwithstanding the introduction of federal matching funds, primary candidates on average raise the majority of their own pre-nomination campaign chests from individual contributions and other sources, so an effective primary campaign still requires an effective fund-raising effort. In 1996, the twelve major and minor party presidential candidates who spent more than $1 million, and who did not choose effectively to finance their campaigns out of their own fortunes, raised over 65 per cent of their receipts from individual contributions, with a further 30 per cent coming in federal matching funds. A total of $5.38 million was transferred from surpluses left from prior campaigns, $4.78 million of this being in the Gramm campaign. This leaves only just over 2 per cent of contributions raised from other sources, such as PACs.

Direct contributions by PACs are lower at the presidential level than in other federal elections. Some candidates, especially Washington insiders, may attract a degree of PAC support. In 1996 Bob Dole received $1.2 million from PACs, Gramm $0.4 million and Alexander $0.28 million. Clinton attracted just over $40,000 in PAC contributions.[8] Some PAC presidential contributions come after candidates withdraw their candidacies, as PACs helped them to retire their campaign debts, and return their attention to their former political roles; this may be seen as an extension of the PACs' legislative presence. In any case, these contributions form only a small proportion of the total raised by any of the candidates, and some candidates, for example 1988 Democratic nominee Michael Dukakis, have preferred to refuse to accept any PAC money, thereby liberating themselves from the potential (even if undeserved) accusation of being in thrall to PAC 'special interests', at the expense of losing access to what has proved to be a very modest campaign resource.

That having been said, it is important to remember that PACs and individuals are free to spend what they wish in support of, or against, a candidate at pre-nomination and general election stages, as long as this spending is done independently of the candidate's own campaign effort. In 1992 over $2 million was spent by independent sources in favour of George Bush, and under $35,000 against him. Bill Clinton met balanced support and opposition, with just over half a million dollars spent for him and an equal amount against.[9] Candidates with a long-term strategy have also found that forming their own leadership PACs and tax-exempt foundations can provide a tool for the promotion of their policies, as well as an opportunity to increase name recognition. Many presidential candidates have found these channels of support very useful in their campaigns, and the search is always on for creative development of new channels. Lamar

Alexander established a non-profit corporation, the Republican Exchange Satellite Network, to produce and distribute his own monthly television broadcasts on policy issues, an activity that does not count as election-eering, for all its value to the candidate.[10] In the run-up to the 2000 election Alexander was again on the cutting edge, discovering ways of transferring unrestricted PAC donations from state committees to his federal committee to cover overhead expenditure.[11] Such creative accounting is not without its risks. GOPAC, the leadership PAC of former Speaker Newt Gingrich, was involved in cross-financing an education foundation that broadcast Gingrich's lecture course 'Renewing American Civilization'. This may have appeared an efficient expenditure to improve the profile of a politician looking for major national office, and hoping to place himself for a future presidential run, but the arrangement fell foul of finance rules, and Gingrich received a reprimand and a $300,000 fine from the House of Representatives as a result.

The most significant financial steps of 1996 were taken by and in support of the Democrats. Both parties offer returns to big donors in terms of access to political leaders, often through meetings that mix the social and business atmosphere. President Clinton and Vice-President Gore took a very active role in raising soft-money contributions for the party and its committees. Many Democratic contributors were entertained at the White House, and there has been concern expressed that some forms of Clinton–Gore financial solicitation may have breached federal law.[12] Mean-while, the US labour movement was raising and spending an estimated $35 million to advertise its stand on issues. The expenditure was success-fully defended as a non-partisan voter education campaign, and as a communication between the unions and their members, thereby avoiding campaign finance regulation. Republican sympathisers, led by the Cham-ber of Commerce, rapidly grouped to form 'the Coalition' in order to counter the labour campaign, indicating the speed with which initiatives cross political lines. All these moves were aimed at providing funds for media campaigns, and were integral to developments in media strategy.

The pre-nomination campaign: media strategies

The presidential election provides the biggest opportunity to observe the modern media campaign in action. Through a year or more of active campaigning, in every state of the nation, the candidates within both major and minor parties produce advertising, compete through media events to attract the attention of news editors and through sound bites try to define direction of their analysis, accept invitations to interviews, chat shows and candidate debates, and hone their skills to undertake these challenges. The professionals in the campaign, informed by all the polling

information they can afford to obtain, take decisions regarding which
media market would represent the most vote-effective spending, what
issues must be addressed, how the campaign agenda might be shifted to
their candidates' advantage, when to recommend attack and when to
insist on vigorous defence.

The management of such a campaign is very complex, and the unpredictable can always happen. Strategies that involve high advertising
spending early in a campaign leave the candidate cash-poor and in trouble
if the strategists were mistaken. Candidates whose faith in the fair-
mindedness of an informed electorate prevents them from responding in
kind to a wave of ruthlessly negative advertising can undermine the power
of their own campaign. Campaigns that cover such a spread of time and
space run the risk of chronic decentralisation on the one hand, or of
failing to use all the available talent on the other. Subtle media management is altogether a difficult problem.

In 1996 Bill Clinton, advised by consultant Dick Morris, held the
opinion that an early media strike would be important, but the FEC
campaign spending limits initially appeared to cramp this approach. Hard
money spent on an early campaign blitz would deplete the potential for
rapid reaction in case of difficulties later in the campaign. In addition, a
strident shift into early mass media campaigning would threaten the
detached, public interest, presidential image that Clinton was seeking to
establish. Fortunately for Clinton the loopholes that campaigners had been
exploring in campaign finance limitations had by 1996 widened to allow
an ever more entrepreneurial approach to the funding of the candidate's
message.

The political media firm Squier Knapp Ochs was retained by both the
Democratic national committee and the Clinton/Gore campaign to handle
media projection. They began, using national committee money, with a
first advertisement running on 27 June 1995. This and further such
advertisements, characterised as 'party building' messages, could be
funded by soft money, and the value of the incumbent President as money
magnet became apparent. The money financed a series of advertisements
that painted a positive vision of President Clinton's record on highly
salient issues – crime, education and Medicare. The advertisements portrayed Clinton as protector of the public interest, and the Republicans as
its enemies. 'The Republicans are wrong to want to cut Medicare benefits,'
said the voice-over of an advertisement launched in August 1995, 'And
President Clinton is right to protect Medicare, right to defend our decision,
as a nation, to do what's moral, good, and right by our elderly.' There was
little hesitation in this script in reaching fairly literally for the moral and
policy high ground, while faded, monochrome pictures of then Speaker
Gingrich and Senate Majority Leader Dole indicated the lack of moral
fervour in Republican ranks to do the right thing by the country and its

elderly (and, incidentally, high voter turnout) population. According to Bill Knapp, the advertisements consciously defined Republican policy threats as 'a violation of our duties and our values'. This definition of 'values' had extra worth in being used at a later stage to try to defuse the potential to use personal character attacks against President Clinton.

Clinton's approval ratings gradually and steadily rose during the next twelve months. There is no doubt that a relatively buoyant economy, low unemployment and the lack of major national crisis to test the President were all very important – the Clinton campaign was not far from the mark in 1992 when it placed at the focus of the campaign the expletive 'It's the economy, stupid!'. The campaign to inform the public of Clinton's good points nevertheless played its part. At the time of the Democratic national convention in August 1996, pollster Peter Hart recorded Clinton's public opinion approval rating at 53 per cent. This compares favourably with Reagan's 54 per cent and Nixon's 57 per cent at a similar stage, and easily outstrips Carter (32 per cent), Bush (40 per cent) and Ford (45 per cent). One has to go back to Eisenhower's approval rating in August 1956 (67 per cent) to find a substantially better score.

The Democratic advertisement campaign was extensive, but went little reported through 1995. The United States is divided into about 200 media markets. Major metropolitan areas like New York, Chicago and Los Angeles are in the top ten. An extensive area based on Waterloo/Cedar Falls in north-east Iowa ranks in the eighties. The Clinton image was massaged only in the more modest media markets – the top-ranked, expensive, media-rich communities were excluded from this part of the campaign. The American media, being essentially local (even its most prestigious newspapers), made little or no comment on the campaign for months. By the time they had picked up on the phenomenon, and called it the 'stealth campaign', it was estimated that at least $25 million had been spent. Bob Squier, finding the 'stealth' label risible (though admitting that this had been a conscious effort to avoid journalistic responses), pointed out that advertisements had been placed in 42 per cent of the US media market.

On the Republican side, the media campaign also started early for the 1996 nomination, with each candidate attempting to define the ground on which they would all compete. The Iowa caucuses have for some years attracted a great deal of on-the-ground activity by presidential hopefuls, but television advertising has generally been kept back until the January of election year. In the election cycle for 1996, Lamar Alexander opened the bidding with a television spot advertisement aired on 19 June 1995. Other candidates followed suit later, but it was the entry of the self-financed candidate Steve Forbes, with a television blitz starting on 22 September 1995, and an expenditure in Iowa alone estimated at over $4 million, that gave the citizens of Iowa a sense of being carpet bombed with political advertisements. The leading candidates – Gramm, Buchanan, Forbes, Dole, Alexander – along with other Republican hopefuls, exposed the raw nerves of Republican Party differences.

The early caucus and primary races are crucial in large part because of the huge media coverage that they attract nationally and internationally. In a barn on an agricultural show field in north-east Iowa, waiting for a Steve Forbes event, the author bumped into the *New York Times* correspondent R. W. Apple, together with correspondents from the *Washington Post*, and national network television presenters. Television crews from Belgium, Holland, France and Singapore were in evidence. A reporter from a Kansas station reacted vigorously when asked whether politics was her usual 'beat', pointing out emphatically that she was an 'air personality', covering the election as a favour to her station manager. When Forbes arrived, an hour late, the waiting crowd was ignored for a further half hour while the press pack was serviced with sound bites by the side of the campaign bus.

In front of these local, national and international audiences Republican candidates spent the primary season arguing bitterly among themselves. The tax code featured heavily. Dole moved towards the 'flat tax' position, but given the evidence of his political career this was viewed with scepticism. Forbes attacked Dole as a political insider, with 'Washington values'. Dole's events were designed carefully for media coverage, with stage parties ranged behind the candidate for the benefit of television cameras, featuring loyalists of varying ethnicity, race and age (but especially young people, to counter the danger of Dole – who was seventy-three at the time – being classed as an elderly candidate). Lamar Alexander sported a plaid shirt and at many events found a piano on which to play 'Alexander's Rag Time Band' in the attempt to establish a down-home, state's rights brand marque. Buchanan appealed to conservatism, to a particular definition of public morality and to fears of the burden on Americans of national and international government. Gramm covered similar ground to Buchanan, but without the evangelical fervour.[13]

Most of the Republican candidates relied to some extent on federal grants. While government money was subsidising the media bloodletting in the Republican Party, it was also contributing to a Clinton Democratic walkover. Although only facing the challenge from fringe candidate Lyndon LaRouche, Clinton was able to collect and spend to the legal limit during the primary season. The primary money picked up where the party-financed issue-advocacy campaign left off, undeflected by internal party divisions, projecting the candidate as presidential, protective of the national interest, and presenting a stark difference to the shrill aggression of the ongoing Republican media battle. This was a luxury previously afforded to President Reagan during his re-election campaign, at which time he too had the opportunity to define some contours of the campaign to his advantage while his opponents were otherwise engaged. In the 1996 case, Clinton ran a virtually unchallenged media campaign for re-nomination lasting over a year. Even after it was clear from the primary results that Dole would be the Republican nominee, his campaign was unable to make a very effective immediate media response, having had its coffers drained by the vigorous Republican primary battle early in the year. The airways from then until the national conventions were left a relatively free range for the Clinton campaign.

Getting nominated: the primary strategy

The nomination contenders run the gauntlet of a nationwide series of state primary and caucus competitions. Held over a period of about four months, on different dates, with widely differing rules, these primaries and caucuses mean that any reasonable nomination strategy involves getting to grips with a mass of complex information. Elaine Ciulla Kamarck, a veteran of Democratic presidential campaigns, says of her invitation to this level of politics, 'I became an expert in the statutes, rules and regulations that govern delegate selection in the Democratic Party. This involved reading hundreds of state statutes and delegate selection plans and then translating these into easily understood state plans and strategies.'[14] Such detailed knowledge is essential for success, but has to be researched independently every four years, since much of the regulation of the local process for the selection of delegates to the major party national conventions is performed at state level, and in any period of four years some states will change their regulations in some way.

Simply making an appearance on the ballots requires a comprehensive knowledge of the myriad state rules and filing dates. States may choose delegates to the national convention using primary elections, or caucuses, or some combination. Delegate nomination may be tied closely to the voting for favourite national candidates, or may be subject to a separate selection process. Voter participation in delegate selection is restricted to declared party members in some states, open to independents in some, and in other states a voter can take part in either primary without declaring any affiliation. The Democratic primaries and caucuses generally allocate delegates according to a form of proportional representation, though usually with a minimum percentage requirement, to benefit leading candidates and disadvantage the runners-up. While the Democrats have tended to initiate the reforms in their nominating procedures from the centre, Republicans have left more decisions to the individual states, and therefore a greater variety of methods governs the allocation of delegates in the Republican contests. State parties as well as national party organisations have moved along similar lines towards a more representative and transparent presidential primary system, but the more common use of winner-take-all rules in the Republican Party has been especially advantageous to any candidate capable of stringing together a series of early successes. It is impossible in this complex political environment to make a reasonable campaign effort without the kind of single-minded research that Kamarck identifies.

The aim of the presidential primary season is to give party activists nationwide the opportunity to choose the delegates who will attend the national nominating convention. By far the majority of delegates are chosen at the state level, but other groups come from associated territories such as American Samoa. Since 1984 the Democratic Party has included a category of 'super delegates', not required to commit in advance to a particular presidential hopeful. These super delegates are made up of the party's congressional officeholders, governors and the members nominated to the national committee by the state parties, and act as a voice for the party establishment. In 1996 they made up about 18 per cent of the delegates to that year's Democratic national convention, held in Chicago. The size of individual delegations is governed by party rules, which reflect the size of states, and the state parties' history of electoral success, as well as priorities such as the representation of national party aims and objectives.

Insofar as a presidential campaign is designed to achieve the nomination of a particular candidate, the primary strategy must be to ensure that a majority of the convention delegates chosen are committed to its own candidate. Campaign strategists, working with limited resources, and restricted by campaign finance law, have to use these resources carefully to ensure a reasonable chance of victory. States with large convention delegations are obvious targets for substantial investment of a campaign's effort, but there are other criteria governing the choice of these states where the campaign will make a disproportionate effort to gain public support. But the nationwide credibility of a campaign may demand a strategy that emphasises performance in particular states in order to demonstrate support across different regions of the nation, to confront and defuse potentially damaging issues, to attract national media attention at crucial points in the campaign, or to attract particular population groups into the candidate's electoral coalition. After the pre-primary manoeuvring and muscle-flexing, it is generally important that a candidate gets a good start to the primary season proper. What is meant by a good start depends on the level of public expectation. What is meant by the start of the primary season is subject to some adjustment.

It is tradition that New Hampshire holds the first primary elections, a spot it has held since 1920, and the events here are guaranteed national attention. The 1996 New Hampshire primary was held in mid-February. This small New England state was the unrivalled starting post for the presidential race until 1976. The Jimmy Carter campaign had noted that Iowa held its initial caucus meetings before the New Hampshire primary. Iowa, a Midwest agricultural state with a relatively small and widely dispersed population, was not an attractive campaigning proposition, especially in winter, and its caucuses (meetings of self-identified party supporters) were only the first step in a complex and lengthy state delegate-selection process. Presidential candidates, devoting almost all their efforts to gaining a favourable launch in New Hampshire, traditionally devoted little attention to Iowa. Since nothing much ever happened at the Iowa caucuses, little coverage was devoted to its campaign, or its results. The Jimmy Carter campaign strategists felt in 1976 that 'no news' Iowa would become 'big news' Iowa if a rank outsider could pull off a surprise success. Carter put considerable effort into the state, including many personal appearances in the year running up to the caucuses. Carter's excellent showing in Iowa, unexpected by the pundits, did indeed help him become front-page news, and gave the campaign momentum that carried him to victory in New Hampshire, and ultimately in the November general election.

From that time Iowa has joined New Hampshire as part of the 'start' of the campaign. Subsequent candidates have recognised the importance of both states. Hopefuls exploring the possibility of a presidential run start their groundwork in these states years in advance. As soon as one election has finished, sightings may be made of potential candidates for next time, making political contacts and public friends in these key strategic locations. Hopefuls who are still in the running a year before the general election put in dozens, even scores, of days campaigning in these sparsely populated states. Iowa received a total of 520 days of visits from Republican candidates between the inauguration of President Clinton in January 1993 and caucus day in February 1996. Senator Arlen Specter (Pennsylvania) and Governor Pete Wilson (California) visited Iowa thirty-seven times between them before withdrawing from the race.[15]

There are continuing challenges to the starting point, both from states wanting to share in the spoils brought by massive campaign coverage and from campaign strategists hoping to steal a march on their opponents. The national rules of the Democratic Party define the time window in which primaries must take place, and help protect the role of Iowa and New Hampshire. The Republican rules are not so definitive, and it is difficult to stop entrepreneurial states. In 1996 Alaska, Guam and Hawaii began their caucuses before Iowa, but the Louisiana Republican Party, with a peculiar primary/caucus hybrid to choose a proportion of its national convention delegates, made the most concerted challenge to the Iowa/New Hampshire axis.[16] Most Republican candidates co-operated in a pact not to campaign in Louisiana. Candidates from the moderate part of the political spectrum had little to gain from a contest in a very conservative state. Candidates with moderate means did not want to risk their campaign funds in an untried competition. However, Pat Buchanan and Phil Gramm, campaigning to the conservative end of the Republican spectrum and, especially in Gramm's case, campaigning from a position of financial strength, did not resist the opportunity to face off against each other and to steal a march on their opponents. The Louisiana result, a small, but surprising, victory for Buchanan, demoralised the Gramm campaign, energised the Buchanan supporters, and helped propel the former Reagan speech-writer to a very strong second-place showing to the favourite, Bob Dole, in Iowa, followed by a startling, if very slim, victory over Dole in New Hampshire.

By the end of the New Hampshire primary in 1996, the Republican hopefuls had been reduced to four candidates with real potential. Bob Dole, winning in Iowa, close second in New Hampshire, had failed to live up to his reputation as the front-runner, but was still strong. Buchanan had established his position as the candidate of the ideological and cultural right wing. Steve Forbes, using his fortune to run a high-impact media campaign, had emerged as the champion of tax reform. Lamar Alexander, a solid third in both Iowa and New Hampshire, was hanging on as a possible compromise candidate. Delaware and Arizona, immediately following New Hampshire, gave Forbes two victories. Again, Dole held on to a clear second place in both states. Buchanan's third in conservative Arizona was disappointing, and Alexander's support was slipping markedly as party voters focused on the leading contenders.

The primary season has become increasingly front-loaded in recent years. In 1976 it took eleven weeks of the primary season to choose 50 per cent of national convention delegates appointed in this fashion, and fourteen weeks to get to 75 per cent. Twenty years later, 51 per cent had been chosen by week four, and 77 per cent by week six.[17] This effective abbreviation of the primary season appears to advantage front-runners with considerable campaign resources. Candidates showing unexpected strength in the early weeks do not have the time to capitalise on these victories in fund-raising, media purchases and campaign development before the bulk of delegate competitions are upon them. Front-runners with big war chests and established field operations can ride out early setbacks as long as they are not humiliated, scoring repeatedly in the second phase of the primary season, when candidates with later-developing campaigns are too stretched to cover all the campaign ground. In 1996 there were nineteen Republican primary elections and three Republican caucuses in the two weeks 5–19 March, in which over 7.6 million citizens took part. Dole rolled up victories in every one of these contests save one (Missouri), as his campaign showed its firm and widespread foundations in states as various as Texas, Florida, Illinois, Connecticut and Washington.

The primary season will constantly be reshaped under the influence of state and campaign entrepreneurship, and national party attempts to construct a mechanism to maximise its eventual nominee's chances. California shifted its primary to 26 March in the season for 1996, but still found this too late substantially to increase its clout in the nomination process. The state legislature chose an earlier date still for 2000, only for a 1998 initiative proposition to be passed in the state that undermined the importance of the California primary in choosing national convention delegates. In the immediate wake of the 1998 result there was a scramble to the courts to try to sort out this matter in favour of a strong and early California primary. Such moves are indicative of the shifts that will continue to make the selection process change and evolve. All candidates must design an efficient route through this maze, conserving their resources when possible, expending them effectively where necessary, to get the best possible bandwagon rolling.

The route chosen will vary according the campaign organisations' perceptions of their strengths and weaknesses. One 1988 candidate, Albert Gore, Jr, then US Senator for Tennessee, recognised that neither Iowa nor New Hampshire offered him very fertile soil. Gore claimed to be 'sitting out' the early contests, saving his strength for the later sweep through the southern states. In fact Gore spent heavily in both Iowa and New Hampshire, but he effectively managed to limit public and media expectations of substantial success. This novel approach was, on the surface at least, not an unreasonable effort. The strategy prevented him being written off immediately, but it nevertheless allowed other candidates to develop the momentum that made life difficult for a late entrant. The fact that a strategy did not work does not mean that it is fatally flawed, though with the increasingly front-loaded primary calendar the flexibility of approach seems more limited.

Expectations have helped and damaged candidates before. Low public expectations of Jimmy Carter's chances made his 1976 Iowa showing newsworthy. In 1984 the expectation was that Walter Mondale and John Glenn would be the major Democratic players. When Glenn slipped to fourth spot in Iowa the newsworthy story was not that Mondale had won convincingly, but that Gary Hart, in a distant second place, was the new challenger, a boost that helped him to victory a few days later in New Hampshire.

In 1992 expectations were strongly influenced by President Bush's public opinion approval in the wake of the Gulf War. In June 1990 an Iowa poll identified eight Democrats as potential nominees, but in face of the received wisdom that Republican incumbent Bush was going to steamroller to victory, almost all of these major figures chose not to run, leaving the field open for a group of little-known Democrats to fight for the right to lose the general election to George Bush. Tom Harkin, US Senator from

Iowa, swept the other candidates aside in Iowa, but the fact that he was a locally based candidate, a 'favourite son' of the state, diminished the impact of this event. Paul Tsongas, former US Senator from Massachusetts, won in his neighbouring state of New Hampshire, but again the momentum that might have been gained from this victory was diminished by comments that he too could almost be considered a 'favourite son' choice. Clinton showed strongly in second place in New Hampshire. He might have done better, but for accusations of Vietnam draft-dodging and sexual infidelity aired on television and in the press at that time. A television appearance by Clinton and his wife Hillary on *Sixty Minutes* may have saved the campaign in the long run, but the boat had been very firmly rocked, and only the ballast provided by an excellent early fund-raising campaign and a well formulated field campaign kept the Clinton effort afloat.[18]

Tsongas, Harkin, former California Governor Jerry Brown and Clinton all had victories in early contests, but the one with the pull in the South was Clinton, then incumbent Governor of Arkansas. In 1984, Democratic Party organisers, looking for a nomination process likely to produce a candidate more attractive to the American electorate than most of the Democratic presidential candidates of the previous two decades, had come up with 'Super Tuesday'. It was hoped that inserting a large wedge of southern contests relatively early in the process would increase the weight of moderate southern opinion, and simultaneously, by selecting a large number of delegates on a single day, eliminate weak candidates and reduce the potential for long and damaging intra-party warfare. It is difficult any longer to speak of Super Tuesday, but in this innovation lay the seeds of the front-loading that has gradually filled early and mid-March with the bulk of the delegate selection, and in 1992 the primaries on 10 March in Florida, Louisiana, Mississippi, Oklahoma, Tennessee and Texas gave Clinton huge victories. While his primary strategy did not mimic that of Gore in 1988, the design of the Clinton route to the nomination ended up looking much as Gore would have planned for himself. The primary system provides a dynamic political structure in which there will always be room for a new approach.

Campaign managers faced with such a complex primary programme have to make difficult and interrelated decisions about how to conduct a campaign to gain momentum, control the issue agenda, forge an electoral coalition and rack up the delegates to capture the party nomination. Campaigns may front-load their effort, or rely on a late surge of support, depending on their assessment of their and their opponents' chances at all stages of the primary battle. Campaign expertise and legislative knowledge are essential, but efficient recruitment and deployment of labour are also crucial. Delivery of literature and videos, intensive telephone campaigning, construction of Internet sites, solicitation of funds and the many other features of a national campaign rely on attracting thousands of volunteer helpers, and on the skilled management of these resources. Delegate tracking is just one example of an administrative chore which is nevertheless crucial to a national campaign. As the campaign moves from state to state, the headquarters must keep as accurate as possible a record not just of the numbers of convention delegates selected, but also of who they are. During the course of the campaign those delegates committed to a candidate may need reassuring, while uncommitted delegates and those freed from their loyalties by the withdrawal of candidates from the competition may be capable of persuasion. If the race is close as the convention approaches, delegate tracking can be particularly important, helping campaigns to marshal their forces for the battle on the convention floor.

The national conventions

The primary season culminates with the parties' national conventions. In 1996 the Republicans met at San Diego, in the key state of California. The Democrats returned to Chicago for the first time since their disastrous 1968 convention in that city, when internal divisions over Vietnam erupted in the convention hall and on the city streets. There is more federal funding allocated for this part of the campaign, with each of the major parties receiving $12.36 million in 1996. These grants are supplemented by funds raised from many sources by a local host committee, including business leaders of all political persuasions, pleased to attract the international publicity that comes from these media-saturated conventions, and not unaware of the value of their contributions in underpinning important political contacts. The Philip Morris Company donated $677,500, three-quarters to the Republican convention. Just over half of Microsoft's $557,319 went to the Democrats. AT&T, the largest single contributor, put almost 83 per cent of its $3.2 million into the San Diego meeting. Well over $30 million was raised in cash donations, and many millions more by in-kind contributions to the conventions.[19]

The parties wish to use the conventions to inspire enthusiasm among the delegates who are about to return to the field for the general election campaign, and to showcase their chosen candidates while they have the undivided attention of the media. Consequently a great deal of effort goes into organising and producing the event. In 1996 the Republicans invested in providing extensive live coverage of the convention on those cable television channels with a Republican-oriented audience. The Democrats established a comprehensive array of localised links through a media centre constructed at the convention site. Pre-packaged clips of Clinton and the convention could be delivered to the hundreds of local outlets around the country, fronted and narrated by officeholders and delegates relevant to that local community. The myriad small television and radio stations and their viewers thereby had the benefit of their own piece of convention coverage, albeit through the intermediary of the party. The Internet access provided by both major parties was particularly useful to journalists looking for easy copy.[20]

By the time of the major party national conventions in mid-summer, it is usually clear who the nominees will be, and party and campaign leaders give every attention to gaining the maximum benefit from the television coverage. The 1996 Republican convention featured Liddy Dole, wife of the candidate, and an impressive public figure in her own right, in a remarkable, relaxed performance eulogising her husband, for which she repeatedly received the accolade of favourable comparison with talk-show megastar Oprah Winfrey. An array of reliable spokespeople appeared on stage at key times, and the less reliable were kept at bay, or relegated to the shadows of the unbroadcast schedule. The firm management of the Republican convention had journalists breathless for lack of stories. The major channels had already decided to cut their coverage to one hour per night, and even so the audience turned off in droves – the audience was around 25 per cent lower than in 1992.

After the Republican convention was characterised as a four-day info-mercial, Democratic leaders cheerfully introduced the Democratic meeting as a four-day press conference. This Chicago convention was designed to sail without a hitch. Presidential incumbency was used to attract media attention to the presidential candidate. Three bills were signed in the Rose Garden in the week before the convention, and an attack on tobacco was launched by the President, all as part of a well planned, news-grabbing foundation for convention coverage. Inside the convention hall another parade of reliable speakers addressed the assembled delegates, alternates (reserve delegates), corporate guests, journalists and hangers-on, for most of the time a fairly uninterested audience. The party activists used the opportunities inside the convention and in the surrounding hotels to rally the troops for forthcoming congressional and state-level races, to look for jobs in government or in some form of political consultancy, to renew old acquaintances and make new ones, and generally to engage in all the professional necessities of networking at a major national conference that is central to one's interests and perhaps to one's career. The television audience for the Democratic convention also fell significantly, but project-ing the party and its candidates to the remaining television viewers was taken very seriously. In the hall, at appropriate times, interns tasked with the job of on-the-ground crowd management would appear with large black plastic bags full of signs, to distribute to conventioneers, complete with instructions on when to wave, and towards which television camera. One speech and one designer wave over, those signs would be dropped, and a different set, with new instructions, would arrive at the end of the row.

The lower television audience was claimed by party managers to be of little concern – regardless of the lower media audiences, each candidate received the lift of a traditional public opinion bump after the convention. The party leaders appeared to share a belief that the conventions were in the final stages of evolution towards ratification ceremonies, and that this would probably lead to shorter conventions in the future, even more directed towards a showcase role. But this is a significant change. Conventions have not gone beyond one nomination ballot for more than a generation, but they have been places for choice and debate. In truth, the party with most vociferous debate on show has generally gone on to lose the election, so the reason for the party management to welcome an evolution towards coronation is evident. The 1996 conventions were carefully choreographed, with the delegates playing the most modest of bit parts. Alistair Cooke once called the US political convention 'a chess game disguised as a circus'. In 1996, political consultant Ken Bode referred to them as 'summer camps with booze'.

Perhaps the fact that conventions are increasingly stage-managed to eliminate controversy has made them less popular viewing, but recent conventions have provided moments of excitement. In 1976 Ronald Reagan's challenge to Gerald Ford lasted into the Republican convention. In 1980 Edward Kennedy reached the Democratic convention with no chance of defeating Jimmy Carter, but with enough delegate support to force issues from his agenda on to the party platform. In 1988 Jesse Jackson came to the Democratic convention in a similar position, not enough delegates to win, but enough enthusiastic support to be able to embarrass the party into agreeing some regulatory changes in return for his co-operation in a peaceful convention. In 1992 Pat Buchanan gained a prime time slot for his endorsement of George Bush, but then disturbed some in the party and the electorate by announcing that the election was part of 'a religious war ... for the soul of America'.

In 1996 Buchanan supporters were causing problems for the Republicans again, managing to influence the platform committee into writing an uncompromisingly conservative statement of policy, when candidate Dole wanted a more tolerant document. When pressed, both Bob Dole and Republican Party chair Haley Barbour made it clear that they had not read the document, and were not bound by it. The 1996 Democratic convention was threatened by allegations that Clinton consultant Dick Morris was a regular client of Sherry Rowlands, a prostitute, who had been given access to confidential communications from the President. Both parties managed to ride out these threats. The Republicans, perceiving the potential platform difficulties, had curtailed the discussion period, thereby limiting the potential for media coverage. The Democrats ensured that

Morris left the campaign team immediately, and limited the damage inflicted.

A strong candidate reaching the convention with an unbeatable lead among the delegates will also have established a degree of control over the rules committee, the platform committee and the floor management of the convention. Such control is important in using the national convention as a celebration of the candidate and a launching pad for the general election. The convention opens with procedural matters, and moves on to a formal vote by the delegates to choose the party's nominee. Only after this does the candidate take part personally. From this point on, the nominee's behaviour is particularly significant. A rousing speech of acceptance is important. A show of solidarity by other defeated hopefuls is valuable. The choice of a vice-presidential running-mate should be made carefully, to balance the ticket by adding further qualities that will attract the support of a broad electoral coalition. Bob Dole's choice of self-styled 'bleeding heart conservative' Jack Kemp in 1996 brought authority to the candidate's conversion to tax reduction and reform long advocated by Kemp.

An unusual addition to the convention calendar in 1996 was that of the Reform Party. Ross Perot, having attracted almost 19 per cent of votes in an independent bid for the presidency in 1992, initiated the creation of the Reform Party on the foundation laid by his earlier run, and invited competitors for the party's nomination. Former Democratic Governor of Colorado, Dick Lamm, entered the lists. In keeping with its name, the Reform Party introduced innovation into the convention and nomination process. The convention met for one day in Long Beach, California, then reconvened for another one-day meeting a week later in Valley Forge, Pennsylvania. Members of the party were invited to vote by mail, telephone or email, but the process was haphazard, ballots were not always received, or were duplicated, and only about 5 per cent of members finally took part. Perot took the nomination. Neither the party nor its candidate gained much credibility from the flawed process, but that is not to say that these innovations may not turn up, more skilfully managed, in the future.

The general election campaign: dollars and sense

Once the nomination is decided, the two major party candidates receive grants from the presidential election campaign fund that are meant to cover all the spending of the official candidate campaigns. Set at $20 million in 1974, cost-of-living adjustments had pushed this figure to $61.8 million for each candidate by 1996. In addition the major parties were allowed to spend $12 million in co-ordination with the presidential campaign committee. Minor party candidates are not automatically eligible for a grant, although if they receive more than 5 per cent of the total vote cast in the general election they will qualify for reimbursement of campaign costs, and will be eligible for a proportionate grant in the next election should the same party run a candidate. John Anderson, a breakaway Republican who ran as the National Unity Coalition candidate in 1980, and gained over 6 per cent of the vote, was reimbursed $4.19 million. Reimbursement was no doubt a relief to Anderson, but it was nevertheless an electoral disadvantage having to spend important campaign time soliciting funds, while the major party candidates, bolstered by their federal grants, could concentrate on getting their messages to the public. Ross Perot's independent campaign in 1992 was not hampered by the problem of fund-raising, since he financed his campaign out of his own fortune. The FEC agreed that Perot's 1992 campaign organisation was the basis of the Reform Party, so Perot's 1992 success in attracting votes was the foundation on which the Reform Party was awarded $29.06 million in federal support for the 1996 election.

The federal grant for the general election campaign is not a matching grant. The law intended that this grant should cover all the costs of the campaign, liberating candidates from the time-consuming and potentially dubious chores of fund-raising, allowing them to spend their time addressing the significant issues of the campaign, and controlling the escalating costs of campaigning at a single stroke. The 1976 campaign was probably the only one that came close to this intent. By the 1980s, greater flexibility in the rules, and the determined search by campaign professionals for loopholes, discussed in chapter 4, had subverted much of the intent of the 1970s reforms. Herbert Alexander characterised the 1988 general election as having consisted of 'at least three distinct but parallel campaigns ... conducted, either by each candidate, or on each candidate's behalf', and these elements are still very evident.[21] The first of these three elements is the legally limited candidate-controlled spending, that is the federal grant plus the national party funds that the law allows candidates to co-ordinate. The second comprises the unlimited categories of spending – soft money spent by state and local committees, funds raised for compliance costs (e.g. the administrative and accountancy expenses in filing the campaign reports required by law) and funds spent on behalf of candidates by allied organisations such as unions. The last is the legal, unlimited spending undertaken by individuals and committees entirely independently of the official campaign organisations. Alexander's conclusion that 'expenditure limits are illusory in a pluralistic system with numerous openings for disbursement sanctioned by law or court decisions' gains in strength with each election.

The party committees in 1996 doubled the amounts they had raised four years earlier, and channelled the hundreds of millions of dollars thus gathered to the various party committees at both state and national level.

The funds financed huge direct-mail efforts, millions of telephone calls, and similar efforts to raise party and candidate visibility, and to get out the vote. Millions were spent on issue advertisements located to benefit the presidential candidates in those states where support needed to be built or solidified. The raising of the money threatened to become a campaign issue, especially when the Democrats were linked to funds coming from dubious sources, in particular donations linked to a large Indonesian company. The Democrats spent the late stages of a campaign in which they had won the spending war scrambling to return illegal and suspect donations, and defending themselves against accusations of selling policy access to foreign interests. This did help to tarnish the Democratic campaign, and its peak of support came before election day. Considering just what might have been, one Democratic leader was quoted on the morning after the election on 5 November 1996 as saying, 'God meant this election to be held on October 22nd'.

The general election campaign: over the airwaves and on television

Agenda-setting is an important part of any campaign's attempt at media management. It is difficult at any stage, but is particularly hard early in the primary season, when there are many voices to be heard. The media need access to candidates to create a news image of the campaign. When many candidates are available, campaigns need to grant relatively easy media access in order to guarantee coverage, but when the field of candidates is small campaigns are sure of coverage, and can control access, minimise the opportunity for error and define more clearly the newsgatherers' delivery of the campaign message.

The 1988 Bush campaign showed an awareness of this when, in the later stages of the campaign, the Republican managers instituted a daily meeting to decide on a theme for the day, a hub to which the complementary spokes of advertising, press releases and speeches by the candidate and entourage could be firmly attached. A series of campaign advertisements promoted George Bush as a trustworthy, gentle, family man committed to a litany of vague but identifiably American values. Complementary to this was a battery of advertisements aimed to redesign the fuzzy image of Michael Dukakis in the public's minds, painting him 'as an out of the mainstream liberal with a soft spot in his heart for criminals, high taxes, and unilateral cuts in national defense'.[22] The Bush media strategy was refined by consultants as the campaign progressed, but some themes of the attack had been decided well before the national conventions, as George Bush confirmed in a May 1988 interview with the *New York Times*.[23]

The 1988 Republican campaign used advertisements to attack Dukakis' record as being soft on crime and weak environmentally. The 'revolving door' spot advertisement, in which prisoners were shown walking freely through a turnstile, pilloried a programme of weekend furloughs for prisoners, including those imprisoned for very serious crimes, some of whom had committed further offences. The 'Boston Harbor' spot advertisement claimed that Dukakis' inaction had left a massive and expensive pollution problem. Dukakis was also attacked for using his gubernatorial veto to stop the passage (in fact because it was possibly unconstitutional) of legislation compelling Massachusetts school teachers to lead pupils in reciting the pledge of allegiance to the US flag. The assault was supplemented by advertisements paid for by independent expenditures committees. The Committee for the Presidency and the National Security Political Action Committee produced spot advertisements concentrating on Willie Horton, an African-American convicted murderer who committed murder and rape when on a weekend pass from a Massachusetts prison. Another independently produced spot advertisement portrayed Dukakis as soft on drugs dealers. It has been said that the candidate himself vetoed a powerful reaction, convinced that a response might give the attacks a credibility they did not deserve, and that no 'intelligent American would fall for' the Bush appeal.[24] Nevertheless, by the time Dukakis began to respond the campaign agenda had been set, to his permanent disadvantage.

The lesson was not lost on subsequent campaigns, where the commitment has been to rapid and vigorous response. In 1992 the Clinton campaign adopted a tight focus, in line with campaign manager James Carville's conviction that the driving issues clustered around 'the economy, stupid'. The Bush campaign, its candidate's poll ratings falling, reverted to the negative style used so successfully in 1988, and attempted to develop the issue of Clinton's character. Groups outside the official campaign pushed some of these issues most strongly. Veiled or direct accusations of draft-dodging, drug-taking, anti-Vietnam activism and Moscow-visiting student days were met robustly by the Clinton campaign, using Hillary as well as Bill as their strongest voices.

There were other media campaign developments in 1992 which turned out to be of varying value to different campaigns. The Clinton campaign made good use of talk show appearances to supplement the paid media strategy, and others played the same suit. Bill Clinton's saxophone playing on *The Arsenio Hall Show* became legendary for its *chutzpah* and charm. Ross Perot's announcement of his candidacy on *Larry King Live* drew further coverage because of its novelty. Perot also made strategic use of thirty-minute 'infomercials', broadcast simultaneously at peak evening viewing times on the major networks. These broadcasts featured Perot lecturing directly to the audience in a distinctive and homely style, and attracted huge audiences. The 1988 abolition, by the Federal Communications Commission, of the 'fairness doctrine', on the grounds that it was contrary to the spirit of the First Amendment to the US Constitution, opened the way for very polemical commentary in the media. Radio talk shows saw the earliest evidence of this, with the growth of shows centred on highly opinionated, usually conservative-leaning, hosts, nicknamed 'shock jocks', who attracted and reinforced substantial audiences of the like-minded. On the technological side, campaigns now delivered advertisements to television stations in advance by satellite. The Democrats realised that they could download their opponents' advertisements before they were broadcast and, when appropriate, could make and broadcast a rapid response spot advertisement, subverting the impact of the Republican attack strategy.

The architecture of the candidates' media campaigns has to include a strategy for the now familiar election debates. Televised debates began in the 1960 Nixon/Kennedy election. Revived in 1976, they have been part of every subsequent election, especially since changes in Federal Communications Commission regulations have simplified the exclusion of minor party candidates. Not every debate produces a significant political moment, but the fact that candidates are, for an hour or so, facing questions in front of millions of viewers, without immediate access to consultants and advisers, presents a greater than usual possibility of throwing a knockout punch or of failing visibly to live up to expectations. In 1976 Gerald Ford twice made the mistaken statement that Poland was not under Soviet domination. In 1980 the Jimmy Carter camp thought that Ronald Reagan would self-destruct, but Reagan's calm, disarming manner enhanced his candidacy. In the 1988 vice-presidential debate, when Republican Dan Quayle compared his own record to that of John F. Kennedy, he withered under Lloyd Bentsen's response, 'Jack Kennedy was a friend of mine. Senator, you're no Jack Kennedy.' The best efforts of Republican Party spin doctors could not disguise this damage, and later strategy was to keep Quayle out of the limelight, and to limit media access. Dukakis' careful and legalistic response to a question that asked for his response if his wife were raped, in the words of former Democratic national chairman Robert Strauss, 'captured the hearts of seventeen lawyers and lost three million voters'.

The 1992 debates had their moments. The Bush campaign was leery of the effect of debates on their efforts, and used various tactics to delay the arrangements. When agreement was reached, it allowed the inclusion of the Perot/Stockdale independent ticket. While retired admiral James Stockdale was embarrassingly poor in the vice-presidential debate, Perot himself performed very well in the presidential debates, and it seems clear that many voters re-evaluated him as a viable and attractive candidate.[25] The organisers of the 1996 debates did not allow the Reform Party ticket of Ross Perot and Pat Choate to take part, and his legal challenges to this decision failed. The television audience for the debates was less than half what it had been four years earlier, and many fewer of these viewers found them useful in making their voting decisions. The Clinton campaign managed to negotiate the number of presidential debates down to two, and Clinton's more relaxed style, especially responding to questions from the floor in the second encounter, gave him a distinct public opinion boost.[26]

The 1996 Dole campaign found it difficult to maintain discipline over the messages that it was trying to get across. Dole refused to watch tapes of his own performance as part of the debate preparation. The Republican campaign team was changed too often. Dole and his vice-presidential nominee rarely appeared comfortable together, and there were reports of Kemp distancing himself from responsibility for the faltering campaign before election day. Late in the day even the national Republican congressional committee was detaching itself from the Dole campaign. On 28 October 1996, they began running a television spot advertisement asking 'What would happen if the Democrats controlled Congress and the White House?... The liberal special interests aligned with Clinton desperately want to buy back control of Congress. If we give the special interests a blank check in Congress, who's going to represent us?' Republican party leaders denied that this was anything but supportive of the Dole re-election effort. Perot was making much smaller waves than he had four years earlier. Having accepted government funding, the Reform Party was limited to a smaller budget than Perot had spent independently in 1992, and, with his infomercials no longer having their earlier novelty value, Perot's audience fell.

Meanwhile the Clinton organisation was helped by the media campaign launched by the major trade union organisation, the AFL–CIO. These 'political education' television spot advertisements used a multimillion-dollar budget to attack Republican stands on sensitive policy issues. They were concentrated in marginal congressional seats, but the effect was to have another voice on the air contributing to the definition of Republican leadership and Republican policy as a malign force. There was almost certainly a positive spin-off for Clinton. Members of union households formed 23 per cent of the turnout in 1996, up from 18 per cent four years earlier. These union-connected voters supported Clinton (59 per cent) above Dole (30 per cent) and Perot (9 per cent). From the start, using Democratic Party money, through the official campaign, and even in the parallel union campaign, Clinton teams remained on message. According to Greg Stevens, a member of Dole's final advertising team, the Clinton campaign 'came out early and defined the race, and defined Bob Dole. They did it in a very disciplined way.'

The general election campaign: the geography and demography of getting elected

Tradition has it that the general election campaign opens on Labor Day, the American public holiday on the first Monday in September, which signals the end of the summer vacation period. In recent years the hiatus after the major party national conventions has been less evident. Even if it takes a while for the official campaign machines to hit top gear there is no slacking as the teams try to capitalise on the boost in public awareness provided by the conventions, and lay the solid organisational foundations on which to build a powerful autumn campaign effort. In particular, the candidate organisation, after the nomination, must co-ordinate fully with the party political organisation. This co-ordination may not be a simple effort, especially if the nomination battle has been fierce.

The 1992 Clinton campaign had been run from Little Rock, Arkansas, and this remained the national headquarters of the Clinton effort even after the convention. There is a danger that such a strategy could under-mine co-ordination between the party headquarters in Washington, DC, and candidate, the two national foci of the campaign. This was evident in the 1988 Dukakis campaign, which maintained its central location in Boston, but the Clinton camp seemed to have learnt from this example, and established a working articulation with the party.

In 1996 Clinton was the incumbent, with no notable intra-party op-position. Serious losses for the Democrats in the 1994 mid-term elections had threatened to destabilise the Clinton presidency, but the potential revolt had failed to materialise as 1995 saw a combination of Republican strategic errors, one national tragedy, a rise in economic indicators, and Democratic campaigning skills help rebuild public confidence in the Clinton administration. The Republicans overplayed their hand in contests between the legislature and the executive branches over policy, appearing petty and losing some public support. The bombing of a federal building in Oklahoma City in 1995 was in some minds associated with the debates of the extreme political right, because of the alleged motivations of the perpetrators. National tragedies bring attention to the President, and Clinton reacted with humility and empathy, giving the public an oppor-tunity to appreciate his leadership. In October 1994 the *Washington Post* was prompted to ask, 'Bill Clinton has: reduced unemployment, tamed the deficit, checked inflation.... So why doesn't he get any credit?' While it would appear that the American public was still concerned about the reliability of these economic developments in 1994, they were confident enough to reward them in 1996. Party–candidate campaign co-operation was firmly established in the Democratic camp at an early stage, and contributed to a steady rise in Clinton's public opinion standings.

After their success in the 1994 mid-term elections, many Republicans felt that their party's presidential nomination was the only game in town. As Clyde Wilcox points out in his analysis of the 1994 elections, 'In late November of 1994, many political analysts had already written off Bill Clinton, and seemed convinced that the Republicans had a lock on the presidency in 1996.'[27] The launch, and failure, of an attempt at complex health reform allowed Republicans to attack Clinton as an old-style tax-and-spend Democrat, who supported intrusion into citizens' lives. Arguments over how to deal with gays in the military and how to protect minority voting power by redesigning constituency boundaries were left unresolved after rancorous public discussion. A deficit-cutting bill was successfully propagandised by the Republicans for the tax increase it imposed on some affluent voters. By autumn 1994, Clinton's approval ratings were polled around 40 per cent, some 15 per cent below the average for other Presidents at the time of mid-term elections.[28] This encouraged a considerable field of candidates to announce their availability for the nomination, contributed to expensive intra-party bloodletting, and limited the opportunity for the eventual nominee and the party organisation to combine their campaigning efforts at an early stage. The Republicans had thought that Clinton's failures as an incumbent were going to subvert his re-election chances, but they found that he was able to build on incumbency advantages in a very traditional manner.

Strategy over the last months of the campaign involves further skilled use of the important resources of the campaign, based on informed advice and polling evidence, aimed towards forming an electoral coalition that will lead to victory in November. Once again the rules of the game lend it a particular structure, and the overarching structural influence is the existence of the Electoral College. Victory in the presidential election is not decided by a straightforward tally of the citizens' votes. Instead, and in keeping with the federal structure of the United States, the votes of members of the public are counted at the state level, and the public vote decides which states have been won by each of the candidates, and no more. Each state, plus the District of Columbia, is allocated a specified number of Electoral College votes. For the states this number equals the total congressional representation of the state (although members of Congress are constitutionally excluded from membership of the Electoral College), so in 2000 Alaska, with one Representative and two Senators, has three votes in the Electoral College, while California (fifty-two Representatives and two Senators) has fifty-four Electoral College votes. The District of Columbia has an Electoral College value of three. This means that there is a total of 538 Electoral College votes nationwide.

In effect the public vote is tallied separately in each state, and the Electoral College value of that state is then awarded to the state-wide victor on a winner-take-all basis. National victory in the election goes to the candidate who gains 50 per cent or more of the Electoral College votes, that is at least 270 votes. The procedure is an adaptation of that designed by the Founding Fathers of the US Constitution, who felt that direct election of the President would not serve the young nation best. The original plan had state legislatures choosing the member of the Electoral College, and these persons casting the states' Electoral College votes for the executive offices. Before the middle of the nineteenth century most states allowed a public vote, rather than the state legislature, to inform the way that the Electoral College votes would be cast between the candidates, and gradually the tradition of 'winner take all' was established.[29]

Although the public vote is now expected to determine the way the states' Electoral College votes are cast, the eighteenth-century institution still exists. Each state chooses a number of members ('Electors') for the quadrennial Electoral College. Often alternative slates of respected political activists are nominated by the parties and, depending on the public vote, the winning party's supporters go through the motions of casting the states' Electoral College votes. According to the formula laid out in the Constitution, they meet in the state capitals to cast their votes, which are then transported to Washington, DC, to be counted by the president of the US Senate. Occasionally in recent years individual Electors have been known to reject the decision of a state's citizens, and such individuals are called 'faithless Electors'. The force of tradition has made the problem of the faithless Elector small, though it is embarrassing to the candidate. In 1988 one West Virginia Elector cast a presidential vote for Lloyd Bentsen instead of Michael Dukakis, and in 1976 a Washington Elector voted for Reagan instead of Ford. In 1972 an Elector from Virginia cast his vote for John Hospers, the Libertarian candidate, instead of Richard Nixon, the Republican winner. That Electoral College member, Roger MacBride, went on to be the Libertarian presidential candidate in 1976.

Under the Electoral College system the only thing that counts towards victory is winning states – a close second is a total loss. Technically it is possible to win in the Electoral College while coming second in the nation-wide popular vote, since marginal victories in enough states will give victory even if counterbalanced by massive losses in the rest of the nation. There has been no clear-cut case of this happening in over a hundred years, but in 1876 and again in 1888 the presidential victors received a majority in the Electoral College while their opponents had received the greater number of popular votes. In recent years the 1960, 1968 and 1976 elections were close enough to inspire pre-election concern that the vagaries of the Electoral College system might install to a President who had not received the most popular votes, but in each case the numbers lined up in the right columns in the end.

In such a system minor party challenges have little chance of break-through unless they are strongly regional in character (table 8.1). A classic example can be seen in 1948, when Henry Wallace, a former Democratic Vice-President running for the presidency as a Progressive, left-wing candidate, and Strom Thurmond, a former Democratic Senator running as a States' Rights Party, right-wing candidate, each received about 2.4 per cent of the national popular vote. Wallace's support was,

Table 8.1. *Presidential election result, 1996*

Candidates	Party	Popular vote	Per-centage	Electoral College vote
Clinton/Gore	Democratic	47,401,185	49.24	379
Dole/Kemp	Republican	39,197,469	40.71	159
Perot/Choate	Reform	8,085,294	8.40	
Nader/La Duke	Green	684,871	0.71	
Browne/Jorgensen	Libertarian	485,759	0.50	
Phillips/various	US Taxpayers	184,656	0.19	
Hagelin/Tompkins	Natural Law	113,667	0.12	
Moorehead/La Riva	Workers World	29,082	0.03	
Feinland/McClatchy	Peace & Freedom	25,332	0.03	
Collins/Giumarra	Independent	8,941	0.01	
Harris/Gorza	Socialist Workers	8,476	0.01	
Peron/Trout	Grassroots	5,378	0.00	
Hollis/Chester	Socialist	4,765	0.00	
White/Mazelis	Socialist Equality	2,438	0.00	
Templin/Van Horn	American	1,847	0.00	
Dodge/Kelly	Prohibition	1,298	0.00	
Crane/Chandler	Utah Independent	1,101	0.00	
Forbes	America First	932	0.00	
Birrenbach	Independent Grassroots	787	0.00	
Masters	Looking Back	752	0.00	
Michaels/Northrup	AIDS Cure	408	0.00	
Miscellaneous write-ins		24,518	0.02	
None of these candidates (Nevada)		5,608	0.00	

Source: FEC, http://www.fec.gov./pubrec/summ.htm, published 16 January 1997.

however, distributed nationwide, and delivered him no Electoral College support, while Thurmond's support was concentrated in the South, where he captured four states, and thirty-nine Electoral College votes (including one from a faithless Tennesseean, who diverted his support away from Harry Truman). The Electoral College votes won by George Wallace (American Independent) and Robert La Follette (Progressive) in 1924 also show regional strength. Theodore Roosevelt's 1912 'Bull Moose' Progressive campaign is the only minor party presidential campaign of this century that can be said to have had nationwide appeal both in the popular vote (23 per cent), and in the Electoral College (88 votes). Ross Perot, with almost 19 per cent of the popular vote in 1992, and 8.5 per

Table 8.2. *States in order of number of Electoral College votes, 2000 election*

State	No. of votes	State	No. of votes
California	54	Kentucky	8
New York	33	Oklahoma	8[a]
Texas	32[a]	South Carolina	8[a]
Florida	25	Iowa	7
Pennsylvania	23	Mississippi	7[a]
Illinois	22	Oregon	7
Ohio	21	Arkansas	6
Michigan	18	Kansas	6[a]
New Jersey	15	Nebraska	5[a]
North Carolina	14[a]	New Mexico	5
Georgia	13	Utah	5[a]
Virginia	13[a]	West Virginia	5
Indiana	12[a]	Hawaii	4
Massachusetts	12	Idaho	4[a]
Missouri	11	Maine	4
Tennessee	11	Nevada	4
Washington	11	New Hampshire	4
Wisconsin	11	Rhode Island	4
Maryland	10	Alaska	3[a]
Minnesota	10[b]	Delaware	3
Alabama	9	District of Columbia	3[b]
Louisiana	9	Montana	3
Arizona	8	North Dakota	3[a]
Colorado	8	South Dakota	3[a]
Connecticut	8	Vermont	3
		Wyoming	3[a]
Total Electoral College vote			538
Minimum Electoral College vote needed for victory			270

[a] These states, totalling 126 Electoral College votes in 2000, were won by the Republican presidential candidate in every election from 1980 to 1996.
[b] These states, totalling 13 Electoral College votes, were won by the Democratic presidential candidate in every election from 1980 to 1996.

cent in 1996, appears to be one of the most successful minor party candidates in US history, but he failed to gain any Electoral College votes. His support in 1992 did vary from 4.3 per cent in Washington, DC, to 30.6 per cent in Maine, but the total almost twenty million votes in 1992 were distributed evenly enough to prevent Perot gaining anything better than a second place position in Utah and Maine.[30]

Playing to win state by state also affects major party strategy, especially in a time of limited campaign resources. Investment must be channelled towards those states where a victory is possible, and the list of states so targeted must add up to an Electoral College total greater than 270 votes. Table 8.2 lists the states by the size of their Electoral College value in 2000. In the crudest terms, any candidate who could win the eleven largest states would have 270 votes, and presidential victory. After the census of 2000 there will be a redistribution of Electoral College votes to reflect changes in population. For example, California, Texas and Florida are likely to gain votes, while New York, Pennsylvania and Illinois will lose, but the combined position of the large states will remain much the same.

While the numbers are very important, however, no candidate would take a campaign approach so directly based on the arithmetic of the system. Campaign appeal has to be built on the candidate's attraction to a mixture of groups within the electorate who will together form a victorious coalition of voters. This appeal, hopefully containing a number of mutually supporting issue positions, will be likely to attract groups who have some elements of background, status, or endeavour in common. Immigrant communities, people of modest income, or persons engaged at all levels of particular industries are the kind of groups that might find elements in the campaign positions that cause them to coalesce with other groups in supporting one candidate. These groups exist across state barriers, but are not randomly distributed. Therefore a candidate who pitches an appeal to the interests of industrial manufacturing is likely to receive a more positive hearing in states like Michigan and Ohio, while one who stresses support of the oil extraction industry and its spin-offs will be appreciated in such states as Texas and Louisiana. The candidate must therefore heed the advice of consultants in identifying those states where policy positions are likely to attract the best popular support. These states are likely to have a regional base, given that many issues, whether cultural or economic, have a region-wide significance. They are also likely to be states where previous party candidates have performed successfully, given that the major parties have at least a modicum of policy and ideological coherence over time and, anyway, it is useful to know if people are in the habit of voting for the party's candidate.

The search for a vision that will appeal to the electorate is likely to be productive only if it is conducted without too much damaging infighting, and in an atmosphere that does not obscure the need to get on with laying the foundations of future campaigns within the framework set by the Electoral College. All candidates are forced to make campaign choices based on a clear assessment of which states can be won given the electoral appeal of the ticket, the platform and the party traditions competing in any particular year.

John Marttila, a veteran Democratic consultant who worked on the 1988 Dukakis campaign, points out that while a campaign can create 'no substitute for a clear vision that addresses [the] country's future', nevertheless any presidential campaign must follow several imperatives.[31] The major tactical challenge faced by the Democrats, according to Marttila, 'is to figure out which states the party's next nominee has a legitimate chance of winning'. Republicans undoubtedly feel the same way. The last presidential candidate to campaign personally in every state was Richard Nixon in 1960, and fulfilling his pledge to do so tied him into an exhausting and inflexible campaign schedule. It is increasingly important for campaigns to marshal all their resources, including the personal time of the candidate, to maximum effect over the whole length of the campaign. Rather than taking a blunderbuss approach, the modern presidential campaign must identify specific targets, and develop a strategy that allows flexibility of response to political developments. Over a twenty-year period from 1968, Republican candidates established a consistent record of success at presidential level. The Democratic victories of 1992 and 1996 have altered the landscape, but it is still true that fifteen states, with 126 Electoral College votes, voted consistently Republican from 1980 to 1996, while only Minnesota and Washington, DC, with 13 votes, were equally loyal to the Democrats. The Republican Party would like to see its support as the bedrock for an era of Republican presidential success. The Democrats would prefer to interpret the figures as underpinning a period of party competitiveness in which they have a good chance of victory.

The growth of Republican attractiveness in the South has made victory in California imperative for a Democratic presidential victory. Democrats also have to foster their pockets of support in the Northeast and the industrial Midwest, while Republicans build on their apparent strength in the agricultural Midwest and in the Mountain states. Both parties have to look beyond these boundaries to build a winning coalition. In 1996 Republican policy statements helped Democrats make inroads into significant voting groups. Fear of threats to Medicare and social security undermined the faith of some elderly voters in Republican management. The attachment of Republicans to bills aimed at limiting immigration, and limiting immigrants' access to welfare, and to moves to abolish affirmative action, stimulated Hispanic and African-American voter turnout, and pulled substantial numbers of Hispanic votes to the Democratic ticket. Clinton's victory in Florida was only the second for a Democratic presidential candidate in the second half of the twentieth century, and his was the only Democratic victory in Arizona over the same period – Hispanic and elderly voters played no small part in each of these states. Both parties must have the foresight and flexibility to restructure their voting coalitions by developing policy, and to take their message to all those parts of the Electoral College that their adapting message allows them to reach.

Here's to the next time

While some analysts are still undecided whether there was a realignment of voting patterns in the 1960s, as posited in chapter 3, or indeed whether the concept is too worn to be useful, others are of the opinion that the US is experiencing its sixth party system – a period of government divided between parties – and are wondering whether the early years of the twenty-first century will see a new realignment. The Republicans have been looking forward to a period of party dominance for some time, frustrated variously by Nixon's failure, the tenacious incumbency of Democrats in Congress and latterly by Clinton's electoral success. The twenty-first century is opening with the two major political parties in a competitive position. Both parties will hope that the presidential candidates they nominate in the elections of the early twenty-first century have coattails – that is, a depth of public appeal that will bring votes to the party's candidates for office further down the ballot. Growing Republican strength in the southern states could be a pillar to a realigned system in favour of that party. Renewed Democratic vigour in the West could stop any such realignment in its tracks, and leave analysts looking for different models of future party competition.

In the early years of the twenty-first century, as ever, candidates will be dealing with a constantly changing political environment. The policy agenda shifts, sometimes in unpredictable ways. Alterations to election law can alter the shape of the playing field. The primary season is becoming ever more front-loaded, putting the emphasis on early victory and heavy start-up spending. The financial structure of the campaign is regularly remoulded by legal challenges and legislative redefinition. Also on the horizon is the prospect that the presidential matching fund may not meet campaign demands, as taxpayers' willingness to donate dollars to the fund fails to keep up with campaign costs. In 1976, 28 per cent of Americans filing tax returns checked off a dollar to the fund. By 1995 the proportion had fallen to 13 per cent, and even with the donation increased to three dollars there is a danger that a busy race will stretch the fund beyond its limits.[32] Campaign strategists at national level, as at all the others, will continue to have their work cut out maintaining their understanding and skills from election to election. Simultaneously, voters at all levels will continue to have their work cut out sorting through the strategy in the process of making a well informed voting choice.

Notes

1   See Edward Pessen, *The Log Cabin Myth: The social backgrounds of the presidents* (New Haven, CT, Yale University Press, 1984).

2   Quotation from David Mervin, 'The brains behind Mr. Bumble', *Times Higher Education Supplement*, 10 May 1991, p. 16.

3   Bill Clinton was active in the failed 1972 presidential campaign of George McGovern, and in 1974 failed in his challenge against an incumbent US congressman in Arkansas. But these experiences gave him extensive contacts and considerable credibility with his party colleagues. He was elected Arkansas state Attorney General in 1976 and Governor in 1978, but was defeated after only one term, in 1980. He bought television time to apologise for his mistakes as Governor, and came back to take the governorship again in 1982, and held on to that office in subsequent elections in spite of allegations of sexual infidelity. Elected to the presidency in 1992, Democrats blamed their extensive losses in the congressional elections of 1994 on Clinton's mismanagement of his first two years in office. A powerful campaign brought Clinton back to victory in the presidential race of 1996, but he was facing investigation on a number of fronts by special prosecutor Kenneth Starr, and in 1998 his sexual liaison with White House staffer Monica Lewinsky was exposed, and impeachment hearings were launched in the House, leading to predictions of a Democratic meltdown at that year's mid-term elections. The electorate instead rallied to Clinton's party, the Democrats made a virtually unprecedented gain of seats in the US House, and Clinton again seemed to be safe in office.

4   *Buckley* v. *Valeo*, 424 US 1 (1976).

5   Figures from FEC press release, 'FEC announces 1996 presidential spending limits', 15 March 1996. A review of current finance laws can be found in Anthony Corrado, Thomas E. Mann, Daniel R. Ortiz, Trevor Potter and Frank Sorauf (eds), *Campaign Finance Reform: A sourcebook* (Washington, DC, Brookings Institution Press, 1997). See especially pp. 5–24.

6   Harold W. Stanley and Richard G. Niemi, *Vital Statistics on American Politics: 1997–1998* (6th edn, Washington, DC, Congressional Quarterly, 1998), pp. 84–6.

7   Clifford W. Brown, Jr, Lynda W. Powell and Clyde Wilcox, *Serious Money: Fund-raising and contributing in presidential nomination campaigns* (Cambridge, Cambridge University Press, 1995), p. 26.

8   Stephen J. Wayne, 'Interest groups on the road to the White House: traveling the hard and soft routes', in *The Interest Group Connection* (P. S. Herrnson, R. S. Shaiko and C. Wilcox, eds, Chatham, NJ, Chatham House, 1998), p. 71.

9   Herbert E. Alexander and Anthony Corrado, *Financing the 1992 Election* (Armonk, NY, M. E. Sharpe, 1995), p. 247.

10 Jason DeParle, 'The first primary', *New York Times Magazine*, 16 April 1995, p. 33, cited in Wayne, 'Interest groups', p. 68.

11 Craig Crawford, 'Lamar's loophole', *National Journal*, 15 August 1998, p. 1944.

12 See, for example, Roberto Suro, 'Sorting out the campaign finance mess', *Washington Post National Weekly Edition*, 18 May 1998, pp. 11–12.

13 See, for example, Philip John Davies, 'The Iowa caucuses and the US presidential election', *Talking Politics*, vol. 9, no. 1, autumn 1996, pp. 57–63; Hugh Winebrenner, *The Iowa Precinct Caucuses: The making of a media event* (2nd edn, Ames, IA, Iowa State University Press, 1998); Niall A. Palmer, *The*

New Hampshire Primary and the American Electoral Process (Westport, CT, Praeger, 1997). The quotations from campaign advisers in this section are taken from the *New York Times* coverage of the election results on 7 November 1996.

14   Elaine Ciulla Kamarck, 'Political scientists in presidential campaigns', *PS: Political Science and Politics*, vol. 23, no. 3, 1990, p. 430.

15   Winebrenner, *Iowa Precinct Caucuses*, p. 236.

16   Paul Abramson, John H. Aldrich and David Rohde, *Change and Continuity in the 1996 Elections* (Washington, DC, Congressional Quarterly Press, 1998), p. 21.

17   William G. Mayer, 'The presidential nominations', in *The Election of 1996: Reports and interpretations* (Gerald M. Pomper, ed., Chatham, NJ, Chatham House, 1997), p. 23.

18   See, for example, Paul Abramson, John H. Aldrich and David Rohde, *Change and Continuity in the 1992 Elections* (Washington, DC, Congressional Quarterly Press, 1994), chapter 1, and Ryan J. Barilleaux and Randall E. Adkins, 'The nominations: process and patterns', in *The Elections of 1992* (Michael Nelson, ed., Washington, DC, Congressional Quarterly Press, 1993), pp. 21–56.

19   See, for example, Larry J. Sabato (ed.), *Towards the Millennium: The elections of 1996* (Boston, MA, Allyn and Bacon, 1997), especially chapters 4, on the conventions, and 10, on campaign finance.

20   Much material was collected by the author at a visit to the 1996 Democratic convention, when he was supported by the United States Information Agency and the Nuffield Foundation.

21   Herbert E. Alexander, 'Financing the presidential elections, 1988', paper presented at the conference of the International Political Science Association, September 1989, pp. 4, 31–4.

22   Marjorie Randon Hershey, 'The campaign and the media', in *The Election of 1988: Reports and interpretations* (Gerald Pomper, ed., Chatham, NJ, Chatham House, 1989), p. 83.

23   Tom Wicker, 'Sowing the whirlwind', *New York Times*, 8 November 1988, p. A23.

24   Hershey, 'The campaign and the media', p. 86. See also Chris Black and Tom Oliphant, *All By Myself: The unmaking of a presidential campaign* (Boston, MA, Globe Pequod Press, 1989).

25   F. Christopher Arterton, 'Campaign '92: strategies and tactics of the candidates', in *The Election of 1992* (Gerald Pomper, ed., Chatham, NJ, Chatham House, 1992), pp. 93–6; Kathleen A. Frankovic, 'Public opinion in the 1992 campaign', in *The Election of 1992* (Gerald Pomper, ed., Chatham, NJ, Chatham House, 1992), pp. 119–21.

26   Michael Nelson, 'The election: turbulence and tranquillity in contemporary American politics', in *The Elections of 1996* (Michael Nelson, ed., Washington, DC, Congressional Quarterly Press, 1997), pp. 70–2; Marion R. Just, 'Candidate strategies and the media campaign', in *The Election of 1996: Reports and interpretations* (Gerald Pomper, ed., Chatham, NJ, Chatham House, 1992), pp. 88–91; Anthony Corrado, 'Financing the 1996 elections', in *The Election of 1996: Reports and interpretations* (Gerald Pomper, ed., Chatham, NJ, Chatham House, 1992), p. 127.

27   Clyde Wilcox, *The Latest American Revolution?* (New York, St. Martin's Press, 1995), p. 28.

28   Wilcox, *Latest American Revolution?*, p. 9.

29   See Walter Berns (ed.), *After the People Vote: A guide to the Electoral College* (Washington, DC, AEI Press, 1992).

30   I have been unable to devote very much space to minor parties in this work. They are nonetheless a fascinating part of the political landscape, with a literature of their own. See, for example, Steven J. Rosenstone, Roy L. Behr and Edward H. Lazarus, *Third Parties in America: Citizen response to major party failure* (Princeton, NJ, Princeton University Press, 1984); Frank Smallwood, *The Other Candidates: Third parties in presidential elections* (Hanover, NH, University Press of New England, 1983); J. David Gillespie, *Politics at the Periphery: Third parties in two-party America* (Columbia, SC, University of South Carolina Press, 1993).

31   John Marttila, 'A daunting task for Democrats', *Boston Sunday Globe*, 10 March 1991, pp. A25, A27–8.

32   Rodney A. Smith, 'White House auction', *Washington Post National Weekly Edition*, 3 August 1998, p. 26.

Index